Scientific
Thinking

Scientific
Thinking

By Robert M. Martin

broadview press

Canadian Cataloguing in Publication Data

Martin, Robert M.
    Scientific thinking

Includes index.
ISBN 1-55111-130-6

1. Induction (Logic). 2. Science–Methodology. I. Title.

BC91.M37 1997   161   C97-930386-9

Broadview Press Ltd., is an independent, international publishing house, incorporated in 1985.

North America:
P.O. Box 1243, Peterborough, Ontario, Canada K9J 7H5
3576 California Road, Orchard Park, NY 14127
Tel: (705) 743-8990; Fax: (705) 743-8353
E-mail: customerservice@broadviewpress.com

United Kingdom:
Turpin Distribution Services Ltd.,
Blackhorse Rd, Letchworth, Hertfordshire SG6 1HN
Tel: (1462) 672555; Fax: (1462) 480947
E-mail: turpin@rsc.org

Australia:
St. Clair Press, P.O. Box 287, Rozelle, NSW 2039
Tel: (02) 818-1942; Fax: (02) 418-1923

www.broadviewpress.com

Broadview Press gratefully acknowledges the financial support of the Ministry of Canadian Heritage through the Book Publishing Industry Development Program.

PRINTED IN CANADA

To Fran

Contents

CHAPTER **0**

Not Your Usual Introduction

0.1 Read this Chapter: It's not the Usual Silly ████ Introduction

Science is vitally important to our civilization, and you need to know how it works, blah blah blah. Most textbooks start with a lot of hype about how important the subject-matter of the book is. You're not interested in being told that, are you? I didn't think so. Instead of all this, let's get down to business.

But wait. There are a couple of things you should know first.

0.2 What this Book is About ████

It's about scientific thinking: the rules that govern good scientific procedure.

Some people are interested in science, and some people aren't. In case you're one of the second group, you should know right now that although there's a lot in this book that's about the kinds of thinking people in laboratories and university science departments do, there's also a lot in here about the kind of thinking done by us non-scientists in ordinary life. So maybe you'll find this discussion interesting and relevant after all.

Those of you with science or math phobias need not worry. To understand the basic methods of science, you'll need to know a little arithmetic, logic, and philosophy; it's also helpful to know a little science, of course. But this book presupposes no such knowledge: you'll be told anything you need.

As examples of the sort of scientific thought I'm talking about, I've included a number of accounts of scientific reasoning in this book. Real science is often complicated and subtle, and what really happened in many scientific investigations is a long story. While these long stories are often interesting (to some people), this is not the place to tell them. I have restricted myself to short and simple stories. Sometimes I've had to shorten and simplify the real accounts a bit. Sometimes my examples are entirely fictitious—designed by me to provide a clear, simple, and forceful illustration of the point at issue, and not to distract you with a large number of irrelevant details which would have had to be included to give a real-life example. In order to avoid the misconception that the scientific discoveries I've made up are real ones, I've indicated, in each case, when an example is real and when it is fictitious. The real-life examples are usually gleaned from newspaper or magazine articles, rather than from scientific journals. Newspapers and magazines simplify matters significantly, but sometimes get them not precisely right. Well, never mind. The point of this book is not to provide you with a substantial and detailed knowledge of the history of any particular discoveries in science: the point is to teach you how scientific thought works in general. If you're interested in finding out more about any of the real-life bits of science I mention, there's no substitute for looking at what's actually written by the scientists involved.

0.3 Some Advice to Readers

As you can tell already, this book is written in a sort of casual, conversational tone, rather than in the formal, pompous style you'll usually find in textbooks. I'm writing it this way on purpose, to make it easier and more pleasant to take. What I say will often—I hope—sound simple and obvious. But don't be misled: there is a serious purpose behind this book, and there's a good deal of fairly complicated content in here. We'll get into some deep waters eventually, so you shouldn't approach this book with the attitude you have when reading the sport pages or looking at music videos. I'm going to go slowly and repeat things a bit to make sure that nobody gets lost. You might be tempted by the slow pace and repetitions to skip over some bits, or to glance through things lightly instead of reading them carefully. But you'll miss important things that way. Please be patient and pay attention.

Scattered throughout this book you'll find exercises. These will usually be followed by answers. You'll see a big question mark next to the beginning of each EXERCISE section, and a big stop-sign symbol next to the beginning of each ANSWER section. These symbols look like this:

> The EXERCISES and ANSWERS are in a different typeface and appear in boxes, like this.

Don't ignore these parts, or skim over them; they form an essential part of the book, and it's important that you read them carefully, and think about them. Try to answer exercise questions before you read the answers provided. Because the answers are sitting right there following the exercises, you'll be tempted to cheat and read the answers right away, before you try to figure them out for yourselves. This is a bad idea. You'll get a much better grasp of what's going on in this book (and prepare yourself much better for class evaluations, if you're using this book as a class textbook) if you don't "cheat" like this. STOP!! before you get to the answer. Try to figure out what it is yourself. Then read on to see if you agree with the answer given by the book. Often the exercises will be quite easy. They're designed that way. Do them anyway; they'll serve to make sure that you've mastered what you're supposed to, and to rub it in.

Here and there throughout the book you'll find technical terms—jargon words, or words used in a special sense for our purposes. It's important that you learn the meanings of these terms, because they serve as useful shorthand abbreviations for complicated concepts, or because you'll find them in scientific reports. **THE FIRST USE OF EACH OF THESE TERMS WILL BE HIGHLIGHTED IN THIS BOOK BY PRINTING IT IN A SPECIAL TYPEFACE LIKE THIS WITH A DOUBLE UNDERLINE**. When you encounter one of these terms, make sure you pay attention to it and understand exactly what it means.

Okay, *now* we can get down to business.

PART I

Induction, Proportions, Correlations

CHAPTER 1

Galileo and Mrs. Smith

1.1 Mrs. Smith ▮▮▮▮▮▮

My first high school science class was taught by a loveable woman named Mrs. Smith. On the first day of class, she told us what science was all about. This enthusiastic account was exciting to me and the few other future science nerds in the class. I'm going to tell you what she told us, because her view nicely summarizes the Modern Official Position on the nature of science.

Here's what she said.

In bygone days, from the time of the Ancient Greeks through Galileo, they didn't know how to find out things about the world. They thought that scientific knowledge came from two sources: from Divine Revelation, as revealed by the Bible and by Church authorities, and from sitting around in an armchair in your living room thinking hard about things. But they were wrong. Scientific knowledge comes from an entirely different source: from observation. The revolution in thought which made real science possible, and which alone has been responsible for all the wonderful scientific knowledge we have today, is based on a simple idea: we have to look at things to find out about them.

Now, looking at things comes naturally to us, and it seems like a pretty simple thing to do, but you have to learn how to really look. Most of us walk around in the world not really noticing things, but we start to be scientists when we learn how to observe things carefully. When you walk home from school today (Mrs. Smith urged us), start to *look*. For example, pay attention to those birds. How many different ones can you find? See if you can carefully describe the size, shape, and colouration of each one. What are they doing? Are they mostly walking around on the ground, or do they perch on trees or telephone wires? What are they eating? What noises are they making? (Don't just look—listen too, and use your other senses.) Your job as newly minted miniature scientists (she told us) is to collect observations.

Mistakes in science arise, Mrs. Smith told us, when people rely on authority or on accepted general views. The old saying is "birds of a feather flock together," meaning that birds group themselves by kinds. But is this really true? Take a look at groups of birds: are they all the same, or are there different kinds in the same group? Everyone knows that birds live in nests in trees, which they build out of twigs, right? Well, that's what you learned from your Grade Three teacher, but is it true? Forget what you were told: the only way you can find out is by following birds home and looking at where they live. In order to be a real scientist, Mrs. Smith insisted, we need to be strongly skeptical of accepted wisdom; we need to find out for ourselves, by observation. Forget everything you already believe; ignore everything they told you. Cleanse your mind of every preconception and prejudice. Let the world show you the way it really is. Because science is the search for truth, real scientists should be *open-minded*— or perhaps "empty-minded" is a better term. We were happy to hear that everything we were supposed to have learned earlier should be ignored. Most of it had already been forgotten anyway, or else not learned in the first place.

Mrs. Smith loved nature and tended to concentrate on the prettier parts of it, like birds and flowers. Nevertheless, she warned, nature is not always pretty, and some aspects of it are not very nice. Nature can be cruel, and it may tell you things you don't like. Our ideas of the way things *ought* to be have no place in science; in fact, they can interfere with our search for how things *are*. Just as real scientists ignore all preconceptions about what the facts are, so too must they ignore any values they might have.

So, Mrs. Smith reasoned, the only motive appropriate for scientists is the pure, disinterested search for truth. What sorts of things might motivate scientists? Maybe they have an axe to grind. Maybe they desire personal advancement, or a Nobel Prize, or maybe they want to make money out of their discovery. Perhaps they want to be famous, or to get revenge on some hated colleague by getting there first or by showing that the colleague was wrong. Any of these less than noble aims will result, from time to time, in a scientist's making premature or unjustified claims. Scientists with an axe to grind may prematurely or even fraudulently present their cherished beliefs as established. The only appropriate motive for a scientist is the desire for truth.

Mrs. Smith's views on science and scientists were inspirational, and the ideals she emphasised, of objective observation and desire to find the truth, are clearly very important to science. This is part of the Modern Official Position about what good science is like. Most people think of science the way Mrs. Smith did—that it is a fairly simple and naïve version of what philosophers call **EMPIRICISM**. Empiricism is the view that knowledge comes from experience. The view that science is a sort of naïve empiricism has been conventional and dominant for centuries.

Nevertheless, over the past 40 years or so, most of the philosophers and scientists who have been thinking about how science works have become convinced that this view is not exactly right—that it's hugely oversimplified, or at least misleading, in many respects. The rest of this book can be seen as correction to Mrs. Smith. We'll be filling in details where this view is over-simplified, and correcting it where it's wrong. It can't be denied, however, that Mrs. Smith had the right sort of idea in general, and we'll keep in mind the correct—even inspiring—Smithian overview.

We're going to start out with some stories from the history of science. As you read these, see if you can pick out who is thinking in the right way, according to the Official, Smithian position, and who is thinking in the wrong way. Also, see if you can say why. These stories are the sort that are told to illustrate and reinforce the Official View. Even while we examine these, however, you'll see some problems with this View developing.

1.2 Galileo and his Telescope

Around 1609, the telescope was invented in Holland. In Italy, Galileo made one of these new instruments for himself, adding some improvements which made it useful for astronomical observation. One of the things he looked at in the night sky was Jupiter. He was surprised to observe four tiny spots of light nearby which slowly changed position relative to the planet: first moving closer to it, then invisible (as if behind or in front of it), then reappearing on the other side, moving away for a while, then moving back toward Jupiter, and so on. Galileo could see what was going on here: these small spots of light were moons going around Jupiter.

This was a very important discovery. The reason why it was so important was that it was inconsistent with the view of the structure of the universe that was current at that time—the view developed by the Ancient Greeks, and incorporated into official Christianity. This view, associated with the

Second Century A.D. Greek astronomer Ptolemy and the Fourth Century Greek philosopher Aristotle, held that the Earth was motionless and at the centre of the universe. The sun, moon, planets, and stars moved around the earth. Why didn't they fall down to earth, as everything else did which was above the ground and not held up? Well, they must be held up there, by something invisible to us: transparent crystal glass spheres surrounding the earth, on which they were imbedded. Everybody could see that the stars appeared to move together around the earth, stationary relative to each other, but the planets, moon, and sun appeared to move in different ways relative to the background of the stars: so each of them must be imbedded on a different crystal sphere, of a smaller radius than the one supporting the stars, with each sphere moving in its own way.

But Galileo's observation showed that there was something drastically wrong with this view. If Jupiter was imbedded on a crystal sphere, it couldn't have moons going around it, because these moons wouldn't be able to get through Jupiter's crystal sphere. Worse still, if there were moons rotating around Jupiter, then the view that everything in the universe circled around the Earth must be wrong. But, as everyone knew, God created the heavens and the Earth, and made the Earth a special place where He put humans, so everything must circle around the Earth.

Galileo began publishing his revolutionary views on astronomy, much to the displeasure of the thinkers of the time. Here's a dramatization of a discussion between Galileo and some of these thinkers, as imagined by the German dramatist Bertolt Brecht:

GALILEO: There are star movements for which Ptolemy's system has no explanations. None at all. Such are the movements of four small stars around the planet Jupiter, newly discovered by myself. Gentlemen, I suggest you begin by looking at these satellites of Jupiter, the Medici stars....

PHILOSOPHER: I fear nothing is that simple, Signor Galilei. Before we apply ourselves to your famous telescope, we beg the pleasure of a disputation. The theme—can such stars exist?...

GALILEO: Why not just look through the telescope and see they exist?...

PHILOSOPHER: Yes, yes.... The cosmos of the divine Aristotle with its mystical, music-making spheres, crystal domes and the gyration of its heavenly bodies...is an edifice of such order and beauty, that we would do well to hesitate before disrupting such harmony.

GALILEO: What if your Highness, this minute, looks through the telescope and sees these impossible and unnecessary stars?

MATHEMATICIAN: One might be tempted to reply that if your telescope shows something that cannot exist, it can't be a very reliable telescope, eh?

GALILEO: And what do you mean by that?

MATHEMATICIAN: It would be more productive, Signor Galilei, if you told us the reasons why you claim that, in the highest sphere of the immutable heavens, stars can float about freely in space?

PHILOSOPHER: Reasons, Signor Galilei, reasons!

GALILEO: Reasons? When one glance at the stars demonstrates the truth? This disputation becomes fatuous.

MATHEMATICIAN: At the risk of exciting you further, one might say—what is in your telescope and what is in the heavens, may be two different things. *

After a few years of lively controversy, Galileo was summoned to Rome to face the Inquisition, where he argued in favour of his views. When it became clear he couldn't win, and was faced with torture and death if he didn't recant his views, Galileo did the sensible thing and proclaimed his error. He was sentenced to life imprisonment, although he was allowed to live out of prison.

---

* The Life of Galileo, translated by Howard Brenton (London, Methuen London Ltd., 1980), Scene Four, pp. 27-9.

1.3 Bacon and the Holes in Your Head

A few years later, the English scientist Francis Bacon (1561-1626) added his thoughts to the controversy. He argued that what Galileo saw couldn't have been moons around Jupiter. Seven "planets" (meaning "heavenly bodies") were already known: the sun, the moon, Mercury, Venus, Mars, Jupiter, and Saturn. If what Galileo saw were really moons around Jupiter, then there would be more than seven "planets" up there. But:

> There are seven windows given to animals in the domicile of the head, through which the air is admitted to the tabernacle of the body, to enlighten, to warm and to nourish it. What are these parts of the microcosmos: Two nostrils, two eyes, two ears and a mouth. So in the heavens, as in a macrocosmos, there are two favourable stars, two unpropitious, two luminaries, and Mercury undecided and indifferent. From this and from many other similarities in nature, such as the seven metals etc., which it were tedious to enumerate, we gather that the number of planets is necessarily seven. *

1.4 The End of the Story of the Number of Planets

The controversy about whether there were more than seven heavenly bodies, and about whether the Earth is the centre around which everything else revolves was, of course, settled a little later. Although it wasn't until 1992 that the Pope got around to making an official announcement that Galileo was right about those moons.

What's the moral of this story?

EXERCISE
The questions we started with are: who is reasoning well, and who isn't? Why? Stop now and try to answer these questions. I'm not asking who came up with the correct answer: we all know this. I'm asking why one methodology was the right one, and the others wrong.

---

* Francesco Sizzi, *Dianoia Astronomica*, Optica, Physica, Florence, 1611.

ANSWER **STOP!**

It's probably clear to you that you're being pushed into answering these questions as follows: The Ancient Greeks, the Renaissance Catholic Church, Francis Bacon, and Brecht's Philosopher and Mathematician were all wrong; Galileo was right. Galileo used his senses to look and see how the universe worked; everyone else just tried to figure it out on the basis of abstract reasoning.

EXERCISE **?**

Thank you for letting yourself be pushed into that answer. Now list the general kinds of "abstract reasoning" which is involved in doing things the wrong way.

ANSWER **STOP!**

Religious principle; moral ideals; philosophical views; relying on sanctioned authority; reasoning from analogy.

Don't be too sure that things are as simple as this, however. The story as I've been telling it is rather oversimplified, and historians say that the issues were nowhere near as cut and dried as I've been presenting them. Well, this doesn't matter much for our purposes. What we're interested in is the philosophical positions that these historical events represent. But these are somewhat oversimplified too. As we'll see, there's a much more complicated story to be told about the proper place of observation—and of abstract thinking—in science. But first, some more history.

1.5 Falling Bodies

In the Fourth Century B.C., Aristotle produced what was to become a hugely influential theory of physical motion. There is no motion without a cause, he reasoned, so nothing can start moving, or continue to move, unless there is a cause—a source of this motion. The stars move around in the heavens because the crystal glass sphere they're embedded in is continuously pushed by an invisible "mover"; this is a case of an external source of motion. Unsupported bodies fall toward the Earth because of a continuous internal source of motion in them: it is part of the nature of things to "want to" fall downwards; their "natural place" is down, and they seek this place with a force that varies according to their weight, which is a measure of how much they want to go downwards. Thus their speed of fall depends on how much weight—internal downward force—they contain, as well as how much resistance to fall is imparted by the medium through which they fall. So the speed of something falling through the air is directly proportional to its weight and inversely proportional to the density (the resistance to motion) of the air through which it falls.

Aristotle was one of the most brilliant thinkers of all time. But the trouble with his ideas about motion is that, as you know if you've learned any physics, they're dead wrong.

Throughout antiquity, and into the Middle Ages, there was lively debate about the theory of falling bodies, and various theories gave various different calculations of this speed. This seems a bit goofy to us: instead of trying to derive the speed of falling bodies from abstract philosophical reasoning, why didn't they *measure* the speed of some real ones? More examples of bad scientific reasoning—bad not just because it comes up with the wrong answers, but because it uses the wrong methods: abstract philosophical principle rather than observation. Occasionally the Ancients and Medievals came up with the right answers, but this was more or less by accident (according to the Official Modern View).

Some of the consequences of ancient physics seem quite absurd to us now. For example, it appears to follow from Aristotelian theory that a body falling through a vacuum, with no resistance from the medium, would have infinite velocity. But Aristotle thought that *infinite* velocity was absurd, and from this he concluded that a vacuum could not exist! Here's another example: the Aristotelian theory of the flight of a rock thrown through the air was roughly that the push when you throw it gives the rock an internal "momentum" - an inner source of motion - which runs counter to its natural tendency to fall toward the earth, and makes it go upward and sideways. The resistance of the air depletes this quantity of internal momentum, and when the momentum runs out, the rock will suddenly stop going upward and sideways, *turn a corner*, and head downward toward the Earth. The reason this view is crazy is that anyone who has ever looked carefully at the path of a thrown rock or baseball or whatever can *see* that its path is nothing like this. It's obvious that none of these things turns a corner in flight.

The Official View draws the moral here, as before, that the ancient approach of science-as-philosophy was seriously impeded by its methodology of deriving knowledge about the world from abstract philosophical principle, rather than from observation. It was not until the Renaissance that the idea that observation is necessary began to get currency. Leonardo da Vinci (1452-1519) argued that deduction from theory was the wrong way to answer questions about scientific matters. Around 1586, a Dutchman named Simon Stevin threw some doubt on Aristotelian theory of falling bodies by dropping two pieces of lead of different weights simultaneously from the same height, and by noticing that the sounds of the lead weights hitting the ground seemed to be simultaneous.

1.6 Galileo on Falling Bodies

But it was our old friend Galileo whose work (before he became distracted by his new telescope) was the most detailed and influential. Galileo noticed that the longer and further something fell, the faster it fell. Did the speed of fall depend on the duration of fall, or on the distance fallen? Did it have anything to do with the weight of the falling body? Galileo tried to answer these questions in a variety of ways. As you read the following accounts, pay close attention to whether, and where, they rely on observation.

Galileo considered Aristotle's position: that the velocity of a falling body depended on its weight. Galileo reasoned as follows: suppose Aristotle were right. Then a big heavy cannonball would fall faster than a lighter musket ball. But imagine that these two balls were connected by a chain, and both were dropped from a height. The cannonball would try to fall faster than the musket ball, but would be held back by the attached musket ball which would be trying to fall slower. The fall of the musket ball would be sped up by the pull of the cannonball. So the end result, according to Aristotelian theory, would appear to be that the two balls plus the chain would fall at an intermediate speed: slower than the cannonball when it fell alone, but faster than the musket ball.

But on the other hand, the two balls connected by the chain now constitute a large object (ball + chain + ball) which is heavier than either ball alone; so Aristotelian theory tells us that this combined new object must fall *faster* than either ball alone.

So Aristotle's theory results in two conclusions about the speed of the fall of the two-balls-plus-chain: that it falls at a speed intermediate between the speed of the unattached cannonball and that of the unattached musketball, and that it falls at a speed faster than either of them. These results are contradictory. Any theory that gives contradictory results must be false.

EXERCISE
Is this right? Has Galileo proven this? Is this observation or abstract reasoning?

ANSWER
This reasoning seems to be correct; but never mind. The interesting part for us is that Galileo seems to have proven (or at least, to have attempted to have proven) something by abstract reasoning alone. Maybe he's not such a hero of observational science after all. If this is good science, then maybe good science has a place for abstract reasoning after all.

Galileo examined the hypothesis that the speed of a falling body might be the same whatever its weight, but might depend instead on the distance fallen. The problem with this seemed to be that in the beginning, a body has fallen zero distance and has zero velocity; but it can't travel a distance until it has a velocity, but if velocity depends on distance, then it can't get a velocity until it's fallen some distance. It thus appeared to be proven that velocity can't depend on distance.

EXERCISE
Is this right? Has Galileo proven this? Is this observation or abstract reasoning?

ANSWER
It's unclear whether this reasoning proves what it's supposed to, but again, it's abstract reasoning rather than experimental observation.

Having rejected the idea that the speed of a falling body depends on the distance fallen, Galileo guessed instead that velocity of a falling body increases simply in proportion to the duration of the fall. This can be expressed by the equation $v = gt$ where v stands for velocity, t for duration of time of fall, and g for a constant representing the force of gravity. Was this right? Galileo decided to put it to an observational test.

You may have run into the story of Galileo's dropping things off the Leaning Tower of Pisa in order to observe how they fall. This story (along with the other famous falling-body story in which Newton gets klunked on the head by a falling apple) is probably false. What historians think went on is this: in Galileo's time, the instruments for measuring time were very crude, and they weren't up to the delicate task of giving good measurements for freely falling bodies. However, Galileo had the brilliant idea that he could get relevant information by rolling balls down an inclined plane. These traveled much slower than freely falling objects, and their speed at various times could be calculated with the aid of the crude time-measuring device he used (essentially a water-bucket with a hole in the bottom: water drained out of it at a constant rate, so you could tell how much time had passed by looking at the level of the water). As a result of his experiments, he concluded that the velocity of a falling body increases at a constant rate, and that this increase was the same for anything, regardless of weight.

EXERCISE
Is this conclusion right? Has Galileo proven it? Is this observation or abstract reasoning?

ANSWER
You've learned in high school physics (remember??) that this conclusion is right. But aren't you substituting reliance on authority for your own observation? Haven't you noticed that light things like feathers fall much slower than heavy things like bowling balls? (Maybe you know what's going on with feathers and bowling balls, but we'll ignore this problem for the time being.) Anyway, it seems clear, at last, that Galileo is in some sense relying on experimental observation rather than abstract reasoning.

▇▇▇▇▇ 1.7 Abstract Reasoning or Observation?

One of the cracks that has appeared in the Official View of science has to do with Galileo's use of abstract reasoning, as opposed to observation, in some of his science. On the one hand, this can be seen as an inevitable leftover of the primitive bad science that Galileo was instrumental in replacing, and we can still view him as a hero of the genuine new observational science while forgiving his backsliding. Historical scholars have often pointed out that the story of Galileo and the Inquisition, as Brecht tells it, and as it has become entrenched in the mythology of modern science, is hugely oversimplified, and that the church was not as foolish, nor Galileo as idealistically devoted to pure observation of pure truth, as the mythology would have it.

But this is just a matter of history. What we're more interested in is whether scientific empiricism—Smithian Official Science—as represented perhaps historically inaccurately by Galileo, is the only good science.

The story of Galileo does raise some interesting concerns relevant to this question. We've noticed that at least some of the abstract, non-observational reasoning attributed to Galileo seems to be scientifically acceptable. If this is the case, then, although Mrs. Smith was certainly right in thinking that observation plays a large part in science, the impression she gave us that that's all there is to it is wrong.

Here's another apparent example of abstract non-observational reasoning in science. It's a lot like Galileo's cannonball example.

Following are two "laws of shadows." I'll bet you believe both of them.

(1) Shadows do not pass through opaque objects.

Imagine a light source on your left, and a wall on your right. Then, of course, your shadow falls on the wall. Now imagine putting a large, opaque screen between you and the wall. Your shadow now falls on the screen, but it couldn't fall on the wall, because it can't pass through the opaque screen.

(2) If light doesn't fall on something, then it doesn't cast a shadow.

Imagine again a light source on your left, and a wall on your right. Now put the opaque screen between you and the light, so that no light falls on you. Your shadow couldn't fall on the wall then, because you're not illuminated by the light.

Both of these are correct principles of the way shadows work, right? Well, consider this example. Imagine, as before, a light source on your left and a wall on your right. Now hold up a small opaque object—a coffee mug, for instance—to your right, between you and the wall, so that it is completely within your shadow. A shadow matching your shape falls on the wall, but consider that part of the shadow which is on the imaginary line you might draw from the light source through your body, through the coffee mug, to the wall. That place on the wall is in shadow, of course, but is that part of the shadow cast by your body or by the coffee mug?

Principle (1) tells us that that part of the shadow isn't cast by your body. The opaque coffee mug is between your body and that part of the shadow. Your shadow falls on the coffee mug, but it can't pass through it to the wall.

But Principle (2) tells us that that part of the shadow isn't cast by the coffee mug either. The coffee mug is completely shaded by you. It isn't illuminated by the light, so it doesn't cast a shadow on the wall.

It appears that if Principles (1) and (2) are both correct, then that part of the shadow isn't cast by anything. But that's absurd. Every part of a shadow must be cast by something.

What has gone wrong here? I guess we have to say that Principles (1) and (2) can't both be true. If we reject (1), then we're free to say that that part of the shadow is cast by you *through* the mug. If we reject (2), then we're free to say that the unlit coffee mug casts a shadow. Both of these options look absurd because both (1) and (2) seem so obviously true. This is a genuine problem. *

In this case, as in the case of Galileo's cannonball thought experiment, it might be concluded that mere thought, without observation or experiment, can establish a conclusion about the way the world works. In both cases, we have shown by mere abstract reasoning that a theory results in a contradiction, and thus that the theory can't be true.

Is this an example of valid scientific thought not based on observation or experiment? Perhaps. If it is, then it's only of a very limited kind. In both this case and in the case of Galileo's cannonball, we're able to show something false by deriving a contradiction from it. But we don't have any case of determining the truth of a true theory merely by abstract reasoning. It appears that this is where observation and experiment must come in.

---

* The shadow problem was discussed by Bas C. van Frassen in Chapter 9 of *Laws and Symmetry* (Oxford: Clarendon Press, 1989), although he says he didn't invent it.

But even the examples we've been looking at—examples which are supposed to reinforce the Smithian view—suggest some further ways in which this view is inadequate. Here are some of them.

1.8 Scientists Don't Just Look: They Experiment

Mrs. Smith's simple instructions to her budding scientists involved merely opening our eyes and observing the way things are. How might one do this to find out about falling bodies? I suppose this would involve looking around until something happened to be falling, and watching it to see how it worked. Galileo didn't do this, and if he had it wouldn't have worked very well. One obvious reason is that things don't fall down very often in the normal course of events, and we'd have to walk around with our eyes open for a long time before we happened to see something falling. The solution to this, which Stevin already thought of, was to do an experiment: *make* something fall. So he dropped things. This involves doing something—making something happen—and not just passive observation of what happens all by itself.

This is not to say that passive observation is unimportant in science. Galileo's observations of the moons of Jupiter were of course merely passive: it's impossible for anyone to make anything happen up there. That's why *experiment* has limited applicability in astronomy, and much more applicability in, say, the physics of falling bodies. (But perhaps there is room even in astronomy for experiment. We'll see how this might be the case later, in 22.2.)

Similar difficulties in passive observation arise even in the scientific research programs Mrs. Smith recommended to us. For example, inspired by her introductory lecture, I actually did try to observe what sparrows ate. I spent the next few days looking for sparrows. These are the most common birds where I was living, and I actually did manage to spot a few. But the ones I saw were just standing around, or flying; none of them was eating anything. I realized that it would be a daunting, time-consuming task, perhaps even an impossible one, to determine what sparrows ate this way, and I began to have doubts about my ability to make any scientific breakthroughs in this area.

An efficient solution to my problem (had I had the time, resources, and inclination—none of which I actually did have) would be to do an experiment: I might have trapped a bunch of sparrows, and put them into a cage, in which I also put measured quantities of worms, seeds of various sorts, assorted bugs and flies, and so on. Then I could watch, or come back later to see what was left.

Suppose I had performed this sparrow experiment: would this give me any reason to come to valid conclusions about what sparrows ate in the wild? How might I have set up this experiment to make it more probable that my conclusions were true? What constitutes a valid experiment is something we shall consider later.

1.9 It's Not Just What You See

Mrs. Smith told us to go out and collect facts by observing them. But Galileo was doing much more than this. When he looked through his telescope, what he saw were little spots of light near Jupiter, changing positions in certain ways from night to night—regularly moving closer or further away from Jupiter, disappearing and reappearing. Were he to have restricted his conclusions to just what he saw, he might have said only that there were these little spots of light etc., and he probably wouldn't have gotten into so much trouble with the Inquisition. But Galileo took these little spots of light to be things rotating around Jupiter—moons. And he went further, recognizing that this would be inconsistent with the Aristotelian universe of crystal spheres, and he drew this conclusion too.

Similarly, Galileo's experiment rolling balls down an inclined plane does not merely result in conclusions reporting what was observed. All he observed, after all, was the behaviour of a few little balls rolling down a particular inclined plane. The conclusions he drew were far more significant and far-reaching, and turned out to be fairly central to classical physics. Peculiarly, the conclusions he drew were not even about balls rolling down planes at all, but about freely falling bodies: a different thing altogether. In this respect he again went beyond what was observed.

The conclusions I might have drawn from my hypothetical sparrow experiment would have exhibited a similar characteristic. Suppose I observed that the three sparrows I kept in a cage ate no worms; that 20% by weight of what they ate was small bugs; that they ate no seeds larger than 2 mm; and that 80% by weight of the diet was seeds 2 mm or smaller in size, of whatever variety I provided. Were I to stick merely to what I saw, I would report that three sparrows kept in a cage ate no worms, etc. But this would be of no significance in itself. The question I started with was: what do sparrows eat *in the wild*? Presumably, my observations have some relevance to the answer to this question; later on, we'll see exactly how this relevance might be established. But note for the moment merely that in this case too, science does and should go beyond mere observation to draw conclusions beyond what is merely observed.

1.10 Not Just Observation—Also Measurement

When Galileo rolled the balls down the inclined plane, he didn't merely look and see what happened. He very carefully measured the distance traveled and the time it took to travel that distance. From these measurements, he calculated the speed of travel. What he came up with was a mathematical equation relating numerical quantities. We can imagine that when he observed the moons of Jupiter, he didn't merely see some spots at various different places from night to night: he kept track of where the spots were, compared their positions from night to night, and perhaps did some calculations intended to compute what path they were traveling, to find out that their change in apparent position was consistent with their being bodies moving around Jupiter. Similarly, in my hypothetical bird experiment I imagined myself as a budding junior scientist weighing the stuff I put into the cage and calculating percentages by weight of what was eaten. It's obvious: numbers are important to science. Scientists measure and calculate; they don't just observe.

1.11 Hypothesis Sometimes Precedes Observation

The story of Galileo's experiment with the inclined plane illustrates something very important and non-Smithian about the thought-processes of scientists. *Before* Galileo performed the experiment, he already had a hypothesis: that the speed of falling bodies depended on the time of falling. Maybe he got this hypothesis from observations of things that he dropped or observed falling all by themselves; maybe it was just a hunch. One reason he decided this one was worth testing was that he had already reasoned purely abstractly that some alternative hypotheses were impossible. Anyway, the important feature of this Galileo story to notice now is that he thought up this hypothesis and decided that it was worth testing before he did the observations that tested it.

My hypothetical sparrow experiment shows a similar feature. *Before* I performed this experiment, I must have had at least a general hypothesis about what sparrows ate. Notice what stuff I put into the cage for the sparrows to eat: seeds, bugs, and worms; and what stuff I didn't put in: for example, cups of hot coffee, pencils, baseballs. In choosing the materials to try the sparrows on, I already have some idea of what sparrows might eat, and I design the experiment to test what I have already decided are plausible hypotheses.

The important moral of this example is that Mrs. Smith's idea of scientific procedure has it wrong in several respects—at least in some cases. The important observations scientists make are often done *after* they have decided on one or more plausible hypotheses. The observations or experiments are designed specifically to test these previously-arrived-at hypotheses. Thus, in the case of these observations at least, scientists don't arrive at their observations with the blank minds Mrs. Smith said they do. Often (at least) they already have hypotheses in mind to test with these observations.

To see how this works, let's compare two hypothetical ways of answering another Mrs. Smith question: where do sparrows live? Here are two ways I might go about answering this question:

A: I might walk around at random until I happen to spot, entirely by accident, something which is clearly a sparrow's home (where its eggs are, where it comes back to at night, etc.)

B: I might decide, before even looking around at all, that it's a plausible hypothesis that sparrows nest in trees. (Why would I decide this?) Then I would test this hypothesis not by wandering around looking at things at random, but rather by looking in trees and seeing if I could see any sparrow's nests there.

Plan B is not guaranteed to work. For one thing, if my hypothesis is right, but I don't happen to look in the right sort of tree, or in the trees where sparrows are in fact nesting, or if I don't recognize a sparrow's nest when I see it, I won't find the answer to my question. And if my hypothesis is wrong, and sparrows don't in fact nest in trees, I will spot no sparrows' nests, and I won't find out anything about where sparrows live, other than the negative fact that they (maybe) don't nest in trees. But nevertheless, B is clearly a superior strategy to A. Imagine that I look for sparrows' nests really at random, with no preliminary hypothesis at all: I would look inside the trunk of my car, under my bed, and inside my microwave oven; I'd dig holes in the back yard, and put on my scuba-gear to have a look under water at the beach. This sort of utterly random search is entirely unlikely to give me any answers to my question at all.

Very often then, hypothesis precedes observation, and it should—although not always. Occasionally, interesting results might just pop up entirely on the basis of random observation. For example, years ago, it was thought that a very primitive family of fish, the coelacanth, which had been seen only in fossil form, was long extinct. Nobody was looking for one. One day in 1938 however, a member of one species of coelacanth turned up, just by accident, in a fisherman's net, and alert observers identified it, to everyone's surprise. And Galileo, it appears, just happened to bump into those moons around Jupiter.

1.12 You Start With a Question

Mrs. Smith's sample questions for little scientists show that she's not quite right about the empty mind with which scientists must begin. She was not, despite her words to the contrary, instructing us to go out into the world with completely vacant minds, and just to look at whatever swam into our field of vision. She was actually suggesting some questions which would guide our observation: questions which would constitute some mental content prior to observation.

This is as it must be. For imagine what it would be like to look at some part of the world with nothing in your mind to guide what to pay attention to. Suppose, for example, that the first thing that you notice when leaving school is a bird. Your Smithian instructions are to observe carefully; but what facts do you take note of? You might note that there's an animal in front of you, or that it's a sparrow, or that it's facing north, or that it's on the ground, or that it's a sparrow on the ground, or that it's a sparrow on the ground on Tuesday, or that it's brown, or that it's brown and it's 4 PM, and so on and so on. There are in fact an *infinite* number of facts you might take note of, and if you've followed Mrs. Smith's instructions, and have emptied your mind of everything, you'd have no questions or interests to guide your observation. You'd have your choice of any of this infinite list to take note of. Where should you begin? Nothing is any more important or relevant than anything else. I suppose all you could do would be to try to note as many of these facts as possible. Most of them would have no importance to anyone at all; why are you making this random collection? No scientist—in fact, nobody halfway sane—approaches the world in this way.

If Galileo hadn't already been trained in conventional astronomy, he wouldn't have realized the importance of those little spots around Jupiter. They would have been just as interesting (or boring) as any of the other things he observed. Nothing would have been more or less important than anything else.

It's clear that any scientist must begin with some motivation—at least, with the desire to try to answer some questions rather than any of the infinite number of others. Where does this motivation come from? It can come from any source.

Perhaps some of the story about Galileo's discovery of the moons of Jupiter is simply a matter of random accident. It was just an accident that the telescope was invented when it was, and that one happened to fall into his hands. Perhaps he was just looking at bright things in the sky more or less at random when he bumped into the little spots around Jupiter. But there had to have been all sorts of motives in his psychology for being interested in looking at the night sky, and for being struck by those little spots, and for thinking about them hard, and for drawing anti-Aristotelian conclusions from them, instead of just ignoring them as uninteresting moving spots. Maybe Aristotle reminded him of his hated father, so he had a psychological motive for proving him wrong. Maybe something in his experience as a child turned him against the church, and he harboured a subconscious desire to destroy its teaching. Maybe he wanted to impress his girlfriend with his radical position; maybe he thought that a new astronomical discovery would make him rich. Who knows! And who cares! The point here is that there has to be more in the story than simply an empty-minded desire for truth.

1.13 You Can't Be Completely Open-Minded

Brecht's mathematician who suggested to Galileo that something was wrong with his telescope was basing his view on his prior assumption that there just couldn't be moons going around Jupiter. This is, of course, objectionable closed-mindedness. But note that the alternative to this is not that we should discard every past belief we've ever taken for granted, and merely look. Galileo's observation meant to him that there were moons around Jupiter only *given* his assumption that his telescope really was showing him accurate pictures of things far away, invisible to the naked eye. If Galileo had discarded the assumption about what telescopes do, and the assumption that his was working right, then his experience of looking through the telescope would have meant nothing to him. It can't be that we're supposed to come to each scientific observation completely devoid of any prior belief; if we did, no observation would mean anything at all.

Of course, Galileo's faith in his telescope wasn't exactly a matter of *faith*: it was established already on the basis of other observations. Remember that the telescope was new then, and people had only recently come to believe that it actually showed them enlarged images of otherwise invisible things far away. How did they find that out? We can imagine, for example, that people looked through it at things on Earth, and then went closer to check out directly whether what the telescope showed them was right. It seems funny to us now to wonder about the workings of a telescope and to have to check them out by direct observation, but remember, the telescope was new then. We take it for granted that telescopes do this only because it's been so thoroughly checked out by observations in the past.

But consider this argument. Suppose that it's true that you already have to know something in order for any observation to mean anything to you. Of course, we use knowledge gotten from earlier observations to make later ones meaningful; but those earlier observations themselves presupposed pre-existent knowledge, and so on, all the way back. In order to get started, as infants just beginning to experience the world, we must already have known something, or else those sense-experiences wouldn't have told us anything. And this something could not have come from experience. This line of reasoning appears to prove that not all knowledge comes from sense experience.

1.14 Science is Often More than Just a List of Observed Facts

Once a scientist has chosen a question, and perhaps guided by one or more preliminary hypotheses which might answer this question, observation and experiment are undertaken. What is the result of all of this? Well, a sample question from Mrs. Smith is "What do sparrows eat?" and as the result of our experimental observation, we might decide that they eat mostly small seeds and some bugs. I've noted above that even this conclusion goes some-what beyond what was given in the observation in that it uses measurement and calculation, and that it generalizes beyond what is directly observed. But it doesn't go very far beyond this. What we've learned is a general fact about what sparrows (in general) eat, and while this might be interesting to some people for some reason, it's not representative of the sort of thing that science does at its most basic, important and significant level.

Compare the results of Galileo's observations of the moons of Jupiter, and of his experiments with balls: these led him to develop some very basic *theories* of physics and astronomy, which served to *explain* a great deal of what happens in our world.

What's a theory? What's an explanation? In later chapters, we'll go into these matters.

1.15 Conclusion

I hope it's clear from this introduction that Smithian naïve scientific em-piricism—the conventional position on scientific methodology—has a core of truth to it, but that it's not quite right, and that there are a lot of things to be done to fix it up. Keep it in mind as we proceed through the rest of the book, where we'll be working toward a more adequate view of how science works.

CHAPTER 2

Induction, Deduction, Confirmation

2.1 The Mysterious Box of Coins ▮▮▮▮▮

Imagine that you're digging a hole in your garden one day, and bump into a large wooden box buried there. You can read, painted on the box, the inscription "PENNIES AND QUARTERS". You unearth the box, and pry the lid open. Inside are about a thousand little lumpy items, of more or less the same size, each one so completely encrusted with dirt and corrosion and deposits from groundwater that it's impossible to tell what it is. You take one of these items into the kitchen and begin to wash and scrape and chip off all the accumulated crud. Gradually, it becomes clearer that it's a coin, and after a good deal of scrubbing with metal polish, you can finally see what it is: it's a forty-year old penny.

You go back to the box and look at the contents more carefully. Now you notice that each item in it looks more or less like the one you took out (before you cleaned it). They're no doubt coins too. But you can't tell what sort of coins they are. You suspect that they are all (as the inscription says) quarters and pennies, but in what proportion? The size of the lumpy dirty objects doesn't give you any clue; they vary in size somewhat, but this may be only the result of different amounts of crud covering them.

Now you're faced with a problem about what to do. If they're almost all forty-year old pennies, it wouldn't be worth the effort to clean off any of them. Forty-year old pennies aren't worth much—even 1000 of them would be hardly worth more than their face value, $10—and the huge effort it would take to clean all these coins off wouldn't be repaid by the result. But if a substantial number of the other coins are old quarters, then you have something of value here. Forty years ago they made quarters out of silver, and they're now worth a good deal more than their face value to coin collectors, so it would repay the effort to clean them off.

Is there a reasonable course of action?

Perhaps you might reason as follows. The one you took out was a penny, so the rest of them must be pennies too. It's not worth the effort to clean any more off, so you might as well toss the whole mess into the garbage and forget about it. But this is not very good reasoning. As far as you can tell by looking at the rest of the lumps, they might be pennies or quarters. There's no reason to think that whoever buried the box would have filled it with mostly pennies or mostly quarters, or any particular proportion of each. You do have a little bit of evidence about the box's content, because you've cleaned off one of them and identified it. But finding out what one coin is does not give you very good evidence about what the other ones are. You're just guessing.

There is a very reliable way to find out exactly what all the other coins are, and that is to clean off each one of them, and then just look and see. This has a clear advantage over the first strategy: now you would have complete and perfectly reliable information about what was in the box. But obviously this strategy is a poor one, in that it involves a tremendous amount of effort, which might not be repaid by the result if it turns out they're mostly pennies.

The best strategy is obviously this: take a sample of coins out of the box, and clean them off. You'll then have somewhat more trustworthy information about what's there, but you won't have to put in all the time and energy that would be involved in looking at all of them.

So you take, say, 99 more coins out of the box, and you clean them off. You find in your sample 49 more pennies and 50 quarters. At this point, you're inclined to conclude that the box contains about half pennies and half quarters.

This kind of thinking, in which you come to a conclusion about what's in the box based on what's in your observed sample, is an example of one sort of scientific reasoning. As you've noticed, it works on the basis of observation—as Mrs. Smith and other empiricists insist that science must—but it also goes beyond what's observed.

2.2 Inductive Reasoning

The process of reasoning you had gone through when you came to the conclusion that the box contained about half pennies and half quarters, on the basis of your evidence from examining 100 of them, is called **INDUCTIVE REASONING**. My dictionary defines 'induction' in its sense in logic as "the principle of reasoning to a conclusion about all the members of a class from examination of only a few members of the class; broadly, reasoning from the particular to the general." This definition is okay: this is the way the term is often ordinarily used, but it is old-fashioned. Modern logicians tend to use the term in a different way, which we'll get to in a moment. Your reasoning in thinking about the coin box is clearly a kind of inductive reasoning, as defined in my dictionary, anyway. You're reasoning to a conclusion about all the members of a class (in this context, 'class' means *collection*), namely the collection of 1000 coins in the box, from examination of only a few—100—of the members of this collection.

There are some features of this sort of reasoning which are pretty obvious, but which deserve explicit mention and attention anyway.

First, notice that this is reasoning *from* the given **EVIDENCE** (that the 100 examined coins—the ones in the sample—are 50 pennies and 50 quarters) *to* the **CONCLUSION** (that the box contains about half and half pennies and quarters). The (one or more) statements which tell the evidence you reason from (in this case there is only one statement) are called **PREMISES**. (This word is plural; the singular is **PREMISE**, though it can also be spelled **PREMISS**.) Premises plus a conclusion constitute an **ARGUMENT**. I'm using the word 'argument' in its philosophical sense. In this sense, the word does not mean a nasty disagreement involving shouting and slamming of doors. An argument, philosophically speaking, is one or more premises intended to support a conclusion.

The important point about inductive arguments is this: it's possible that, even though an argument is a good one, starting from true premises and reasoning in the right way, it can give you a false conclusion. It might just be the case, notwithstanding the fact that all the coins you examined were half and half pennies and quarters, that nevertheless all the rest of the coins in the box were pennies, and that you happened to pick all the 50 quarters that were in there. In that case, there would actually be about 950 pennies and 50 quarters in the box, and your conclusion that there were about half and half would be badly wrong. Or, of course, if all or most of the rest of the coins were quarters, your conclusion would have erred badly in the other direction.

Nevertheless, the inductive reasoning we imagined you just used is of some use. It gives you some reason for believing the conclusion. It's *likely* that the box contains about half pennies and half quarters. The premises make it reasonable for you to believe this, even though it could turn out that this is wrong.

2.3 A Better Definition of 'Induction'

These considerations suggest a better definition of 'induction': a good inductive argument is an argument in which the premises give you good reason to believe the conclusion. This is closer to the definition which is used by modern logicians, and it includes some arguments which the old-fashioned definition would exclude. For example, consider this argument:

> PREMISES: Almost all of Sally's boyfriends have been stupid.
> Seymour is Sally's latest boyfriend.
> CONCLUSION: Seymour is stupid.

Notice first that this fits the modern definition for a good inductive argument. If you believed those two premises, you'd have some reason to believe the conclusion. Of course, you might be wrong: Seymour could turn out to be one of those rare things, a boyfriend of Sally's who wasn't stupid. But those premises give you a pretty good reason to think the conclusion is true.

But notice that the argument doesn't fit the old definition of induction, which I got from my dictionary. It doesn't reason to a conclusion about all the members of a class from examination of only a few members. It doesn't reason from the particular to the general. It's rather the other way around. It reasons about a particular member of a class (the class of Sally's boyfriends) from a general statement about the whole class (that almost all of them are stupid).

The reason I'm carrying on at such tedious length about the difference between the old and new definitions is that a lot of students have come across the old definition, and can't get it out of their heads without a lot of prodding. Consider yourself prodded.

EXERCISE

Following are several arguments. Note that they're not arranged in the neat premise/conclusion form that we have been using. (a) Your first job is to figure out which is the conclusion and which are the premises. (Ask yourself: which statement was it the speaker's main intention to establish? Which statements were intended to be reasons for accepting this conclusion?) Arrange them in the neat premise/conclusion form we've been using. (b) Next, estimate how good this argument is as an inductive argument. Do the premises give a strong or weak reason to believe the conclusion? Or no reason at all?

1. Fred must be at the pub. He's gone there every Friday afternoon for the last three years. It's Friday afternoon.

2. That's Fred's hat and coat, over there, on the pub's coat-rack. So Fred must be here in the pub.

3. I've read what must be hundreds of Superman comics over the past few years. In every one of them I've read, Superman wins the battle over evil at the end. He must win in every Superman comic ever made.

4. Cigarettes can't be all that harmful. Granny Carruthers smoked three packs a day every day till she died. She lived to be 95.

5. In some places in Hawaii, it rains almost every night. So Hemingway's greatest novel is *The Sun Also Rises*.

6. Almost every pig can fly. So it's likely that Porky can fly. Because he's a pig.

ANSWERS

1.(a) PREMISES: Fred's gone to the pub every Friday
                     afternoon for the last three years.
                     It's Friday afternoon.
    CONCLUSION: Fred must be at the pub.

(b) This is a pretty good inductive argument. There's lots of evidence that Fred is in the pub now.

2. (a) PREMISE: That's Fred's hat and coat, over there, on the pub's coat-rack.

    CONCLUSION: So Fred must be here in the pub.

(b) This is a pretty good inductive argument too. Note that there's only one premise. Notice that, as in the case of all inductive arguments, it's possible that the conclusion is false despite the truth of the premise. (Maybe Fred left the pub quickly, leaving his hat and coat behind. Possible, but unlikely.)

3. (a) PREMISES: I've read what must be hundreds of Superman comics over the past few years. In every one of them Superman wins the battle over evil at the end.

    CONCLUSION: He must win in every Superman comic ever made.

(b) Again, a pretty good inductive argument, although things can change in comic book land.

4. (a) PREMISE: Granny Carruthers smoked three packs a day every day till she died. She lived to be 95.

    CONCLUSION: Cigarettes can't be all that harmful.

(b) This case is a lousy inductive argument. One case gives hardly any evidence to believe that conclusion.

5. (a) PREMISE: In some places in Hawaii, it rains almost every night.

    CONCLUSION: So Hemingway's greatest novel is *The Sun Also Rises*.

(b) In this case, the premise gives no evidence at all about the conclusion. It appears entirely irrelevant.

6. (a) PREMISES: Almost every pig can fly. Porky is a pig.

    CONCLUSION: So it's likely that Porky can fly.

(b) In this case, the premises give very good evidence for the conclusion.

There's something very important to note about the last exercise. Despite the fact that the premises give strong evidence for the conclusion, you have no reason at all to believe the conclusion. The reason for this is the obvious fact that the first premise is false. No matter how strongly the premises of an inductive argument support the conclusion, the argument won't be any good if one or more of its premises are false.

What this means is that in evaluating an inductive argument, we have to think about two things: (1) are its premises true? (2) do they strongly support the conclusion? I suppose that we should restrict the term 'good inductive argument' to an inductive argument for which both (1) and (2) are the case. We can instead use the term 'strong inductive argument' to refer to any inductive argument in which (2) is the case, whether or not the premises are true. In the examples above, 1, 2, 3, and 6 are *strong* inductive arguments, although 6 clearly isn't a *good* inductive argument.

So here are the final definitions, the ones you should remember:

A STRONG INDUCTIVE ARGUMENT is an argument in which the premises give strong evidence for the conclusion. (As far as strength is concerned, it doesn't matter whether the premises or the conclusion are true or false.)

A WEAK INDUCTIVE ARGUMENT is an argument in which the premises don't give strong evidence for the conclusion. (The truth or falsity of the premises or the conclusion are both irrelevant here again.)

A GOOD INDUCTIVE ARGUMENT is a strong inductive argument with true premises.

EXERCISES
Provide examples of one-premise arguments of the following sorts:

1. A strong inductive argument with a false premise and a false conclusion.

2. A strong inductive argument with a false premise and a true conclusion.

3. A weak inductive argument with a true premise and a true conclusion.

4. A good inductive argument with a false conclusion.

STOP!

ANSWERS

1. PREMISE: Elvis's fingerprints were discovered on the weapon that killed Nicole Simpson.
   CONCLUSION: Elvis murdered Nicole Simpson.

Stop here and think about the answer provided. Do you see why this is a strong inductive argument? It's because *if* that premise were true, then it would be very likely that the conclusion was true. That premise would provide very good support for the conclusion. Of course, the premise is false, so in fact it doesn't give us good reason to believe that conclusion. The conclusion is also, by the way, obviously false.

2. PREMISE: Elvis showed up in the police station covered with Nicole Simpson's blood, and said, "I murderedher!"
   CONCLUSION: Nicole Simpson was murdered.

Here again, if that premise were true, it would give us a good reason to believe the conclusion. So the argument is inductively strong. But the premise is again false, so this argument doesn't in fact justify its conclusion. The conclusion is in fact true, and we have good reason to believe it. However, the good reason isn't given by this premise.

3. PREMISE: O.J. Simpson owned a white Bronco.
   CONCLUSION: Nicole Simpson was murdered.

Here we already know that the premise and the conclusion are true. However, the premise offers no reason at all to believe the conclusion: it's irrelevant. This is a very weak inductive argument.

4. PREMISE: Sally and Fred both have blue eyes.
   CONCLUSION: All children of Sally and Fred have blue eyes.

You might be aware of the genetic principles involved in this argument that make it very likely that a child of two blue-eyed parents will have blue eyes. But even though it's very likely, it's possible that it's false. In very rare cases blue-eyed parents can have children who aren't blue-eyed. This happens to be one of them: Seymour, Fred and Sally's son, is brown-eyed.

2.4 Deduction

A good inductive argument provides good evidence for its conclusion, but, as we've seen in the last exercise, no matter how good the evidence for the conclusion, it's always possible that the conclusion is false. This is an important fact that we'll be remarking on several times.

There is, however, a different sort of argument in which the truth of the premises doesn't just make the truth of the conclusion more likely—it *guarantees* the truth of the conclusion. In this different sort of argument, if the premises are true, the conclusion *must* be true. Here's an example:

PREMISES: All fish breathe under water with gills.
                     Flounders are a kind of fish.
CONCLUSION: All flounders breathe under water with gills.

When you're thinking about this example, ignore whether or not the premises are true, or what evidence there is for them. Concentrate on the fact that if those premises are true, then that conclusion would have to be true also. It's logically impossible that the premises be true while the conclusion is false.

Here are some more examples of this sort of argument:

PREMISES: If it rains on Tuesday, the picnic is off.
                     It's raining.
                     It's Tuesday.
CONCLUSION: The picnic is off.

PREMISES: None of Fred's skateboards is cool.
                     Sally has borrowed a cool skateboard.
CONCLUSION: The skateboard Sally has borrowed isn't Fred's.

PREMISES: The filling in this Twinkie tastes wonderful.
Real whipped cream tastes terrible.
CONCLUSION: The filling in this Twinkie isn't real whipped cream.

Notice again that as far as "the logic" of these arguments is concerned, it doesn't matter whether any statement in them is actually true or false. All that matters is whether it's the case that *if* the premises were all true, then the conclusion *couldn't* be false.

All of the above are examples of deductive reasoning. In a good deductive argument, true premises guarantee a true conclusion. Now look at this argument:

PREMISES: All chickens are mammals.
All mammals are green.
CONCLUSION: All chickens are green.

You know that all the premises in this argument are false, and so is the conclusion. Nevertheless, the "logic" of this deductive argument is okay: if the premises were true, then the conclusion would have to be true too.

So the situation with deductive arguments is analogous to the one already described with inductive ones. Remember that the *strength* of an inductive argument had to do only with the logical relationship between the premises and the conclusion, and ignored whether or not the premises were true. In the case of deductive reasoning, the analogous measure which ignores the truth or falsity of the premises is validity.

An argument is **DEDUCTIVELY VALID** when it's impossible that the premises be true but the conclusion false. That is: in every valid deductive argument, if the premises were true, then the conclusion would have to be true.

As we've seen, we can have valid deductive arguments with one or more false premises. The chicken argument above is an example of this. Despite the fact that this argument is deductively valid, it doesn't tell us that the conclusion is true, because the premises are false. The only deductively valid argument which in fact does guarantee the truth of its conclusion is one in which the premises are all true. An argument of this sort is called a **DEDUCTIVELY SOUND** argument.

Now we've got four technical terms. Please look them over again and try to master them. They all have precise meanings, and we're going to have occasion to use them again.

EXERCISE

Classify each of the following arguments as one of:
  deductively valid
  deductively sound
  strong inductive
  good inductive

1. Polar bears are plentiful in Florida. So we'll bag one if we go hunting there.

2. In leap years, February has 29 days. In 1997, February has 28 days. So 1997 isn't a leap year.

3. The odds of winning a big-payoff lottery are very small. So if you buy a ticket to a big-payoff lottery, you won't win.

4. Toronto has a larger population than Hong Kong. Hong Kong has a larger population than Moose Jaw. So Toronto has a larger population than Moose Jaw.

ANSWERS

1. This is a fairly strong inductive argument: the truth of the premise would be pretty good evidence for the truth of the conclusion. Obviously, however, the premise isn't true, so this is not a good inductive argument. Note that this argument is not deductively valid: if the premise were true, the conclusion could still be false.

2. This argument is deductively valid: if the premises were true, then the conclusion couldn't be false. And the premises are true, so the argument is also deductively sound.

3. This is a fairly strong inductive argument: when the odds of something happening are very low, you've got good reason to conclude that it won't happen. But this conclusion could be false, so this is not a valid deductive argument. The premise is in fact true, so this is a good inductive argument.

4. Be careful on this one. The argument is deductively valid. If A is bigger than B, and if B is bigger than C, then A has to be bigger than C. But one of these premises is false: Toronto does not have a larger population than Hong Kong. This means that the argument is not deductively sound. What may confuse you about this judgement is that the conclusion is true.

EXERCISE

If you're familiar with Sherlock Holmes stories, consider the kind of reasoning he's so good at. He often speaks of his reasoning as "deductive". Is he right?

If you're not familiar with these stories, consider this example, which is rather like the kind of argument Sherlock produced:

> There's a footprint on the floor next to the murder victim made by a very peculiarly-shaped sole.
> The only place you can buy shoes which make that sort of footprint is China.
> Therefore the murderer must have been to China.

Is this deductive reasoning?

ANSWER

No, it's inductive.

Those premises do give evidence for the conclusion, but it's nevertheless possible that the conclusion is false even if (or even though) the premises are true. It's an inductive argument. I suppose, under the circumstances, it's a fairly strong one, although probably not strong enough to convince a jury to convict.

EXERCISE

Is this a valid deductive argument?

> Fred is always either in the library or in the pub at three in the afternoon.
> It's three in the afternoon on Thursday.
> Fred never goes to the library on Thursdays.
> Asunción is the capital of Paraguay.
> Therefore Fred is in the pub.

ANSWER

Yes, it's a valid deductive argument.

What's peculiar here is, of course, that fourth premise. What's it doing in here? Dunno. Nevertheless, if all those premises were true, then the conclusion would have to be true, so it's a valid deductive argument. The fourth premise is, however, irrelevant. If it were left out, the argument would still be a valid deductive argument. This is not the case for any of the other premises. The fact that some premises of a valid deductive argument are relevant while some may not be is one that will be important later. Remember it.

2.5 Why Use Induction?

Deductive reasoning, when done correctly (validly), and when you happen to start with true premises, will guarantee the truth of the conclusion; however, inductive reasoning, when done correctly from true premises, will not. In this respect, deductive reasoning is superior to inductive reasoning. Despite the fact that the premises of a well-constructed (very strong) inductive argument are true, the conclusion might just be false. To return to the example at the start of this chapter, despite the fact that there are half pennies and half quarters in your sample, the box might contain a huge majority of one or the other.

Why use inductive reasoning then? Well, our coin-box case is an example in which a strategy using inductive reasoning is better. What would a deductive argument for the conclusion that there are half pennies and half quarters in the coin box look like? Well, here's one:

PREMISES:	There are 1000 coins in the box.
	Coin #1 is a penny
	Coin #2 is a penny
	Coin #3 is a quarter
	Coin #4 is a quarter
	Coin #5 is a penny
	...
	Coin #998 is a quarter
	Coin #999 is a penny
	Coin #1000 is a quarter
CONCLUSION:	The box contains half pennies and half quarters.

This argument, we imagine, contains 1001 premises; 500 of these premises identify pennies and 500 quarters. (The "..." in the middle marks where I've left out a lot of these premises.) You should be able to see why this argument is deductively valid: if the premises are all true, then the conclusion must be true.

How would we know the truth of all these premises? I suppose we'd just have to take out each of the 1000 lumps in the box and clean off each one.

Now compare this to an inductive argument we might use, in which we reason to a slightly different conclusion, that the box contains *about* half pennies and half quarters, on the basis of a sample of, say, 100 coins. There are two ways in which this is not as good an argument as the deductive one: (1) Its conclusion is weaker than the conclusion of the deductive argument. Its conclusion is that the box contains *about* half pennies and half quarters, whereas the deductive argument permitted the much more precise conclusion that the box contained *exactly* half pennies and half quarters. (2) The conclusion of the inductive argument is made likely by its premises, but it might be wrong (if the sample we cleaned off was highly unrepresentative of the rest of the contents of the box). The deductive argument, however, guarantees the truth of its conclusion.

The inductive argument isn't worthless: it does give us some reason to believe its conclusion. But why rely on induction, when a more precise conclusion can be established with certainty by a deductive argument?

The answer is obvious: practicality. It's far too much trouble—more trouble than it seems to be worth—to examine every coin in the box. We'll get some fairly good information from the small sample, and that's good enough for us.

A sound deductive argument often requires much more information, and it would be too costly, in this case, to get all that information. Science uses inductive reasoning all the time, because the corresponding deductive argument would require information that's unavailable or too costly (and thus not worth it) to obtain.

Here's an example of a very similar sort of inductive reasoning at work in science—an example which, for some reason, shows up very frequently in discussions of the logic of science. Europeans found swans in many countries, and all of them that were observed were white. They concluded on the basis of this sample that all swans were white. This was a completely acceptable form of inductive reasoning, under the circumstances. But it turned out to give a false conclusion: when they explored Australia, they discovered black swans there. Even though it didn't work in this case, inductive reasoning was the proper tool to use, and they used it in the right way. They were interested in finding out what colour swans were, and the deductive argument with a conclusion about what colour(s) all swans were was impossible to obtain, because they couldn't look at *all* swans. They had to reason only on the basis of the information that was available.

2.6 Induction in Science

The kind of inductive reasoning we were looking at in the coin-box case is reasoning from a sample. Science uses inductive reasoning all the time, especially reasoning from a sample. Reasoning from a sample might be used to answer questions like these:

- What percentage of stars exist in double-star clusters?
- What proportion of the voting population in Québec is now inclined to vote Liberal?
- How prevalent is rabies among the raccoon population in Saskatoon?
- How many Catholic couples practise birth control?
- What proportion of Canadian single working women have an income of over $20,000?
- How many North Americans now have the flu?
- Do sparrows eat insects? If so, what proportion of their diet is insects?

And so on. You might try noticing just how often scientific findings are based on this sort of induction by (for example) reading the little reports of social and natural science discoveries in the newspaper. In the process, you might also notice that there are many instances of (nevertheless inductive) scientific reasoning which do not fit the patterns we've been looking at.

2.7 The Imperfection of Science

Induction is the central kind of scientific reasoning. An acceptable inductive argument with true premises may give a false conclusion. These two facts, taken together, imply that acceptable scientific reasoning can, and sometimes does, yield false conclusions. The black-swan case is one of many real-life examples of this. As we've seen, however, a strong inductive argument is one in which the premises give good evidence for the conclusion. Note carefully that we can have good evidence for something that nevertheless turns out, in fact, to be false. So the big news is that science is imperfect: sometimes, even when it's working exactly as is should be, it tells us false things. Well, ho hum, everyone knows this: I'm sure even Mrs. Smith, science's most enthusiastic fan, is willing to admit it.

But this is not a reason to toss science into the trash can. Science does, of course, often give us good evidence to believe its conclusions, and often this is the best, under the circumstances, we can hope for. Good evidence can be very good—so good that everyone ought to believe what it shows. It can be **CONCLUSIVE** —that is, good enough to justify believing the conclusion— so good that rational people can *conclude* an investigation and consider the case settled. Good evidence is certainly much better than no evidence at all. The alternatives to science—for example, the "evidence" of dreams, or of pseudo-sciences like astrology, or mere guesswork—provide no evidence at all. A good inductive argument is much better than any lousy argument. It offers us, under the circumstances, the best bet at finding out the truth (though not a sure bet). And, as Mrs. Smith insisted, truth is what we're after.

2.8 Stronger and Weaker Inductive Arguments

Let's return to our coin box. The strategy we were considering involved drawing a conclusion about all the coins in the box from an examination of 100 of them. These 100 coins provide some evidence about the rest of the coins in the box, but you might (if it were worth the trouble) have gotten better evidence than this by examining more coins. If you examined 200 coins and found that about 100 of them were pennies and about 100 of them quarters, you'd have stronger evidence that the coin box contained about half and half. Conversely, if you had examined only 50 coins and found 25 pennies and 25 quarters, your evidence that the box contained about half and half would be weaker. We can say, then, that inductive arguments come with various degrees of strength: some are stronger than others, in that the premises make the conclusion more probably true—they give stronger evidence for the conclusion.

This feature of inductive arguments is not, of course, shared by deductive arguments. A valid deductive argument (with true premises) always gives perfect assurance of the truth of the conclusion: there is no question of degrees of strength of evidence in deductive arguments.

The size of the sample affects the strength of the evidence we have. But there's another factor that affects the strength. Suppose that all 100 of the coins you examined were taken off the top of the pile. Maybe whoever put the coins in the box put mixed pennies and quarters on top, but all quarters on the bottom. So the sample you took off the top would have contained half and half, and would not be representative of the total content of the box, which would be mostly quarters. The evidence you have for the half-and-half conclusion would be better if you took coins from all over in the box: if you took some from the top, some from the bottom, some from the middle, and so on.

Two factors, then, influence how strong the evidence is: the size of the sample, and the "representativeness" it's likely to have of what's in the box. You can increase the strength of your evidence by taking a larger sample, or by taking pains to make sure your sample is likely to be representative. We'll discuss each of these matters separately, and at length. But before we do, it's worth noting that although each of these would give you better evidence for what's in the box, it's not necessarily a good idea for you to do either. Taking a bigger sample would involve more work cleaning off the lumps, and even though the evidence you'd get would be better, this might not be worth the effort. Suppose that all the lumps in the box are firmly stuck together, and it would be much more trouble to get ones out from the middle or the bottom of the box. Or suppose that the grayish lumps were much harder to clean, so you didn't want to look at many of them. Because it's not at all sure that the color has any relation to the contents, it might not be worthwhile to make the effort to clean more of them.

More evidence usually comes at a cost, and maybe it's not worth the cost. There are all sorts of considerations to be taken into account when calculating what's worth the cost and what's not. Under the circumstances, the evidence you get from looking at 100 small lumps from the top might be good enough, and better evidence about what's in the box might not be worth the trouble. There's a trade-off here: better evidence against more trouble collecting evidence. You need to make some sort of decision about how far to go to increase the strength of the evidence you will get.

There's more to be said about the sort of selection procedure which will improve the strength of the evidence, and much more to be said about the relation between sample size and strength of evidence. These will be discussed in chapters to come.

2.9 Confirmation

CONFIRMATION for a statement is reason to believe it. A statement is confirmed to the extent that there's reason to believe it, to the extent that there's something that makes it likely (or certain) to be true. You can get confirmation just by looking and seeing that something is the case. For example, when I look out the window, I have confirmation that today is sunny. Looking at what's inside each lump in the coin box confirms that the box contains half pennies and half quarters. But you can also get indirect confirmation. This is when you have evidence, when you use an inductive argument. The premises of an inductive argument provide confirmation for the conclusion. Thus, the 100 coins you examine from the box confirm that the box contains half pennies and half quarters, indirectly, from inductive evidence.

The word 'confirmation' as used by philosophers and scientists is a technical term. Its implications are somewhat different from those you might associate with its ordinary use.

First of all, in ordinary talk when you say that something is "confirmed" by evidence, you tend to mean that it's something that was already suspected, and that the evidence gives more reason to think it's true. But the way we're using the term, it's not necessarily the case that what's confirmed by evidence is something you already suspected. When evidence is found about who did the murder or about the prevalence of rabies in the raccoon population, the conclusion that's inductively supported might have previously been unsuspected, although one can also speak about finding confirmation for what is already believed or suspected.

Secondly, the word 'confirmation' might suggest to you that what is said to be confirmed is shown to be definitely true—to be made *certain* by evidence. The way philosophers use this term, however, the evidence which constitutes confirmation of a statement need not make that statement *certainly* true. A very strong inductive argument whose premises are quite certain will give enough evidence to satisfy anyone that the conclusion is true:

it may be "conclusive" in the sense that the investigation can be concluded, and we can believe the conclusion without doubt. Remember, however, that where there's only inductive evidence for a conclusion, there's always some possibility that the conclusion is false despite the truth of the premises. Some statements are conclusively confirmed by evidence (although they just might be false). Some statements are only weakly confirmed by evidence. Not every inductive argument gives conclusive justification for its conclusion. Where the premises give relatively weak evidence for the conclusion, or where the truth of one or more premises is itself in some doubt, then there's rational doubt about the conclusion. But when there's some evidence for a conclusion, even when that evidence is weak, then we say that the evidence confirms the conclusion, if only weakly.

A third point to notice about confirmation is that philosophers speak of confirmation of a statement even when that statement is false. There can be evidence for false statements, as readers of detective novels are aware. Even after we find out that a statement is definitely false, we nevertheless admit that there was some evidence in its favour, and that it was to some degree confirmed.

2.10 Confirmation and Disconfirmation ████████████

Getting evidence that a statement is false is called **DISCONFIRMING** it. You should note carefully that disconfirming a statement is different from merely failing to confirm it. Imagine, for example, that you suspect you left your keys in a drawer, so you open it and push all the mess inside around a bit trying to find them. If they appear, then you've gotten conclusive confirmation of your suspicion. But suppose that after a few seconds of moving things around, they don't appear. Then you've failed to confirm your suspicion, but you haven't disconfirmed it—not to any large extent, anyway, and surely not conclusively. They might be in that huge pile of stuff in the drawer anyway. Maybe they came into view but you didn't notice them. Maybe you just didn't look long enough.

Sometimes confirming a statement calls for different procedures than disconfirming it. In order to disconfirm the statement that your keys are in the drawer, a thorough search, not just a random shuffle-through, might be necessary.

It's not always the case (as it is here) that confirming a statement is easier than disconfirming it. You can easily disconfirm the statement that today will be sunny all day by looking outside right now and seeing that it's cloudy and rainy. But if that statement is true, you'll have to observe the weather all day long. Notice that statements which claim the existence of something are often confirmable by a single observation—when you see it— whereas a longer and more thorough search is necessary to disconfirm it. General statements of the form "Every X is a Y" may be disconfirmed easily by finding one X which isn't a Y, whereas a more thorough search may be necessary to confirm them.

2.11 Indirect and Direct Confirmation and Disconfirmation

The simplest way to disconfirm (or confirm) any statement is simply to look and see if it's false or true. This is sometimes possible. But sometimes instead of direct observation, we must use indirect methods which accumulate evidence for the statement's truth or falsity. These are cases in which what is confirmed will be the conclusion of an inductive argument, with the premises stating the evidence. The coin box we've been thinking about is a case in which getting indirect evidence for the proportion of quarters and pennies in the box is more practical than looking and seeing what's inside each lump.

Consider this example. Suppose you're thinking of going to the pub this afternoon, but you think it might be closed. They have no phone, and you don't want to walk over to see—to confirm or disconfirm the statement that it's open *directly*—because it's a long trip and you don't want to run the risk of walking over there without a cold beer at the end. You believe that Seymour will be in the pub if it's open. You can easily telephone his house; if he's home, this will provide conclusive indirect confirmation for you that the pub is closed.

EXERCISE
If Seymour's at home, this confirms that the pub is closed. If he's not home, does this disconfirm that suspicion?

ANSWER

No. Remember, all you know is that Seymour will be in the pub if it's open. If it's closed he might be at home, but he might be somewhere else too. The fact that he's not at home doesn't show that it's false that the pub is closed.

STOP!

So your telephoning him may provide conclusive confirmation that the pub is closed, but it can't provide anywhere near this strength of evidence to disconfirm this suspicion.

Indirect confirmation or disconfirmation often is more dubitable than direct. Observing that Seymour is home provides confirmation for you that the pub is closed, but it does so only given the **SUBSIDIARY INFORMATION** you believe: that he'd be in the pub if it were open. If you have any doubts about this subsidiary information, then you should also doubt the conclusion you draw, that the pub is closed. There's a possibility that this subsidiary belief you have is wrong; and this possibility transfers to the conclusion that you think is sufficiently confirmed by your evidence.

I'm not implying that every process of direct confirmation is utterly doubt-free. People are sometimes mistaken also in what they think they find out directly. For example, you might look at someone and think it's Zelda, but it's not. Maybe it was too dark for you to get a good look. Maybe you're not very good at identifying people. Maybe you're hallucinating, or dreaming. But usually we take information we get from direct observation to be reliable, and usually it is. When conditions of observation are good, and it's the sort of thing we think we're reasonably skilled at finding out by looking, then to harbour doubts about it would just be neurotic. Reasonable people take direct observation, under these good conditions, to be conclusive (that is, to be good enough to warrant concluding the investigation). Sometimes they're wrong, but usually they're right.

Direct observation isn't perfect, but it's often more reliable than indirect confirmation or disconfirmation. Notice that when we indirectly confirm or disconfirm something, we're going to have to do some sort of direct observation anyway. When you find out that the pub is closed indirectly, you have to find out that Seymour is home by direct observation, by seeing that he's there. So both direct and indirect confirmation/disconfirmation share whatever doubts are raised by the fallibility of direct observation. But indirect confirmation/disconfirmation has an additional source of fallibility: maybe the subsidiary belief is wrong. Nevertheless, the practicality of indirect confirmation/disconfirmation, compared to the direct method, often makes it preferable.

You have an enormous pile of particular beliefs. They may include the following:

- Baltimore is in Maryland.
- The First World War killed a lot of people.
- Brazil produces coffee.
- Your great-grandmother was born in Europe.
- There's a spiral nebula in Andromeda.
- Your car contains a driver's side air bag.

It's probable that you believe these things, and a whole lot of other things, because somebody you take to be reliable told you they were so. This is, of course, another kind of indirect confirmation, and there's nothing wrong with it. Think of how impoverished your beliefs would be if you restricted yourself to direct confirmation (or disconfirmation).

The comparative practicality of indirect confirmation/disconfirmation of particular statements is one reason we sometimes use it. There are other reasons: it's impossible for you to have direct confirmation/disconfirmation of statements about what happened before you were born, or about what's going on in places you can't get to. Some statements require expertise on the part of the observer, and if you don't have that expertise, you're just going to have to confirm/disconfirm them indirectly, on the basis of what that person says, or in some other indirect way.

2.12 Indirect Confirmation/Disconfirmation in Science

Consider how Galileo found out that there were moons around Jupiter. Did he do so directly, just by looking and seeing? Well, in a sense he did: he just looked through his telescope. But in another sense, he didn't. His evidence that there were moons there depended on subsidiary information about how a telescope works. If Galileo didn't think that telescopes provide enlarged views of distant things, then he wouldn't have come to the conclusion he did. In a sense, then, what he "directly saw" were little white spots in the image given by his telescope. Given his subsidiary information, he took this as evidence that there were large moons out there, near Jupiter.

A good deal of what scientists observe is done by means of instruments. Imagine a scientist collecting observations: you'll probably see, in your mind's eye, a person in a laboratory or in the field surrounded by measuring and recording instruments. This scientist is performing indirect confirmation/disconfirmation, and this is the rule, not the exception, in real science.

A scientist might, for example, find out that the pressure inside a container is 1850 kg/sq. cm, but this wouldn't be found out by simply "looking and seeing" the magnitude of the pressure, or even by "feeling" it. It would be determined indirectly.

EXERCISE

A scientist directly sees the dial on an instrument pointing to 1850 kg/sq. cm. What subsidiary information is involved in the inference that the pressure inside the container is 1850 kg/sq. cm?

ANSWER

- The mechanism inside this sort of measuring device makes the pointer on the dial move in a way corresponding to the pressure in the container it's connected to.
- This measuring device is working.
- The device is connected in the right way to the container whose pressure we want to measure.

This subsidiary information is not always something that can be taken for granted. There's a story circulating around my university about a scientist here who years ago got a surprising reading off his instruments. Assuming that the instruments worked the way everyone thought they did, and that they were in working order and connected correctly to what they were measuring, this would confirm a statement in conflict with some basic scientific beliefs. Sensibly, he decided that there was something wrong in these subsidiary beliefs, so he tried to fix his instruments, and adjust how they were measuring things. But he had no success: those strange readings kept turning up. He eventually abandoned the project as a failure. Another scientist, a little later, got the same readings, trusted his instruments, and got the Nobel Prize for revolutionizing a basic area of this science.

CHAPTER 3

Sampling

3.1 Reasoning About Proportions

Recall the list of sample scientific questions given in the last chapter:

- What percentage of stars exist in double-star clusters?
- What proportion of the voting population in Québec is now inclined to vote Liberal?
- How prevalent is rabies among the raccoon population in Saskatoon?
- How many Catholic couples practise birth control?
- What proportion of Canadian single working women have an income of over $20,000?
- What proportion of the sparrow's diet is insects?
- How many North Americans now have the flu?
- And, of course: what percentage of coins in the box are quarters?

These questions have a couple of things in common:

(1) they ask us to consider a certain group of things:

- stars
- the voting population in Québec
- raccoons in Saskatoon
- Catholic couples
- Canadian single working women
- the sparrow's diet
- North Americans
- coins in the coin box

We're going to call the general group of things which is relevant to a particular question the **POPULATION**. Note that 'population' does not refer merely to a group of people: it can be a group of anything. We're going to call the things which make up the population **INDIVIDUALS**. Of course, these 'individuals' can be things other than people.

(2) they ask us to consider a certain characteristic which may be had by some percentage of individuals in a certain population:

- being in a double-star cluster
- being inclined to vote Liberal
- having rabies
- practising birth control
- having an income of over $20,000
- being an insect
- having the flu
- being a quarter

We're going to call the characteristic in question a **PROPERTY**. All these questions, then, ask what proportion of individuals in a population have a property. In some cases, the answer might turn out to be 100% or 0%; in many cases, the answer, we expect, would turn out to be somewhere in between.

One of the questions, "How many Catholic couples practise birth control?" might be construed as asking for a number; for example, '5 million', rather than a percentage, such as '54%'. But it turns out that in order to answer this question, we're first going to have to get an answer in terms of percentage; and then, if we know how many Catholic couples there are, we can calculate the number.

It's conceivable that someone might try to answer each of these questions in a Mrs. Smithian sort of way by just looking at every individual in the population. But some of the populations are too large to make looking at every individual possible. If there are lots of raccoons in Saskatoon, you won't be able to look at all of them. In some cases, we lack the technology to look at some members of the population (we can only "see" a limited number of stars). In some cases, we might, if we wanted to, look at every member of the population, but it would be too costly in terms of money or trouble or time to do so, and probably not worth it. (The coin box is an example of this.)

So the sensible way of going about trying to answer these questions is to look at a limited number of individuals in the population: we observe a **SAMPLE** of the individuals in the population. We use the observed information about the proportion of the property in the sample as inductive evidence about the proportion of the property in the population.

3.2 A Sample of Stars

As we've already seen, inductive evidence can have degrees of strength. In the sort of case we've been looking at, the inductive evidence is the information about the sample. This is evidence for the conclusion about the proprotion of the property in the population. The evidence the sample gives us for a conclusion about the population might be weaker or stronger. And one factor that would make evidence stronger or weaker is the degree to which the sample is representative of the population. It might be so weak that we would say that it's just about no evidence at all.

A **REPRESENTATIVE SAMPLE** is a sample that is likely to have close to the same proportion of the property as the population.

Imagine that you're an astronomer who is trying to figure out what proportion of stars are in double-star clusters. You pick a convenient small region of the sky, where you can see, say, 1000 stars through your telescope, and you count how many of these stars are in double-star clusters. Suppose that 50 of them—5%—are in double-star clusters. You conclude that about 5% of stars—of *all* stars, not just the ones you observe—are in double-star clusters. Now, it's obvious that this conclusion might be badly wrong if the sample was not representative of stars in general. Maybe the particular region of the sky you happened to look at was particularly rich, or particularly poor, in double-star clusters. This possibility undermines the evidence somewhat, and other astronomers might object to the conclusion as being insufficiently justified by the evidence you have given.

One way you might provide a conclusion on the basis of better evidence is to look at more than 1000 stars. But even with a sample of just 1000 stars, you could get better evidence. You could pick your 1000 stars from several regions of the sky. You can travel to Australia, to include some stars in your sample that were invisible from the Northern Hemisphere. That might serve somewhat to alleviate doubts that you had happened to choose your sample from a region particularly poor or rich in double-star clusters.

But other questions can be raised. Suppose, for example, that you chose to take a look at only brighter stars, because those would be the ones you could survey using a conveniently short exposure on the photographic plate attached to your telescope. Now, the stars that look brighter from Earth are the ones that are closer to us or are brighter in themselves (in "absolute" brightness). It's possible that the region nearer the Earth is richer or poorer in double-star clusters than other regions; and it's possible that the stars with greater absolute brightness tend to occur in double-star clusters more or less often than others.

Well, you could do something to make your evidence stronger in these respects too, though it might take more money and time. Instead of examining only the brightest ones your telescope could see, you could pick the stars to examine without regard to brightness. You could, for example, pick your sample so that it contained stars with a wide variety of brightness; you could even pick them so that they were representative (to some extent) of the distance and absolute brightness of all the stars visible from Earth. Of course, there's a limit to how representative you could make your sample in this respect. Some stars are simply too far away or too dim to be seen (or, even if they can be seen, they're too far away or too dim for you to tell whether they're in double-star clusters or not). This produces a limit on how good the evidence can be, and you can't overcome this limit; better technology will, presumably, make for better evidence in the future.

Remember, however, that getting the best evidence you can is not necessarily a good idea. Maybe it would take such high-technology techniques, or such involved and lengthy procedures, to include certain very dim stars in your sample, that it simply wouldn't be worth it. It would cost too much money, and take up too much time, to produce what might be only a small improvement in the strength of your evidence. As always, there's a trade-off between strength of evidence and cost. Every scientist must make a decision on where the appropriate solution to this dilemma lies.

3.3 Polling Québecois

Here's another example to illustrate the same thing. Imagine that the Liberal Party of Québec hires you to find out what proportion of Québecois of voting age are now inclined to vote Liberal. You don't have the time or budget to ask all of them—there are millions—so you decide to pick a sample of 1000, to get inductive evidence about the whole population. (Is 1000 a good number to pick? Later on we'll talk about the significance of sample size.) How should you pick your sample?

Suppose you spent several Saturdays hanging around the shopping mall near your home in suburban Montréal, stopping passing people and asking them how they would vote if the election were held now; and you did this until you got 1000 people who would answer you. You find that 421 of them would now be inclined to vote Liberal, so you report to the Party that about 42% of the voting population are now Liberal-inclined.

EXERCISE
Is the evidence you've obtained strong evidence?

ANSWER
No. (Think about why before you read on.)

It's quite clear that your scientific technique has much to be desired here—that your conclusion is based on evidence that is quite weak—because there are good reasons to think that your sample is unrepresentative.

When we say that your sample is 'unrepresentative', what we might mean is that the proportion of Liberal voters in it is quite different from the proportion in the whole population in question. This, of course, makes your sample worthless. However, you can't directly go about making your sample 'representative' in this sense by insuring that it shows the same proportion of Liberal-inclined people as the whole population, because you don't know what the proportion in the population is. That's what you're trying to find out. Similarly, your critics can't object that your sample is unrepresentative because it contains a different proportion of Liberal-inclined voters than the whole population, because they don't know this either. Everyone must base their judgment of the representativeness of your sample—and thus on the strength of your evidence—on other, more indirect considerations. Like what?

Here are some suggested criticisms. The way you chose your sample means that it's likely that it contains a much higher proportion of middle-class people than the population as a whole, because this mall contains mid-range stores likely to be avoided by both rich people and poor people. Why is this criticism relevant? Because one might suspect that voting patterns tend to differ according to economic class: rich people, middle-class people, and poor people might tend to have different proportions of Liberal-inclined voters. Your sample might very well consist of a far higher proportion of middle-class people than the population as a whole, and it might by consequence show a far different proportion of Liberal-inclined voters than the population as a whole.

It's easy to think of other properties whose proportion in your sample may differ considerably from the whole population.

EXERCISE
Try to make a list of some others.

ANSWER
You may have included some of the following in your list. There may be some items on your list which are good ones, but which I haven't mentioned.

- Because women go to malls more than men, maybe your sample contains a higher proportion of women than the voting population as a whole.
- Because, as we all know, teenagers are notorious mall-rats, your sample may contain a larger proportion of teenagers than there is in the voting population in Québec.
- Because this mall is located in suburban Montréal, it may contain a larger proportion of suburbanites, and of city-dwellers, than the whole population.
- It almost certainly contains a larger proportion of people who have their homes near Montréal than the whole population.
- Perhaps it contains a smaller percentage of farmers, and a larger percentage of middle-management people, than the population.
- Maybe this mall contains a higher (or lower) proportion of French-speakers than the general Québec population; if so, your sample might contain a proportion of French speakers far from the proportion in the population.
- Because you speak English much better than you speak French, probably you got more English-speakers to answer your question than French-speakers.

This list consists in what I shall call **SECONDARY PROPERTIES**. These are properties other than the one in question (the **PRIMARY PROPERTY** —the one we started off being interested in—in this case, disposition to vote Liberal). It's not hard to construct a list of secondary properties like this, but the important point for our purposes is to see exactly why and how secondary properties are relevant. To do this, let's consider a secondary property whose proportion in your sample certainly differs from its proportion in the whole population: being out of one's house on a Saturday. It's certain that 100% of the people in your sample left their homes on Saturday, and it's also certain that less than 100% of the voters in Québec did. But this isn't a relevant consideration. Why not? Because there's no reason to think that the percentage of Liberal-inclined people among those who left their homes that Saturday would be higher or lower than among those who didn't.

What we're doing then, when we're raising relevant criticisms of the representativeness of the sample, is finding secondary properties which, it's reasonable to think, are like this:

(1) The proportion of that secondary property may be somewhat higher or lower in the sample than in the population; *and*

(2) individuals with that secondary property may be either somewhat more, or somewhat less, likely to show the primary property.

Sometimes, it may be *known* that some secondary property has both characteristics (1) and (2). For example, it's quite clear—nobody could doubt—that the mall will contain a higher proportion of people who live in or around Montréal than the general population. Similarly, it has been very well established by past voting statistics that the population living in or around Montréal has a larger proportion of Liberal voters than the general population of Québec. When (1) and (2) are both known about a certain other property, and when the differences in proportion in (1) and (2) are large enough to make an appreciable difference, then pointing this out will be a definitely relevant and often devastating criticism. The fact that your sample contained only people in a mall in Montréal, then, is a criticism which shows that your evidence for your conclusion is so weak that it gives no grounds at all for believing your conclusion.

At other times, however, it is just *suspected* that the secondary property has both characteristics (1) and (2). It might be the case, for example, that your sample contains a much higher proportion of teenagers than the population as a whole, and it might be the case that teenagers have different voting habits from the rest of the voting population. Nobody knows either of these things for sure. So this objection is not quite so strong: it casts some doubts on your conclusion, but maybe not enough doubt to encourage us to discount it altogether. Because it does raise some doubts, however, it means that we should regard your evidence as weaker, by consequence. Even though it isn't sure that a secondary property has both characteristics (1) and (2), if it's *possible* that it does—if it's reasonable to think that it *might*—then pointing out this secondary property does cast some doubt on the strength of your reasoning, and justifies us in thinking that it's somewhat weaker. Only when we're pretty sure that a secondary property doesn't have both (1) and (2) is it irrelevant.

3.4 One Way to Get a Representative Sample

Well, all these criticisms made you see that your poll was really not much good, so you've decided to do it again, better this time. It's possible to do this in two ways. In this chapter, we'll consider one of these ways; the second will come up in Chapter 4.

Now you make a list of secondary properties which it's reasonable to think might affect voting preference (that is, of which (2), above, is possible), and you decide to choose your sample carefully, so that it contains close to the proportion of each of these properties which is shown by the general population of Québec (that is, to make (1) false).

So, for example, you will make sure that your sample of 1000 contains about the same distribution of high, middle, and low incomes as does the population of Québec voters.

First, you need information about the distribution of incomes in Québec. This is presumably available somewhere. This will tell you that (let's imagine) 20% of the people earn more than $50,000 a year, 20% earn less than $7000, and the rest are in between. (I'm just making these figures up: don't take them seriously.) Now you can go back to that same mall and start interviewing again; but you ask everyone what their income is before you ask them about their voting preferences. You want to wind up with a sample that has a similar distribution of incomes to the population as a whole. This procedure is called **SAMPLE MATCHING.**

Now, let's suppose that the people in this mall really do turn out to be predominantly middle-income people (between $7000 and $50,000)—suppose that 95% of them are. In your sample, you'll need 600 people—60% of the sample—to be people who have middle incomes, and it won't be hard to find them. But it will be a lot harder to find people earning less than $7000, or more than $50,000. Pretty soon, you'll have interviews from all the 600 middle-income earners you need, but you'll be far short on your quota of 200 low- and 200 high-income earners. That means you'll spend a long time asking people what their income is, and when (as will happen about 95% of the time) you find out that the person isn't in the high or low ranges you need to fill these quota, you'll have to tell them to go away (or maybe, to be polite, you should continue the interview, but then just throw away the results). This means you'll have to do a lot more than 1000 interviews to get the 1000 individuals you need for your sample.

You'll also have to consider all the other relevant secondary properties of which (2) may be true, and perform sample matching with regard to these too. For example, you'll have to find out what the mother-tongue of each person is, in order to have your sample contain the same proportions of mother-tongue as the general population of Québec. If this mall is in an English-speaking suburb of Montréal, you may have a difficult time filling your quota of French-speakers, and you'll probably have to start discarding the results from English-speakers after a while. Similarly, you want your sample to show a distribution of ages similar to that in the general voting population, so you'll have to ask everyone their age, and if this mall is inhabited by an undue proportion of teenagers, you will have to start discarding the results of interviews from them (or to stop approaching them for interviews in the first place, when you can tell that they're teenagers just from looking.)

Note that you're going to have to do sample matching for *every* relevant secondary property: that is, every one which it seems reasonable might have characteristics (1) and (2).

Here's a further problem we haven't even noticed: suppose that you finally get a sample with 20% of the individuals having low incomes (about the same as in Québec as a whole) and with the same proportion of French-speakers (say, 70%) as in Québec. It doesn't follow from this that your sample has the same proportion of *French speakers with low incomes* as the population as a whole. This complex property is a *different* secondary property from either of the others, and it's reasonable to think that this might have characteristics (1) and (2); so you'll have to do *additional* sample matching for this secondary property too, and for all the other relevant combinations of secondary properties—for example,

- French-speaking-suburban dwellers
- Women-with-incomes-over-$50,000
- English-speaking-suburban-dwelling-high-income-women-aged between-40-and-50

and on and on.

Obviously, this is going to mean a great deal more work for you, to collect a sample of 1000. You'll probably wind up, toward the end, with a number of unfilled quotas, and have to spend a long time looking for people to fill them. You will have a lot of trouble spotting the people likely to fill these quotas, and you'll have to do many more than 1000 interviews to do so. Is the Liberal party paying you enough to justify this very long procedure?

This is starting to look like an enormous job. It may be more than you're able to do. It may even be undoable altogether, for example, if there are no statistics available anywhere about the percentage of French-speaking-suburban-dwelling high-income women aged between 40 and 50 in Québec. But there are ways of getting around some difficulties, at least to some extent.

First of all, it's becoming clear that you are making a mistake in doing all your interviews in that particular mall. You'll be able to do much better by interviewing people in a large number of very different places, and whom you contact in many different ways. This will make it more probable that you'll approach greater diversity of people with regard to the relevant secondary characteristics, and that it will a bit easier to fill your quotas.

A second mistake you made was to keep track of all these complicated quotas as you went along. It would be a better idea for you to do a huge number of interviews in a large variety of ways, and then take the results home and try to sort them out, throwing out some, in a way that will best fill all the quotas. This is a daunting calculational task: what selection of the thousands of interviews you have collected will best fit all those quotas? This is where a computer would come in handy: a huge computational task like this is just the sort of thing they're good at. Now you're getting closer to the techniques used by professional pollsters.

EXERCISE
Imagine that you've been given a small grant by the Saskatchewan government to do a study to determine what proportion of the racoons living around Saskatoon have rabies. On the basis of the (possibly minimal) information you have right now about racoons and rabies, list some secondary characteristics you should consider when you match your sample to the population.

ANSWER
You're going to have to match your sample to the population with regard to several characteristics, for example: where the raccoon lives, its gender, its age, even how hungry it is. Note that traps with food in them are likely to catch only hungry raccoons, and maybe the hungry ones are more or less likely than the rest to have rabies.

3.5 Some Other Problems With Sample Matching

Before we leave the topic of achieving a representative sample by sample matching, we should consider some perpetual difficulties that plague this technique.

The technique we've been talking about involves matching a sample for *all* relevant secondary properties. We imagine that you make a list of all of them you can think of, and try to match their proportions in your sample to the proportions in the population. Now: what makes you sure that your list contains *all* the relevant secondary properties? Well, you can think as hard as you can about what should go on the list, and you can talk to experts about what might be relevant, and read the literature; but it's always possible that you've left something important off the list, either because you've not done enough research, or because you've judged mistakenly that some suggested secondary property couldn't possibly satisfy (2). Imagine, for example, that somebody points out to you that you haven't taken care to match your sample to the general population with regard to the secondary property of shoe size. Is there the same distribution of shoe sizes in your sample as there is in the general population? You decide that this isn't a relevant secondary property: there couldn't possibly be a connection between shoe size and voting preference, and if your sample shows a far different distribution of shoe-sizes from the rest of the population, then that couldn't possibly effect the validity of your conclusion. But you may be wrong! Worse still, there may be secondary properties which really are relevant, but which nobody has even thought of. However careful you are to find out what all the relevant second properties might be—which even have a chance of having characteristic (2)—and to match for them, somebody might later think of one which you didn't consider. There's always this possibility, which would shoot your work down in flames.

This is clearly one of the places where science can fail: what everyone takes to be good evidence actually turns out not to be. Well, you do the best you can, given your resources. All one can ask is that you do the best you can; if your work turns out not to provide good evidence after all, as shown by the suggestion of an additional relevant secondary property you didn't match for, then too bad: them's the breaks.

3.6 Mrs. Smith Again

Remember Mrs. Smith's advice for infant scientists? One of the things she told us was that a scientist must approach reality with a mind cleared of all preconceptions and conventional wisdom: never believe anything anyone thought before; clear your own mind of everything; just look.

The considerations in this chapter show a clear way in which she was wrong. Using the matching technique for producing a representative sample can be good science, but it essentially depends on things already believed. As we've seen, in order to match your sample to the population in question, you have to construct a list of possibly relevant secondary properties. What should be on this list is something you have to have an idea of before you can do the sampling technique for finding out something new. In the case we've been considering, before we can get some idea of how the Québec population is inclined to vote—before we can "look and see" using the sampling technique—we *already* have to have a considerable knowledge of what secondary properties are relevant to voting behaviour. If you clean your mind out beforehand and ignore conventional wisdom altogether, you'd have no idea whatever of what secondary properties you must match in your sample, and this technique would be unusable. Mrs. Smith was wrong, at least with regard to this particular entirely acceptable scientific technique: it depends by its very nature on a considerable body of already-accepted belief.

CHAPTER 4

Random
Samples

4.1 Random Sample Selection ▨

We've seen that sample matching can be a difficult, time-consuming, and expensive procedure, and that there's always the possibility that one has failed to match for every possibly significant secondary property. Fortunately, there is a second sort of way to select a representative sample which, in some situations, can be done much more easily, and may produce more reliable results. This method of selection gets the individuals for the sample out of the population randomly.

To see how this works, let's return to the example of the coin box. As we've seen, just picking the coins to examine from the top of the box may result in an unrepresentative sample, and reasonable doubts can be raised about the strength of the evidence this sample gives. The discussion in the last chapter of the matching strategy tells us why this is so. If you pick the sample off the top, the individuals in the sample all have a secondary property (being on the top of the box); and individuals with this secondary property may well be more or less likely to have the primary quality (being a quarter) than the rest of the individuals in the population. In other words: maybe the top of the box contains a larger, or a smaller, percentage of quarters than the box as a whole. Matching the sample to the population for this secondary property means being careful to take coins, in equal proportion, from every area in the box. But suppose you don't feel like scraping off the more heavily-encrusted coins, so you take for your sample only the more lightly encrusted ones. But this secondary property may also make the sample unrepresentative (if the quarters tend to get more heavily, or more lightly, encrusted than the pennies); so you should make sure that your sample contains about the same distribution of heavily- and lightly-encrusted coins as the whole box has. Similarly, we want to match for the possibly relevant secondary property of being covered with greenish, as opposed to grayish, stuff. And so on. This is the matching strategy in action.

But by now, you've probably thought of a better way to select the sample: mix up the lumps in the box very thoroughly before you pick any items for the sample, and then just pick whatever comes to hand. This very thorough mixture will mean that your sample is a random one, so it's very likely to be a representative one, one which can be counted on to provide good evidence. Picking the sample this way saves us the trouble of thinking of all the possibly relevant secondary properties, and of carefully picking the sample to match all their proportions in the sample to their proportions in the box.

Similarly, in the Québec voters case you could produce a reliable sample of voters in Québec, while avoiding the enormous amount of work it would take to carefully match your sample to the population with regard to every possibly relevant secondary property, if there were a way of choosing them randomly from the population.

EXERCISE
Can you explain why random selection is a good way to produce a representative sample of voters in Québec?

ANSWER
Here's why. The problem with your imagined non-random (non-matched) initial sample from the mall was that this probably resulted in a sample with proportions of relevant secondary properties significantly higher or lower than those in the population, and this might result in a higher or lower proportion of the primary property. Random selection of the sample, on the other hand, would be likely to produce a sample which had the same proportion of any possibly relevant secondary property—and also, of course, of the primary property—as the population. It's an automatic way of making it likely that the sample is representative.

4.2 The Meaning of 'Random'

But what, exactly, does it mean to select the sample 'randomly'? Well, we have a rough idea of what this would amount to in practice, at least in some cases. In the case of the coin box, this means that we should mix it up very thoroughly first, to make sure that the ones we'll eventually pick off the top haven't got an unrepresentative proportion of any property. You could put a stick in there and stir for a long time. Or you could shake the box very thoroughly. This, it would seem, would make the probability-of-being-a-quarter of any coin you pick off the top the same as the probability-of-being-a-quarter of any other coin anywhere else in the box.

Here's another way of putting the same point. Suppose that, when you dug the box up, the quarters just happened to be mostly at the top. If you pick a coin off the top, then it's much more likely that that coin is a quarter than if you picked a coin from somewhere else. So it matters how you pick the coin. But once you've mixed up the coins very thoroughly, the probability of getting a quarter no matter where you pick the coin from is the same. The way the box was arranged at first artificially raised the probability of getting a quarter in your sample above what its probability would have been if you had an equal chance of picking any coin in the box. Mixing it up gives every coin in the box an equal probability of being picked, so it makes your sample more reliable. We can say then that a **RANDOMLY SELECTED SAMPLE** is one in which all individuals in the population have an equal chance of being selected for the sample.

4.3 A Random Sample from the Coin Box?

But how do you get a genuinely random sample from the coin box? Imagine that you decide to randomize your sample of coins from the coin box by first shaking up the box very thoroughly, before you pick the coins off the top.

> EXERCISE
>
> Have you really given each coin an equal chance of being selected for the sample?

STOP! ANSWER
Perhaps not. You might not be aware of it, but shaking a box full of different sized things makes the larger things tend to head for the top of the box. Many people wouldn't guess that this is so: they'd guess that the larger things, probably heavier, would tend to go to the *bottom*; but what really happens is that the smaller things slide into the spaces between the larger ones, so the larger ones tend to move *up*. So shaking the box a lot makes the larger lumps tend to rise, and if you pick the sample off the top, you'd be likely to get an unrepresentatively high proportion of larger lumps. And, of course, being a larger lump is possibly a relevant secondary property: maybe the larger lumps are more likely to be quarters than the smaller ones. So it could be that shaking up the box and picking off the top would result in a larger proportion of quarters than is in the box as a whole. It wouldn't really be taking a random sample.

Something like the following suggestion might have occurred to you: why not reach in and move your hand all over the place among the coins for a few seconds, and then grab whatever coin is touching the tip of your index finger?

 EXERCISE
Try to imagine how this procedure might not produce a random sample.

STOP! ANSWER
The larger lumps take up more space in the box, so the one touching your index finger after a few seconds of random motion is more likely to be a larger lump. If 50% of the lumps in the box are larger ones, this selection procedure might result in a sample with, say, 55% larger lumps. Also: how are you going to move your hand around in the box? Normally people who do this would tend to move their hand around in the middle of the box, avoiding the very top, the very bottom, the corners of the box, etc. This might also influence the sample and make it unrepresentative.

Getting a genuinely random sample can be a tricky matter.

4.4   A Random Sample in an Election Poll?

Now think about our other example of inductive reasoning from a sample: the poll of voters in Québec. Here we found that there were great difficulties and costs in producing a 'matched' sample; why not just get a random one? But how would you get a truly random sample of voters? Think about this.

Here's a real-life example in which the attempt to produce a random sample of voters failed, and the poll's results were badly wrong. In 1936, an American magazine conducted a large-scale political poll to see how Americans were inclined to vote in the next presidential election. Ten million ballots were mailed to people all over the country. The people to whom ballots were mailed were randomly selected from telephone books from every region.

EXERCISE
Stop and think now how you might do a random selection even from one telephone book. Perhaps you would thumbtack every page of the book to the wall, and throw a dart at the book, and choose the person whose name the dart happened to hit. Would this produce a random sample?

ANSWER
Maybe not. If you put the pages up in alphabetical order, and you aimed for the middle, this would make people at the very beginning of the alphabet, and at the very end, less likely to be chosen. So what? Is alphabetical location a possibly relevant property? Well, maybe. The people whose surname begins with 'Z' in my city tend to be mostly of Chinese or Middle-European origin; so this dart-throwing sample selection procedure would produce a sample which would be somewhat likely to under-represent these groups. Ethnicity might be a relevant secondary property, if these groups have different voting dispositions than the rest of the population.

Well, anyway, let's suppose that there were a way to make every name in the telephone book equally likely to be selected, and that the 1936 survey did this for the whole country. Now are you confident that their selection of sample was random? Well, here's what happened. A whopping two million mail ballots were filled in and returned to the magazine; these showed a clear majority for Republican Alfred M. Landon over Democrat Franklin Roosevelt. You probably know that Roosevelt won the real election by a landslide.

EXERCISE
What went wrong? Can you figure it out?

STOP! ANSWER
The problem with this poll was that in 1936, poor people tended not to have telephones, so their names were not selected for this poll in proportion to their percentage in the population. Poor people tended to vote for Roosevelt, and rich people for Landon. The poll selected its sample with a significantly lower proportion of a relevant secondary property: poverty. It was not a representative sample after all, and that's because the method of selection was not random with respect to level of income.

4.5 Abuse Prevalent in Elite Sport, Survey Indicates

This is the title of a newspaper article.* Let's take a look at how this survey worked.

Researchers sent out 1200 questionnaires to members of Athletes CAN, an athletes association in Canada. Of the 266 athletes who replied, one-fifth said they have had sexual intercourse with an authority figure in sport, and 8.6% said they had experienced forced sexual intercourse. One quarter said they were "insulted, ridiculed, made to feel like a bad person, slapped or hit, beaten or punched."

―――――――――――――

*by Beverly Smith, in the (Toronto) *Globe and Mail*, July 17, 1996, pp. A1 and A6.

There's a lot we need to think about in evaluating the results of this survey, and the newspaper article doesn't give us anywhere near enough information for this purpose. As always, if you're interested in the result, you should look at the original report, and not rely on a newspaper's second-hand, or my third-hand, version.

We can raise some doubts, however, on the basis of the details provided by the story.

The researchers here wanted to study the frequency of various "abusive" experiences among elite athletes in Canada. They decided to send questionnaires to the Athletes CAN organization because this organization, we can suppose, has a large representative sample of elite athletes in Canada as members, and offers, through its mailing list, a convenient way to get in touch with them. So far so good. Now, 1200 questionnaires were mailed out (to everyone who is a member of Athletes CAN?) and 266 of them were returned. But a problem arises here. Even if we assume that the membership of Athletes CAN is representative of the general population, can we assume that the 22% of the membership who bothered to fill in and return the questionnaire are representative of the whole?

EXERCISE

Think up some reasons why the athletes who returned the questionnaire might not be representative of the whole group. That is, imagine why this group might have higher (or lower) levels of "abuse" experiences than the general population of membership of the Association.

ANSWER

Here are some grounds for doubt. You may have thought of others:

- Maybe athletes who have been abused are more likely to be upset about the issue than those who haven't, so they're more likely to fill in the questionnaires than the rest. This would result in an unrepresentatively high proportion of reports of abuse in the questionnaires.
- Maybe athletes who have been abused are sometimes ashamed of the incidents, or reluctant to talk about them; so maybe they fill in and return the questionnaires at a lower rate than the rest. The result then would be an unrepresentatively low proportion of reports of abuse.

This survey isn't an example of random sampling. The 266 people who form the sample here weren't selected randomly: they selected themselves. This sort of thing is thus called **SELF-SELECTION**. Whenever there is self-selection, one has to worry that all the usual problems of an unrepresentative sample might arise, and there is always some room for doubt about the conclusions the survey draws. Unfortunately, there's no clear way around this problem in cases such as this. The researchers couldn't choose (say) 266 members of Athletes CAN at random and force them to fill out questionnaires. Especially where people are involved, sometimes the best one can do is to rely on self-selection.

4.6 The General Problem of Sampling

It's starting to look like a difficult problem to produce a really random sample. Here's the problem, in abstract: every selection procedure must use some method or other. Thus, every selection procedure selects on the basis of some property (e.g., being in the telephone book, being on the top of the box after shaking, being in contact with your index finger). If this property happens to be a significant secondary property, then the selection procedure isn't random. To make a genuinely random selection, then, we need to be sure that the property which is the basis of selection is not a possibly significant secondary property. So it seems that we're faced with a problem here related to the central problem we faced in matching the sample: we must judge which secondary properties are possibly relevant.

Of course, in practise, we can perform selection of sample individuals in a way that makes it reasonable to think that the property used to select individuals is not a relevant secondary property. For example, here's a hypothetical way of selecting individuals for our Québec voter's poll. Suppose you could get an alphabetical list of all the people in Québec of voting age; let's imagine there are 3 million of them. Now program your computer to pick a number between 1 and 3 million, at random. (It's easy to get a program by which a computer can pick a "random" number between x and y.) Now count down that alphabetical list that number of names. That person is in your sample. Do this 1000 times, and you have a random list of 1000 people to try to contact.

Your computer program doesn't really generate numbers "at random"—it uses a complicated mathematical way to calculate a "random number". It starts with a number generated from the current date and time, and does a variety of mathematical operations on this, resulting in the "random" output. The point is that this imagined way of picking people to be on our voter's list is picking them on the basis of their having a certain property: being the *n*th person on the alphabetical list, where *n* was generated on the basis of day and time of generation, by a complicated formula, by your computer. The reason that this is a "random" selection procedure is that we can be sure that this property isn't a relevant secondary property. We can be fully confident that this secondary property has no connection at all to voting habits.

Of course, the practicalities of this way of conducting a voting poll need to be considered. Can you actually get such an alphabetical list of all the people in Québec of voting age? It's easy to get a computer to crank out a series of "random" numbers between 1 and 3 million, but it would be hard to count down a list to the 2 millionth name, or to enter all 3 million into the computer which would then do the counting. The point here is that one has to balance costs and benefits. A much more reliably random selection procedure might just be too difficult and expensive.

How do real political pollsters do it? One way they do it is to have their computers crank out a random telephone number, which they call and see if there's someone of voting age there. This might not produce the problem that the 1936 election poll did, because telephones are now owned by a wider economic spectrum of people, but maybe you can think of some other problems that might be raised by this not-very-random procedure. For example: usually a family, no matter how big, shares one telephone number. This means that this procedure makes it likely that the people in the sample live in smaller domestic groups (see if you can figure out why this is so). Maybe this is a relevant secondary property. This way of selecting a sample is probably not too bad, however, and given its practicality and low cost, maybe it's the best way of going about political polling.

Even when the people that the polling group contact are selected "randomly" like this, however, there's still a problem. Not everyone who is contacted will agree to participate in the poll. The ones who do participate are self-selected from the group who are contacted. It's not impossible that the ones who agree to be polled when asked are, for example, likely to be ones who are angry about the current government. So the selection may, after all, be unrepresentative, even after all this careful randomisation.

4.7 Bad Data; Bad Conclusions

Just in passing, we should note a further source of possible problems for this mode of inductive reasoning. We've been concentrating on cases in which we know the proportion of individuals in the sample who have the primary property, and examining whether and when this gives good evidence about the proportion in the whole population. But we should not ignore the further problem that sometimes it's possible that we're not correct about the proportion of individuals in the sample who have the primary property.

The double-star survey can illustrate this problem. Suppose you really have picked a good sample of stars to examine, either randomly or by carefully matching the sample. You want to count the proportion of stars in your sample which are members of a double-star cluster; but maybe you get this wrong. Double stars are stars close to each other in space; but two stars that look like they're right next to each other may in fact be very far apart, one far behind the other as we see them. So what appears to us to be a double star may in fact not be one. On the other hand, some double-star clusters may appear to us as single stars, if the second star is exactly behind the other as we see them, or so close that we can't distinguish the two. Or maybe the second star is just too dim to see in your telescope.

This sort of problem did not show up in our coin-box example. We were assuming that after cleaning, there was no question that could reasonably be raised about whether the object in the sample was a quarter or a penny. So this is not a problem in every example of this sort of inductive reasoning.

This sort of problem might be a real worry in some cases of polling people for their voting preferences, or for other facts about them. In the recent Québec referendum on sovereignty, for example, the polls were criticised on the basis that how people said they would vote might not correspond to how they would actually vote. While many people might secretly be planning to vote against Québec separation, when asked they might reply with what they thought was the more patriotic, more fashionable, more "idealistic" position—in favour of separation. (It turned out, however, that the polls close to the election were remarkably accurate.) This sort of criticism is frequently raised to sample polls about people's sexual habits. When they are asked about this sort of thing, people lie a lot, or give answers they think are correct, but are badly wrong. Of course, the surveys themselves need to be carefully designed so as not to encourage misleading answers, and the conclusions drawn must not go beyond exactly what was asked.

Here's a quote from a review of a book about contemporary sexual politics. * Take a look at what the issues are here.

> In *Lip Service*, Kate Fillion reports on a recent American sex survey, widely touted to be authoritative, in which 22 percent of the women surveyed—by implication 22 per cent of all American women—reported that they had at some point in their lives been "forced to do something sexual that they did not want to do by a man." But according to Fillion, "force" is not defined, so it's impossible to tell whether they were physically forced, threatened, verbally coerced, or simply felt they couldn't say no. It's also unclear whether they communicated their reluctance, or felt forced to kiss a man or have anal sex with him. In written questionnaires given to women, "astonishingly," says Fillion, the word "sexual" was mistakenly dropped from a question that read, "Have you ever been forced by a man to do something that you did not want to do?" It wasn't even clear if the context was sexual. Fillion says some women might have written yes, meaning, "I've felt forced to do the dishes."
>
> "Conclusive" studies such as these form the basis of our public policy about issues like date rape.

The first sentence hints at questions about the representativeness of the sample: do the experiences of the women surveyed represent American women in general? But the main criticism here is that the questions were vague, and the implications drawn from the study unjustified. Defenders of the study might argue that this was exactly the right way to ask the questions: for example, given the subtle varieties of "force" that women are subject to, the word can't and shouldn't be precisely defined. This debate, of course, occurs within the highly-charged value-laden conflict of basic ideologies regarding sexual politics. Whether you view this study as scientifically adequate seems to vary with what ideology you hold. Is there really such a thing as scientific objectivity, divorced (as Mrs. Smith would want it to be) from all ideology and value?

We're not going to go into an argument about date rape here, so you can calm down. If you really want to find out about this study, you should take a look at the study itself, and at its critics. (Don't rely on my discussion of a newspaper review of a book which discusses the study!) My purpose is merely to emphasize that whenever you see an example of research attempting to reach an inductive conclusion, you should consider all these sorts of issues.

---

*The book is by Kate Fillion: *Lip Service: The Truth about Women's Darker Side in Love, Sex, and Friendship* (Harper Collins). The review is by Wendy Dennis, in the (Toronto) *Globe and Mail*, February 3, 1996, p. C8.

4.8 The Basic Problem With Induction, Again

You'll remember that it's always possible, in any inductive argument, that the premises are true but that the conclusion is false. This affects the kind of inductive reasoning we have been considering in a way we have not touched on so far.

Consider again our coin box. Now imagine that you somehow manage to mix things up really thoroughly, and to pick out a sample of 100 lumps really at random. (Maybe the random-number generator on your computer can be used for this.) In your sample there are 50 quarters and 50 pennies. You conclude that there's something like half quarters and half pennies in the box as a whole. But it's possible that your conclusion is badly mistaken. Imagine that what's really in the box is 950 pennies and 50 quarters. The percentage of quarters in the box is actually nothing like 50%; it's really only 5%. Your random sample has managed to get all of the quarters, *just by accident.* It can happen! Nevertheless, you're justified in thinking that your sample gives you fairly good reason to think that the box contains about half quarters; this is perfectly good reasoning, although in this case, it has come up with a really wrong conclusion. The reason this sort of reasoning is good is that we don't expect it to go this badly wrong very often. The sort of accident which made it go so badly wrong this time is very unusual, so the mode of reasoning you've used is one that can be counted on to work most of the time. We'll come back to this idea again.

CHAPTER 5

Imprecision and Confidence Level

5.1 Two Methods of Selecting a Sample

We imagined that in selecting your sample of coins from the coin box, you stirred the box and took ten coins out of the box to examine, leaving the rest behind. You might have sampled the coin box using a slightly different method: take a coin out, clean it, examine it, *then put it back*; stir again; then take a coin out, clean it (if it hasn't already been cleaned), examine it, *then put it back*; stir again, and so on, until you have done this 100 times. This second method of sampling leaves open the possibility of your examining a coin twice or more, whereas the first method, which takes out all 100 coins for your sample at once, does not. The second method of sampling is called **SAMPLING WITH REPLACEMENT**, and the first method **SAMPLING WITHOUT REPLACEMENT**.

In some cases, the strength of the evidence you get for a conclusion would be different if your sample were taken with replacement or without. Suppose, for example, that the whole population of the coin box is only 105 lumps. Now, if you took a sample of 100 of them *without* replacement, that means that you actually look at all but five of them. If these 100 turn out to be half pennies and half quarters, you'd have extremely strong evidence that the whole population contains close to half-and-half. But suppose that you did your sampling from this box of 105 lumps *with* replacement. You'd probably get some of the coins several times in your sample (because you're replacing each coin after you look at it). Your evidence would be somewhat weaker, because you'll probably look at far fewer than 100 different coins altogether. In this case, when the population is only a little larger than the sample size, the strength of the evidence from a sample taken without replacement is much greater than the evidence from a sample taken with replacement.

Now imagine a really huge coin box, containing thousands and thousands of lumps. As before, the sample is 100. If you replace a coin after looking at it, it's not very likely you'll get this coin again, given the large number of things in the box. That means that if you sample with replacement, you'll probably look at 100, or very close to 100, different coins. If you sample without replacement, you'll certainly look at exactly 100 different coins. There probably won't be very much difference, then, if you sample with replacement or without replacement when the size of the population is much larger than the size of the sample.

In real-life cases, the populations being sampled are usually extremely large—much much larger than the size of the sample. For example, the population of people of voting age in Québec numbers in the millions, and we're imagining a sample of 100 or so. The population of stars is quite a good deal larger. So in these cases, it almost certainly makes almost no difference whether sampling is done with or without replacement. Suppose, for example, that you sample the voting preferences of Québecois by getting random telephone numbers from your computer. There's a small chance that you'll get the same number twice from your computer, and that on both occasions when you phone that number you'll speak to the same person. But it's a very small chance.

So in most real-life cases, it doesn't make a difference whether the sample is done with or without replacement.

We're going to begin quantifying matters regarding induction from samples, and it turns out to be somewhat easier to think about this when we're talking about sampling *with* replacement. The reason for this is that when you sample with replacement, *the size of the population is irrelevant* to the strength of the evidence you get. I'll try to make this claim intuitively reasonable. (If, however, I don't manage to make it seem true to you, you'll just have to take my word for it.)

You should be able to see that the size of the population is relevant to the strength of the evidence when we're sampling without replacement. We've already seen that the evidence for a population of 105, given a sample (without replacement) of 100, is extremely strong; but the evidence for a population of 10,000, given a sample (without replacement) of 100, is somewhat weaker.

But (and this is harder to see) the size of the population is not relevant to the strength of the evidence when we're sampling with replacement. A sample of 100 coins of which half are quarters, taken with replacement from a population of 105, gives some justification to the claim that around half of the coins in the population are quarters. And a sample with replacement of 100 coins of which half are quarters, from a population of 10,000, gives *exactly the same strength* of justification to the claim that around half of the coins in the population are quarters. And a sample with replacement of 100 coins of which half are quarters, taken from a population of only 10, gives exactly the same strength of evidence to the conclusion. Note that taking a sample of 100 *without* replacement from a population of 10 is impossible. Note also that it's hard to think of a reason why anyone would try to find out what's in a population of 10 by taking a sample of 100 with replacement. It would give stronger evidence to take a sample of only 10 without replacement—that is, just to look at every lump in the box.

The fact that the strength of evidence is the same for a given sample size when the sample is taken with replacement, no matter what the population size is, makes it simpler for us to deal with. So we're going to look at the simple arithmetic of sampling with replacement. (The arithmetic of sampling without replacement isn't that much harder, but we won't deal with it.) As I've pointed out, the fact that we're looking only at sampling with replacement won't make you less able to deal with real-life science when they do sampling without replacement, since the population sizes are often huge compared to the sample sizes. That means there won't be very much difference in the numbers.

5.2 Imprecision

You may have noticed that when I have drawn general inductive conclusions from a sample, these conclusions have always had a certain imprecision. For example, when we considered your reasoning as an astronomer investigating the proportion of stars in double-star clusters, we imagined that you found *exactly* 5% of the stars in your sample of 1000 were in these clusters, but you concluded that in the general population of stars, *about* 5% of them were. Similarly, from the fact that five out of ten examined coins were quarters, the conclusion was drawn that the box contained *roughly* half quarters.

It might seem that this imprecision is a defect. Mrs. Smith was appalled when I handed in my first bird-report containing the results of my observations. It said that a lot of the birds I saw were sparrows of some sort, of a sort of streaky brownish colour, and that they were hopping around on the ground eating something or other. Precision! advised Mrs. Smith.

My bird reports were, of course, defective; but the imprecision in the conclusions about the proportions of stars and quarters is actually a scientific virtue. This needs some explanation.

To see exactly why this is so, let's look closely at the coin-box case. We're imagining a sample with replacement of 100—50 quarters and 50 pennies. Suppose that there are 1000 lumps in the box. Why not conclude, on the basis of this sample, that *exactly* half of the coins in the population—exactly 500—were quarters? This conclusion would have been more precise than the wishy-washy one we did produce—that about half the coins in the population were quarters. The problem with this more precise conclusion is that it would be less likely to be true than the wishy-washy one we did draw.

Think of the situation this way. How likely is it that exactly 500 of those coins were quarters, given the evidence? Well, it's more likely that exactly 500 of them were quarters than that, say, exactly 10 of them were quarters.

Consider the list of 1001 hypotheses, numbered for obvious reasons from 0 to 1000, about what the box contains. Here is a portion of that list:

0.   There are no quarters in the box.
1.   There is 1 quarter in the box.
2.   There are 2 quarters in the box.
...
499. There are 499 quarters in the box.
500. There are 500 quarters in the box.
501. There are 501 quarters in the box.
...
998. There are 998 quarters in the box.
999. There are 999 quarters in the box.
1000. There are 1000 quarters in the box.

Mathematical techniques involving probability can give us precise numerical values for the probability of each of these hypotheses given the evidence. We won't go into the details of how to calculate these numbers, you'll probably be happy to hear, but you should try to get a rough idea of what these numbers would be like.

None of these hypotheses has a very large probability of being true. Given that there were quarters in the sample, this rules out hypothesis 0 altogether. We're imagining that we're sampling with replacement, so hypothesis 1 is remotely possible, but very very improbable. (For it to be true, you would have had to have picked that lonely quarter out of the box five out of ten times, in a random draw from a mixed-up pile of 1000 lumps. You can see how this is very improbable.) Hypothesis 2 is slightly more probable, and the probability of each hypothesis continues to rise slowly until we reach hypothesis 500, which is the most probable on the list, although it is still has, in absolute terms, very small probability. Then, moving down the list, the probability starts decreasing slowly; hypothesis 999 is barely possible, though just as improbable as hypothesis 1. Given that we got pennies in the sample, hypothesis 1000 is impossible.

Suppose that on the basis of your sample you had to make a guess about exactly how many quarters there were in the box. Which of the 1001 hypotheses would you guess? Of course, you'd guess the most probable of them: hypothesis 500, because it's the most probable on the list. But hypothesis 500 isn't very likely at all. Should you, as a scientist interested in truth, make the claim that exactly 500 of the coins in the box are quarters?

Whenever you use inductive reasoning to support any claim about the proportion of quarters in the box, you might be wrong; this is of course a consequence of the inductive nature of the reasoning. So what you should be worried about is not guaranteed truth, but rather evidence and probabilities. You should say what you think is most warranted by the evidence, what is most likely to be true. Hypothesis 500 is the most likely on the list. But because it's not very likely at all, you wouldn't want to make that claim.

Well, here's how you can get out of this dilemma. Suppose that instead of saying that exactly 500 of the coins in the box are quarters, you say that *about* 500 of them are quarters. What you're doing is collecting together the most likely hypotheses on this list—the ones including and surrounding hypothesis 500, and making the claim that one of these is true, though you're not saying which.

Notice that, roughly speaking, when you say that one of a bunch of hypotheses is true without saying which, you add the probabilities of each of these individual hypotheses. Your new claim then has a probability which is the sum of the probabilities of each individual one. For example, suppose that a weather forecaster thinks that there's 1/3 probability of rain tomorrow and 1/3 probability of snow. It follows that there's 2/3 probability of precipitation (rain or snow). A prediction of rain will probably be wrong. So will a prediction of snow. But the prediction of precipitation (either rain or snow) will likely be right.

So your claim that *around* 500 of the coins in the box are quarters has a probability of truth which is the sum of the small probabilities of the hypotheses around and including hypothesis 500. If you add the small probabilities of enough of these, you get a probability which is quite high. This means that now you're able to make a claim which has a strong likelihood of being true.

I'm belabouring a point here which, put another way, is obvious: the less information there is in your claim, the more likely it is to be true. Of course, if you reduce the information to a minimum, you get maximum probability that what you say is true. If you said that some number of coins between 1 and 999 in the box were quarters, you're saying almost nothing, and your claim will certainly be true. But this would be a very uninformative claim.

What we're faced with, then, is a trade-off: we want to give the most information we can, while still making what we say likely to be true. The smaller the number of hypotheses included in our claim, the more information. So the best way to make a very-likely-true claim that maximizes information is to collect together a bunch of the most likely claims around hypothesis 500, and to claim that one of these is the case. This will produce a claim that is as precise—as informative—as possible, under the circumstances, while being likely to be true. It's a less precise claim than saying that exactly 500 of the coins are quarters, but it is very probably a true claim. Imprecision, then, is a necessary evil.

5.3 Some Technical Terms

There are standard scientific ways to refer to the matters we have been considering, and to give numbers to them, and it's worthwhile for you to be aware of them.

First of all, we've seen that you want to make your claim about the coin box not by claiming that hypothesis 500 is true, but that one of the hypotheses in a range around 500 is true. That is, you want to say that the percentage of quarters in the box lies somewhere in a range around 50%.

Here's a very simple picture to illustrate this: *

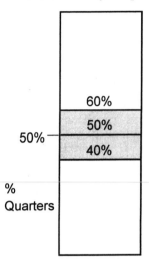

In this picture the rectangle represents the range between 0% at the bottom and 100% at the top. Our sample showed 50% quarters, and this is represented by a line across the rectangle at 50%. What we want to say about the population is that it has a percentage of quarters in it around 50%—in this case, between 60% and 40%. (Later on I'll tell you why I picked these numbers). So there are lines at 60% and 40%, representing the upper and lower limits of the range in which we want to say the percentage of quarters in the population falls, and I've shaded in gray the region between the upper and lower limits of this range.

Let's begin to use some standard statistical terminology. The **SAMPLE SIZE** in this case is 100. In this sample, the **OBSERVED FREQUENCY** of quarters—that is, the proportion of quarters we see in the sample—is 50%, which we can express in decimal form as .50. Note that the graph shows the proportion of the sample that is quarters (50%, .50), not the number (50).

When you make a claim about the frequency of quarters in the population, you'll want to give a range of possibilities around this observed frequency. This range is called the **MARGIN OF ERROR**. It's expressed in terms of a decimal figure "±"—"plus and minus"—that is to be added to and subtracted from the observed frequency. Thus, to state the observed frequency and the margin of error, we might want to say .50 ± .10. This refers to the range from (.50 - .10) to (.50 + .10), that is, from .40 to .60. By stating that the observed frequency is .50, and the margin of error ± .10, we thus claim that one of the hypotheses numbered 400 to 600 is true: that the coin box contains somewhere between 40% and 60% quarters.

Putting all this together, we might say, for example, that our sample size was 100, with an observed frequency of quarters of .50; and claim as a result that the population has a frequency of quarters of .50 ± .10.

Now please go read this section over again. The ideas here aren't very complicated, but you need to master the technical vocabulary.

---

* This style of diagram is adapted from *Understanding Scientific Reasoning* by Ronald N. Giere (Fort Worth, TX: Holt, Rinehart and Winston, Inc., Third Edition, 1991).

? EXERCISE
Take a look at this diagram:

Fill in the numbers:
The observed frequency is _____
The margin of error is _____

STOP! ANSWERS
The observed frequency is .54
The margin of error is ± .05

5.4 Confidence Level

Corresponding to different-sized margins of error, there are different likelihoods of the truth of the conclusion. The probability of truth of a claim is called the **CONFIDENCE LEVEL** of the claim. Thus, for instance, we might make a claim that is more likely than not to be true, but not very likely: one with a confidence level of, say, .67. A different claim might have a confidence level of .95, or of .99. This last confidence level expresses a claim with a very high probability of truth.

What is this thing called 'confidence level'? What does it mean to say that a confidence level is .67 or .95? It may help to look at matters this way: saying that assigning a margin of error of ± .10 around an observed frequency of .50 gives a confidence level of .95 means that it's highly probable, 95% probable in fact, that there are somewhere in between 40% and 60% quarters in the box. Of course, it's possible that there are less than 40% or more than 60% quarters in there, but this is only 5% (100% - 95%) probable—very unlikely. Saying that a claim has a confidence level of .95 can be taken to mean that we're entitled to be 95% sure of it, or that 95% of the time this claim will be true. Thus, we might imagine that if a scientist makes a large number of claims at the .95 confidence level, in the long run 95% of these will turn out to be true, and only 5% of them false. Another way of putting this is that the results are reliable 95 times out of 100, or, in other words, 19 times out of 20.

You probably recognize at least one of these phrases from reports of election polls in the news. A typical report might say something like: "The poll showed that if the election were held today, the Liberals could expect 43% of the vote, plus or minus 3%, 19 times out of twenty." This means that the observed frequency was .43; the margin of error was ± .03; and the confidence level was 95%. Don't panic: I'm going to explain all this.

5.5 How to Pick a Confidence Level

As we'll see in detail, the confidence level you pick will influence the margin of error you must assign, given a sample size; or it will influence the sample size you must use, if you've already decided on the size of the margin of error. Usually, scientists pick a confidence level of .95. Why?

Well, all that can be said about this is that .95 is a very nice confidence level: it doesn't guarantee truth (which can't be guaranteed in inductive reasoning), but it's certainly good enough in most situations to justify belief. It means you'll be wrong only 5% of the time. Scientists are usually satisfied with this, and the general rules understood by practising scientists specify this level.

Nevertheless, the confidence level you'd prefer is a matter of individual evaluation. Suppose, for instance, that you're the kind of person who enjoys going out on a limb, likes to take risks. You might then want to make a claim with more information in it—a smaller margin of error—but with a higher risk of being wrong—maybe only a .66 level of confidence. Or suppose that you're the sort who wants to play things very safe and careful. Maybe then a .95 level of confidence wouldn't be good enough to fit your values: you'd prefer to make, say, 99% sure before you opened your mouth. This seems, to some extent, to be a matter of taste. Even though there are certain standards which scientists in a particular discipline accept and expect from each other—often a .95 level of certainty—there does seem to be some room for different individual tastes.

What's also relevant is how much reliability can be provided by a particular science in a particular context. The weather where I live isn't very reliable. If the scientists who construct the weather predictions here used a .95 level of confidence, they wouldn't be able to say much. They might only be able to predict, for example, that there's going to be rain at least once during the month of April, and that there won't be any snow in August. These boring predictions wouldn't be of interest to anyone. They make more informative predictions, but with a much lower confidence level. They're wrong many more than 5 times out of 100.

In particular cases there might be other sorts of good reasons to choose a level of confidence different from the usual one of .95. When we're indulging in relatively idle speculation, with no particular practical consequences of what we say, maybe a lower level of confidence is justified. When we're going to use our scientific findings for practical purposes, and it will be very costly or disastrous in some other respects if we're wrong, then maybe a higher level of confidence is necessitated. For example, if we're building a rocket to fly past a comet, and we'll only get one chance to do it, and many millions of dollars will go down the drain if something goes wrong, maybe a 95% assurance of our inductive conclusions isn't good enough.

What we have here is a variety of different sorts of situations and values which lead to the use of different confidence levels. Look over what we have just said, and see how often values are relevant to choices of confidence level. Clearly, this is a place in which values and tastes are relevant to what scientific claims can be made. Mrs. Smith, and naïve empiricists in general, insist that science is value-free, that scientists must park their values at the door when they enter their labs, that values and tastes have no part in the scientific enterprise. These considerations show where they're wrong.

CHAPTER 6

Statistical Relations

6.1 Some Functional Relations ███████

WARNING! This section will take a lot of careful attention!

We've said enough in the last chapter for you to be able to see how the various features of inductive arguments based on sampling fit together, but now I'll review them, and collect them together. These can best be seen as "functional relations": what happens as certain numbers get larger or smaller.

Remember first that all these considerations have nothing to do with population size. All numbers are the same regardless of population size (assuming, as we are, that we are sampling with replacement).

The relevant considerations when thinking about reasoning about a population on the basis of a sample are:

- Sample size
- Margin of error
- Level of confidence

Thinking about how these three quantities are related to each other can be confusing. Their relations can be stated briefly, but you'll have to read the following statements slowly, several times, and think about them very carefully to make sure you understand what's going on and remember it.

A larger sample size always gives better information. To see this, imagine comparing a sample of 100 with a sample of 225. Because a sample of 225 gives better information than a sample of 100, the same margin of error around both observed frequencies will give a higher confidence level for the sample of 225 than for a sample of 100. In fact, with a sample of 100, an observed frequency of 50%, and a margin of error of ±10%, there's a 95% confidence level; but with a sample of 225, given the same observed frequency and margin of error, there's a 99% confidence level. *

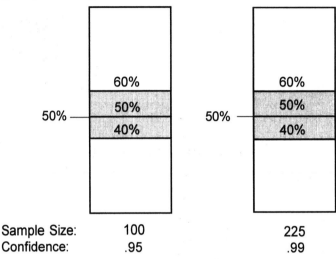

Sample Size: 100   225
Confidence: .95   .99

Alternatively, in order to get the same level of confidence for your conclusion, you'll need a larger margin of error if your sample is smaller. For example, with a sample of 100, achieving a level of confidence of .95 means you need a margin of error of ±10%. But with a sample of 50, achieving a level of confidence of .95 means you need a margin of error of ±14%.

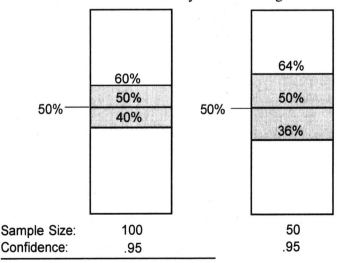

Sample Size: 100   50
Confidence: .95   .95

* Where are these numbers coming from? There's a formula that you can use to get them, and I'll tell you what it is a little later, but don't worry about it now.

A higher confidence level requires better information. For example, compare a confidence level of .67 with a confidence level of .95. With a sample of 100, you'll need to give a wider margin of error to get a confidence level of .95 than to get a confidence level of .67. In fact, the margin of error to give you a confidence level of .95 is ± 10%, but the margin of error to give you a confidence level of only .67 is ± 5%:

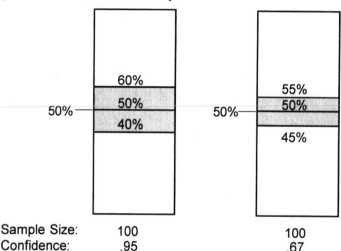

Sample Size:	100	100
Confidence:	.95	.67

Got all that? I didn't think so. Now go back and work your way through all that again, slowly and carefully, making sure you understand each claim. Work your way through these until you can say on your own what would be the result on one number if you changed the second and kept the third one constant. You won't fully grasp all these relations until you can do the following exercises:

EXERCISE
a(i). What change results in the margin of error if you raise the sample size, keeping the level of confidence constant?

ANSWER
The margin of error gets smaller.

How do you figure that out? Well, here's the line of reasoning that is something like what you should go through. Pay close attention. A larger sample size will give more information, so for the same level of certainty, you can be more precise about predicting the frequency in the sample. So it will allow a smaller margin of error.

Now see if you can think your way through the rest of these exercises:

MORE EXERCISES
  a. What change results in the margin of error if you:
  (i) Raise the sample size, keeping the level of confidence constant?
  (ii) Lower the sample size, keeping the level of confidence constant?
  (iii) Raise the level of confidence, keeping the sample size constant?
  (iv) Lower the level of confidence, keeping the sample size constant?

  b. What change results in the level of confidence if you:
  (i) Raise the sample size, keeping the margin of error constant?
  (ii) Lower the sample size, keeping the margin of error constant?
  (iii) Raise the margin of error, keeping the sample size constant?
  (iv) Lower the margin of error, keeping the sample size constant?

  c. What change must be made in the sample size if you:
  (i) Raise the margin of error, keeping the level of confidence constant?
  (ii) Lower the margin of error, keeping the level of confidence constant?
  (iii) Raise the level of confidence, keeping the margin of error constant?
  (iv) Lower the level of confidence, keeping the margin of error constant?

STOP! ANSWERS
  a. (i) smaller
     (ii) larger
     (iii) large
     (iv) smaller

b. (i) larger
    (ii) smaller
    (iii) larger
    (iv) smaller

c. (i) smaller
    (ii) larger
    (iii) larger
    (iv) smaller

6.2 Standard Deviation

The margin of error around the observed frequency which gives you a 67% level of confidence is what's called **ONE STANDARD DEVIATION**.

A margin of error twice as large as one standard deviation is, of course, called **TWO STANDARD DEVIATIONS**. A margin of error that is two standard deviations gives you a 95% level of confidence.

THREE STANDARD DEVIATIONS around the observed frequency—a margin of error three times as large as one standard deviation—gives you a 99% level of confidence.

You should remember these numbers. Here they are, in a table:

Standard Deviations	Confidence level
1 SD	.67
2 SD	.95
3 SD	.99

How big one standard deviation actually is depends (as you now should realize) on the size of the sample. * In a sample of 100, 1 SD is a margin of error of ± .05; 2 SD is a margin of error of twice this, ± .10; 3 SD is a margin of error of ± .15.

---

* It also, strictly speaking, depends on the what the observed frequency is. The numbers we've been looking at are approximately true for observed frequencies in the vicinity of .50, but differ somewhat for much larger or much smaller observed frequencies. This is a complication that makes what we're saying not quite accurate, but we can continue to ignore this (though real statisticians can't).

You can calculate the size of standard deviations using a mathematical formula,* or you can look them up in a table usually provided in statistics texts, or get this information from many pocket calculators with more than the most basic functions built into them. But for our purposes, you don't need the actual numbers. Just to give you a feeling for how the numbers work, here's a very small sample of them. These are approximate numbers, applying to observed frequencies around .50: (I wouldn't advise your trying to remember any of these numbers—unless your sadistic teacher tells you that you have to.)

For a sample size of 100 and a level of confidence of .95 (that is, two standard deviations), the margin of error is ± .10. This means that for example your sample of 100 coins out of the coin box (assuming replacement) containing 50% quarters would have justified (with a 95% level of confidence) the claim that .50 ± .10 of the coins in the box were quarters: that is, somewhere between 400 and 600 of them.

For a sample size of 10 and a level of confidence of .95, the margin of error is ± .30. Of course, as you should have been able to predict by now, a smaller sample size, keeping the level of confidence constant, requires a larger margin of error. This means that, for example, your sample of 10 coins

---

* In case you're interested, here's the formula for calculating the (approximate) size of one standard deviation:

$$1 \text{ standard deviation} = [(f)\ (1 - f)/n]^{1/2}$$

f is the 'observed frequency'; *n* is the sample size. You always wanted to know what that √ key on your pocket calculator was good for, didn't you? It gives the square root (indicated in the equation by the exponent $^{1/2}$). This equation gives you the margin of error which is to be added to, and subtracted from, the observed frequency—the number I've been giving after the '±'. Two standard deviations is just two times this number.

Thus, for example, for a sample size of 200 and an observed frequency of .4, the size of 1 standard deviation is the square root of [.4×.6 / 200], which is about .035. This is 1 standard deviation—a confidence level of .67. For two standard deviations—a confidence level of .95—this number is doubled: .07. So for a sample size of 200, an observed frequency of .4, and a confidence level of .95, the margin of error is ± .07.

I wouldn't advise you to pay any attention to this equation unless you're good at mathematics, or your teacher tells you to. You won't need to know this to understand anything else in this book.

out of the coin box (assuming replacement) containing 50% quarters would have justified (with a 95% level of confidence) the claim that .50 ± .30 of the coins in the box were quarters—that is, somewhere between 200 and 800 of them. This is not a whole lot of information; it's a consequence of the high level of confidence we're imposing and the small sample size. Would this be enough information for you? You could be 95% sure that there weren't less than 200 quarters in the box. This might have been sufficient information to make it worthwhile for you to undertake a thorough cleaning of all the lumps.

For a sample size of 1000 and a level of confidence of .95, the margin of error is ± .03. A larger sample size produces a smaller margin of error. This means that, for example, a sample of 1000 coins out of the coin box (assuming replacement) containing 50% quarters would have justified (with a 95% level of confidence) the claim that .50 ± .03 of the coins in the box were quarters: that is, somewhere between 470 and 530 of them. This is fairly precise information, with a small margin of error and a high level of confidence: a consequence, of course, of the large sample size.

Here's a table of these numbers:

Sample Size	Margin of error (.95 confidence)
10	±.30
100	±.10
1000	±.03

Recall the typical sample of election poll results I presented in the last chapter: "The poll showed that if the election were held today, the Liberals could expect 43% of the vote, plus or minus 3%, 19 times out of twenty." As I mentioned then, this means that the observed frequency was .43; the margin of error was ± .03, and the confidence level was 95%. Now you can estimate how many people were included in the poll's sample.

EXERCISE
Before you read the answer, try to estimate how many people were included in this poll's sample.

ANSWER
It's about 1000.

CHAPTER 7

Correlations
Described

7.1   Proportions and Correlations

What we have been looking at in the last few chapters is inductive arguments which arrive at a conclusion about a *proportion*—a percent—of some
population that has a certain property. Scientists are, however, very often
interested in something a bit more complicated: **CORRELATIONS**. The distinction between a proportion and a correlation is an important one for you to
understand.

For an illustration of this distinction, we'll return to the old coin-box
example. Suppose that you noticed that the lumps in the coin box were of
two kinds. Some lumps were greenish and some lumps were grayish. Now
we can think about the individuals in this population with regard to two categories of characteristics: what colour they are (greenish or grayish) and
what coins they are (quarters or pennies). We can ask, and answer on the
basis of a sample, questions about proportions regarding either category of
characteristic:

- What proportion of the lumps in the box are quarters? What
    proportion of them are not (i.e., are pennies)?
- What proportion of the lumps in the box are greenish? What
    proportion of them are not (i.e., are grayish)?

We can also consider smaller populations of individuals in the box, selected
according to a characteristic in one of these categories, and ask questions
about the proportion of this smaller population which has a characteristic in
the other category. For example, we can ask:

- What proportion of the greenish lumps are quarters?
- What proportion of the greenish lumps are pennies?
- What proportion of the grayish lumps are quarters?
- What proportion of the grayish lumps are pennies?
- What proportion of the lumps holding quarters are greenish?
- What proportion of the lumps holding quarters are grayish?
- What proportion of the lumps holding pennies are greenish?
- What proportion of the lumps holding pennies are grayish?

All of these are separate questions, and the answer to each of these questions might be different. Note, however, that the answers aren't all independent of each other. If you determine that 40% of the greenish lumps are pennies, you can conclude deductively from this that 60% of the greenish lumps are quarters, because everything in there is either (we assume) a quarter or a penny.

You might find some of these proportions relevant to your interests, given the fact that the quarters are worth enough to justify the trouble of cleaning off their lumps. You know that if you pick out the greenish lumps to clean, you'll be rewarded by getting a quarter about 60% of the time—more precisely, 60% ± the margin of error.

But this may not be all you want to know. Suppose that inductive sampling techniques result in your coming to these *two* conclusions:

- About 60% of the greenish lumps are quarters
- About 35% of the grayish lumps are quarters

These two proportions together allow you to *compare* the proportion of quarters in the greenish lumps and in the rest of the box. Together they tell you that quarters occur more frequently inside the greenish lumps than elsewhere. This conclusion is not a simple proportion: it's a comparison of the magnitude of two proportions. It's a **CORRELATION**. What you've discovered is that the property *greenish* and the property *being a quarter* are **POSITIVELY CORRELATED**. What this means is that the proportion of quarters among greenish lumps is larger than the proportion of quarters among the rest (i.e., the grayish). In other words, that quarters are more likely to be found inside the greenish lumps than inside the rest.

7.2 The Importance of Correlations

Under certain circumstances, correlations might give you more important information than either simple proportion alone. In the current case, the positive correlation between the properties of containing a quarter and being a greenish lump tells you that the payoff for cleaning a greenish lump is likely to be greater than for cleaning off a greyish one. Of course, quarters might be worth enough to justify cleaning off both the greenish and the grayish lumps; but assuming that the trouble of cleaning is the same for both sorts of lumps, this information tells you that cleaning the greenish ones is more worthwhile.

Recall the real-life example we looked at in section 4.5, involving the study of abuse in elite sport. One of the results of that survey was that approximately one quarter of the respondents reported that they were "insulted, ridiculed, made to feel like a bad person, slapped or hit, beaten or punched" in the course of their sporting careers. We'll assume that this sample is representative, and justifies to some extent the conclusion that about a quarter of elite athletes suffer abuse like this. This is, of course, interesting information, and is a cause of some concern. But the article goes on to say that the researchers have concluded that "sport is a 'particular subculture' with what they call a 'dome of violence' that allows violence to occur in ways that it could not in ordinary society." * There seems to be an implication (in the article reporting this study anyway, if not in the original research report) that there's something particularly bad about sport—that abuse is worse in sport contexts than elsewhere. That is, there seems to be the claim that the proportion of abuse in sport contexts is greater than its proportion in other contexts. This is a correlation, not a simple proportion. This correlation would be of somewhat greater interest than a mere proportion. It would be much more revealing of something special about sports contexts to show that there's a higher proportion of abuse there than elsewhere. But there's much less of interest here if the study merely gives some evidence about the incidence of abuse in sport—a simple proportion—but no way to say how this compares with other contexts. If it turned out that there was little or no correlation—if abuse in sports turned out to be about the same proportion as anywhere else—this would hardly merit front-page treatment in the newspaper. Or if it turned out that the proportion of abuse in sports contexts was *lower* than the proportion of abuse in other contexts, then we'd be able to come to a different interesting conclusion: that there's something special about sports contexts that *reduces* the incidence of abuse.

---

*"Abuse prevalent in elite sport, survey indicates" by Beverley Smith, *Globe and Mail*, July 17, 1996, pp. A1, A6.

Unless there is evidence indicating the proportion of abuse in non-sport contexts, no claim about a correlation can justifiably be made. And the newspaper report goes on to state that "the survey does not show whether the incidence of sexual harassment and abuse in sport is more widespread than in the general population." But the article singles out sports, as if there is something special about this context that encouraged abuse. In this way, it encourages us to draw a conclusion which the study does not justify. I am not implying that this conclusion is false. My point is that it is really the one we are interested in, and it would be shown by a correlation, not by a simple proportion. Correlations, not merely simple proportions, are often what's important.

7.3 An Uninteresting Child Abuse Figure

A newspaper article reports that 60% of U.S. cases of physical abuse of children take place in families in which both biological parents are present. *

EXERCISE
Explain why this is an uninteresting, useless figure. Say what we want to know instead.

ANSWER
What we (might) want to know is whether rates of child abuse vary depending on whether or not both biological parents are in the family. Are child abuse rates higher or lower in families in which one of the "parents" is not a biological parent (for example, in which the man is a live-in boyfriend)? (The news article in fact goes on to report that they're much higher.) In other words, we want a correlation, not a simple proportion.

7.4 An Astronomical Correlation

Here's an example of a positive correlation. Imagine that you, as an astronomer, are aware of two categories of property as you look at the stars. Some of the stars are dwarf stars, and some are not. Some stars occur in double-star clusters, and some don't. Suppose that out of the 1000 stars you

---

* "Suffer the murdered babies" by Michael Valpy, *Globe and Mail*, August 3, 1996, pp. D1, D5.

look at, only a few of them, say 50 (5%), are dwarf stars; and that say, 89 of them (9%) occur in double-star clusters. You have (some) evidence for two conclusions about simple proportions: 5% of stars are dwarf stars; 9% of stars occur in double-star clusters. This information tells you nothing about the relation—the possible correlation—between the two properties. Now you ask a different question: are dwarf stars more or less likely than the others to occur in double-star clusters? Now you take a look at your dwarf stars: what proportion of these are in double-star clusters? Imagine that 9 of the 50 dwarfs you observe (18%) are in double-star clusters, and the other 41 are singles. Then imagine that 80 of the 950 ordinary stars you observe are doubles (8%), and the other 870 are singles.

Here's a **TREE DIAGRAM** illustrating your findings:

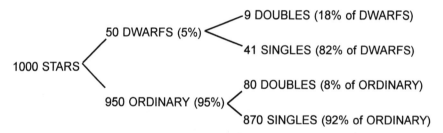

Lots of simple proportions can be derived from this data. But now the question is: in the sample, is being a dwarf star correlated with occurring in a double-star cluster? There would be such a correlation in the sample if the proportion of doubles among the dwarfs is greater than the proportion of doubles among the ordinary stars. In the sample, the proportion of doubles among the dwarfs is 18%; the proportion of doubles among the ordinaries is 8%. There is a positive correlation in the sample.

This may lead you to suspect that there's a positive correlation between being a dwarf star and occurring in a double-star cluster among the population of stars as a whole, and not merely in the sample. But of course it doesn't follow from the fact that we've observed a positive correlation in the sample that we can go ahead and make a claim about a positive correlation in the population. A positive correlation in the sample gives some evidence—maybe only just a tiny bit, or maybe a lot—that there's a positive correlation in the population. We could go ahead and claim that there is a positive correlation in the population if the evidence from the sample is strong enough. Is it strong enough evidence in this case? You may already have an idea of how to answer this question, but we'll return to it later.

Here's something to notice very carefully. To say that there's a positive correlation in a sample between being a dwarf star and being in a double-star cluster is not at all to say that lots of dwarf stars in the sample are in double-star clusters. In fact, in this example, only 18% of the dwarf stars in the sample are in double-star clusters. Most of the dwarf stars *aren't* in double-star clusters. To say that there's a positive correlation between these two properties is *not* to say that the proportion of dwarfs which are doubles is large; it's to say that it's larger than the proportion of ordinary stars which are doubles.

EXERCISES

A. Suppose you discover that a large proportion of women in a sample are worried about their economic futures: 93%. Does this sample exhibit a positive correlation between being a woman and being worried about one's economic future?

ANSWER TO A.
The answer is NOT NECESSARILY. Make sure you understand why.

B. See now if you can say what would show this positive correlation.

ANSWER TO B.
To say that, in a sample, being a woman is positively correlated with worrying about one's future is to say that in this sample the proportion of women worried about their economic future is larger than the proportion of non-women (men) who are worried about their economic future. Imagine, as above, that 93% of sampled women have this worry, but imagine in addition that 98% of sampled men have this worry. The proportion of women who are worried is not larger than the proportion of others who are worried. The statement that in the sample there is a positive correlation between being a woman and worrying about your economic future is false.

7.5 A General Definition of 'Positive Correlation' ▮▮▮▮

Consider a population whose members might have some property P, and whose members might have some property Q. In that population, P is positively correlated with Q just when the proportion of the Qs among the Ps is greater than the proportion of Qs among the not-Ps.

Let's apply this to various examples. If, in the coin box, the proportion of quarters among the grayish lumps is greater than the proportion of quarters among the non-grayish lumps (that is, the greenish ones), then the properties being-a-grayish-lump and being-a-quarter are positively correlated. If, among the stars, the proportion of double-stars among the dwarfs is greater than the proportion of double-stars among the non-dwarfs (that is, the ordinary ones), then the properties of being-a-dwarf and of being-a-double-star are positively correlated. If, among people, the proportion of women who are worried is larger than the proportion of non-women (that is, men) who are worried, then the properties of being-a-woman and of being-worried are positively correlated. If the proportion of women who worry is equal to or smaller than the proportion of men who worry, then there is not a positive correlation.

MORE EXERCISES

Now, to make sure that you have all this straight, you should review the above, and then attempt the following exercises. In each case, you should: (i) draw a tree diagram illustrating what's been found in the sample, including your calculations, in percentage form, of the relevant proportions; then (ii) answer the question about whether there is a positive correlation in each sample or not, and explain why. Note that you're merely being asked about the sample, not about conclusions you might draw about the population as a whole. Thus you don't have to worry about margins of error, levels of confidence, and the like.

C. A researcher interviews 1000 university students. It turns out that of these, 800 have smoked marijuana during the past month, and of these 800, 35 have failed at least one test during that month. The remaining students have not smoked marijuana during the last month; of these, 12 have failed at least one test during the month. In this sample, is there a positive correlation between smoking marijuana and failing at least one test?

D. An agricultural botanist is studying the effects of spraying corn with Vitamin Z. She examines 100 corn plants that have been sprayed, and finds that 10 of these are infected with corn borers. She also examines 50 plants which have not been sprayed, and finds that 5 of these are infected. In this sample, is there a positive correlation between being sprayed with Vitamin Z and being infected?

E. A market researcher hangs around a corner store during a weekend and interviews 100 people who enter. Thirty of these people buy Yummie Cheezelike Goodies, and 10 of these buyers remember having seen the ad for Yummie Cheezelike Goodies on TV. Of the non-buyers, 12 remember having seen the ad. In this sample, is there a positive correlation between buying Yummie Cheezelike Goodies and remembering having seen the TV ad?

ANSWERS

C.

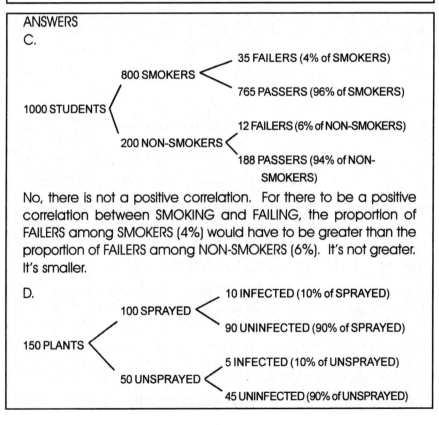

1000 STUDENTS

800 SMOKERS
- 35 FAILERS (4% of SMOKERS)
- 765 PASSERS (96% of SMOKERS)

200 NON-SMOKERS
- 12 FAILERS (6% of NON-SMOKERS)
- 188 PASSERS (94% of NON-SMOKERS)

No, there is not a positive correlation. For there to be a positive correlation between SMOKING and FAILING, the proportion of FAILERS among SMOKERS (4%) would have to be greater than the proportion of FAILERS among NON-SMOKERS (6%). It's not greater. It's smaller.

D.

150 PLANTS

100 SPRAYED
- 10 INFECTED (10% of SPRAYED)
- 90 UNINFECTED (90% of SPRAYED)

50 UNSPRAYED
- 5 INFECTED (10% of UNSPRAYED)
- 45 UNINFECTED (90% of UNSPRAYED)

No, there is not a positive correlation. For there to be a positive correlation, the proportion of INFECTED among SPRAYED (10%) would have to be greater than the proportion of INFECTED among UNSPRAYED (10%). It's not greater. It's the same.

E.

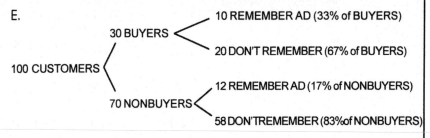

10 REMEMBER AD (33% of BUYERS)

30 BUYERS

20 DON'T REMEMBER (67% of BUYERS)

100 CUSTOMERS

12 REMEMBER AD (17% of NONBUYERS)

70 NONBUYERS

58 DON'T REMEMBER (83% of NONBUYERS)

Yes, there is a positive correlation. For there to be a positive correlation, the proportion of REMEMBER AD among BUYERS (33%) would have to be greater than the proportion of REMEMBER AD among NON-BUYERS (17%). It is greater.

7.6 Another Way of Calculating ██████████

We were imagining that you, as an astronomer, calculated your data in the following order: first, you identified the dwarfs and the ordinary stars in your sample. Then, concentrating on the dwarfs in your sample, you considered each of the individuals in this sub-population, considering whether each of them was a member of a double-star cluster or not. You came up with this:

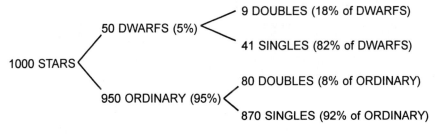

9 DOUBLES (18% of DWARFS)

50 DWARFS (5%)

41 SINGLES (82% of DWARFS)

1000 STARS

80 DOUBLES (8% of ORDINARY)

950 ORDINARY (95%)

870 SINGLES (92% of ORDINARY)

But suppose you thought about this same sample of stars in a different order. Suppose you first identified those stars, among the 1000 in the sample, that were members of a double-star cluster. Then, concentrating on the double-star cluster members in your sample, you considered each of the individuals in this sub-population, considering whether each of them was a dwarf or not. The diagram illustrating your findings would then look like this:

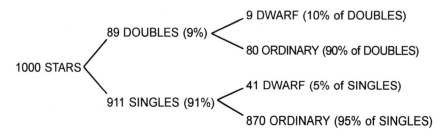

Look carefully to see the difference between these two tables. They are in fact two different ways of displaying exactly the same data. In the first case, represented by the first tree diagram, we compared the proportion of DOUBLES among the DWARFS (18%) to the proportion of DOUBLES among the ORDINARIES (8%). Because the first was larger than the second, we concluded that there is a positive correlation between DWARFS and DOUBLES. In the second case, represented by the second tree diagram, however, we compared the proportion of DWARFS among the DOUBLES (10%) to the proportion of DWARFS among the SINGLES (5%). In this case, the former is larger than the latter, so we concluded that there is a positive correlation between DOUBLES and DWARFS. Examine the two tree diagrams to make sure you see the difference in the way of calculating things.

Is there a difference here? Can there ever be a case in which A is positively correlated with B, but in which B is not positively correlated with A? Do we need to consider the same data in these two different ways? The answer is NO. Whenever there is a positive correlation between A and B, there will also be a positive correlation between B and A. It's possible to prove this point mathematically, but you needn't be worried about this proof. Take my word for it: it doesn't matter whether you set up your data one way or the other. Whenever you get a positive correlation looking at things one way, you'll get a positive correlation looking at things the other way. So in order to avoid confusion, we'll just take it that to say that A is positively correlated with B means just the same thing as to say that B is positively correlated with A: it doesn't make any difference which order things come in. Both of these can equally well be shown by demonstrating *either* that:

• The proportion of Bs among the As is greater than the proportion of Bs among the non-As.

or that:

• The proportion of As among the Bs is greater than the proportion of As among the non-Bs.

STILL MORE EXERCISES
Now consider EXERCISES C, D, and E above, except calculate them the "other way around". Make sure that your answers come out the same as they did the first time.

ANSWERS
C.

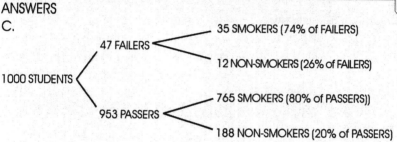

No, there is not a positive correlation. For there to be a positive correlation, the proportion of SMOKERS among FAILERS (74%) would have to be greater than the proportion of SMOKERS among PASSERS (80%). It's not greater. It's smaller.

D.

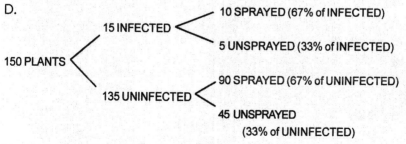

No, there is not a positive correlation. For there to be a positive correlation, the proportion of SPRAYED among INFECTED (67%) would have to be greater than the proportion of SPRAYED among UNINFECTED (67%). It's not greater. It's equal.

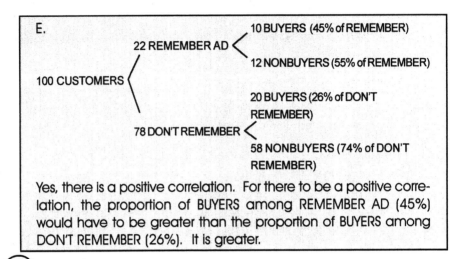

E.

100 CUSTOMERS

22 REMEMBER AD

10 BUYERS (45% of REMEMBER)

12 NONBUYERS (55% of REMEMBER)

78 DON'T REMEMBER

20 BUYERS (26% of DON'T REMEMBER)

58 NONBUYERS (74% of DON'T REMEMBER)

Yes, there is a positive correlation. For there to be a positive corre-lation, the proportion of BUYERS among REMEMBER AD (45%) would have to be greater than the proportion of BUYERS among DON'T REMEMBER (26%). It is greater.

? STILL MORE EXERCISES

F. Suppose that you're interested in possible effects of marijuana smoking on the performance of students in university classes, and imagine someone knew about the results of the scientific study in EXERCISE C above, and told you, "In the group studied, 74% of the people who failed at least one class had smoked marijuana during the past month." You might think: Wow! That's terrible! I'd better stop!

But now, suppose they told you instead, "In the group studied, 4% of the people who had smoked marijuana during the last month failed at least one class." You might then think, "That number is really very small. I guess I don't have to stop."

Both of the facts you might have been told are true about this study. Take a look again at the two answers to EXERCISE C above, and satisfy yourself that they are both right. How come they lead to opposite conclusions? What's gone wrong here?

STOP! ANSWER

What's gone wrong here is that neither of these figures have any-thing to do with what you're interested in.

G. What information about the study might be relevant to your interest?

ANSWER

STOP!

The information that's (possibly) relevant is whether or not there's a positive correlation between smoking marijuana and failing. Note carefully that neither of the figures the person told you give this information.

Now, the information I gave you in Exercise C does tell you that smoking marijuana is not positively correlated with failing at least one class. Before you use this information about smoking marijuana as a practical guide, however, you should keep several things in mind. First, this is information about the sample, not about the population. Information about a sample doesn't tell you anything reliable about the population if the sample is unrepresentative. Was this sample chosen in the right way? You don't know. Second, the lack of positive correlation was discovered in the sample. We still have not considered how to apply statistical information from a sample to a population (involving margins of error, etc.) in the case of a correlation. Third, and most important, this isn't a real study. I just made all this up.

7.7 Another Warning

This chapter is very long and very complicated. If you try to understand what's in it all at one sitting, you'll get overloaded and confused. This might be a good point to stop. Go watch the Bugs Bunny Show on TV instead, and let your brain clear out. Come back later, review briefly the part above, and then continue.

7.8 Negative Correlation

If 93% of women in the sample are worried, and 98% of the others (men) are worried, then, as has been mentioned above, it's false that there's a positive correlation in the sample between being a woman and being worried; what we have here is a **NEGATIVE CORRELATION**. The proportion of women who are worried is *smaller than* the proportion of the men who are worried. This is the same as positive correlation, except we substitute 'smaller than' for 'greater than' throughout.

As before, this can be established in two equivalent ways, by showing either:

- The proportion of worried people among women is smaller than the proportion of worried people among the non-women (men)

or:

- The proportion of women among worried people is smaller than the proportion of women among non-worried people.

7.9 No Correlation

Suppose that in our sample, the proportions of worried people turn out to be exactly the same among men as among women. For example, suppose that 83% of the women in the sample are worried and 83% of the men are worried. This means that there is **NO CORRELATION** between the properties of being a woman and being worried. This is the same as positive correlation, except we substitute 'equal to' for 'greater than' throughout.

As before, this can be established in two equivalent ways, by showing either:

- The proportion of worried people among women is equal to the proportion of worried people among the non-women (men)

or:

- The proportion of women among worried people is equal to the proportion of women among non-worried people.

OH NO! STILL MORE EXERCISES
Now return to EXERCISES C, D, and E; say in each case whether there's a positive, a negative, or no correlation, and say why.

STOP! ANSWERS
C. There's a negative correlation. This is shown in two ways, depending on how you calculate things. In the first way, it's shown by the fact that the proportion of FAILERS among SMOKERS (4%) is less than the proportion of FAILERS among NON-SMOKERS (6%). In the second way, it's shown by the fact that the proportion of SMOKERS among FAILERS (74%) is less than the proportion of SMOKERS among PASSERS (80%).

D. There's no correlation. This is shown in two ways, depending on how you calculate things. In the first way, it's shown by the fact that the proportion of INFECTED among SPRAYED (10%) is the equal to the proportion of INFECTED among UNSPRAYED (10%). In the second way, it's shown by the fact that the proportion of SPRAYED among INFECTED (67%) is equal to the proportion of SPRAYED among UNINFECTED (67%).

E. We've already shown, in two ways, that there's a positive correlation. In the first way, it's shown by the fact that the proportion of REMEMBER among BUYERS (33%) is greater than the proportion of REMEMBER among NONBUYERS (17%). In the second way, it's shown by the fact that the proportion of BUYERS among REMEMBER (45%) is greater than the proportion of BUYERS among DON'T REMEMBER (26%).

CHAPTER 8

Correlations Calculated

8.1 The Selling Power of Green Books ▮▮▮▮

In the last chapter we were concentrating on understanding what correlations are, and on recognizing when they showed up in the sample taken from a population. Of course, the sample from a population is of interest because of the possible evidence it provides about the population. When there's a correlation in the sample, this may be evidence that the population has the same correlation. When is there good evidence for a correlation in the population?

Here's an example we can work through which will answer this question.

A publisher once told me that I shouldn't have a green cover on one of my books because books with green covers tend to have lower sales than other books. Let's imagine a scientific test of this claim.

First we should note that the publisher's statement can be construed as a claim about a correlation in a population. The population in question is books sold in bookstores. We're thinking about these books with regard to their properties in two categories: *colour of cover*; *number sold*. A simple way to arrange things conceptually, for the purposes of our scientific test, is to consider two properties in each of these categories. In the category *colour of cover* it will be convenient to distinguish between books that are entirely or mostly green and the rest—those that are entirely or mostly some other colour. Let's call the books distinguished this way GREEN and OTHER COLOUR. In the category *number sold*, let's distinguish between the books which have sold a lot of copies—call them BEST SELLERS—and the rest—

call them POOR SELLERS. In these terms, we can state in various ways the correlation that the publisher claimed. The most obvious way to state his claim is to say that in the population of books in bookstores,

GREEN is negatively correlated with BEST SELLERS.

In other words, the proportion of BEST SELLERS among GREEN is smaller than the proportion of BEST SELLERS among OTHER COLOUR. For example, we might imagine that 8% of the GREEN books are BEST SELLERS but 12% of the OTHER COLOUR are BEST SELLERS.

You might remember from the previous chapter that there's an alternative way of thinking about the same fact:

BEST SELLERS is negatively correlated with GREEN.

In other words, the proportion of GREEN among BEST SELLERS is smaller than the proportion of GREEN among POOR SELLERS. For example, we might imagine that 6% of BEST SELLERS are GREEN, while 9% of POOR SELLERS are GREEN.

Let's pick one of these (equivalent) claims, and imagine that you go about testing it. You go into your friendly neighbourhood bookstore, where the manager will cooperate with your study. In this bookstore you pick out—at random—*two* samples of 100 books each: 100 GREEN books and 100 OTHER COLOUR books. Now you go into the bookstore's computerized sales records and take a look at how many sales have been made of copies of these books during the past five years. You write down, for each of these 200 books, whether it is a BEST SELLER or a POOR SELLER. (You'll need, of course, to make a decision regarding how many books sold is the minimum to make it count, according to your categories, as a BEST SELLER. It would be best to put that number at a place where many of the books have sold numbers above that figure, and many below.)

Suppose you arrive at these figures:

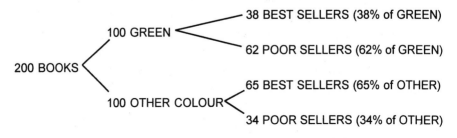

It will be convenient for our purposes to display some of these numbers graphically:

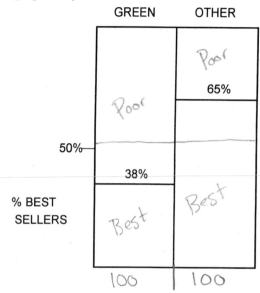

This graph represents the proportions of BEST SELLERS observed in the samples of GREEN and of OTHER COLOUR. Of course, the proportion of BEST SELLERS among the GREEN is lower than the proportion of BEST SELLERS among the OTHER *in the sample,* but what can we conclude from this about the whole population of books?

You can look at our data as giving us evidence about two simple proportions from different populations.

(1) We have examined a sample of GREEN and found out the proportion of BEST SELLERS in this sample. This gives us some evidence about the proportion of BEST SELLERS among GREEN books in the whole population.

(2) We have examined a sample of OTHER COLOUR, and found out the proportion of BEST SELLERS in this sample. This gives us some evidence about the proportion of BEST SELLERS among OTHER COLOUR books in the whole population.

In both cases, we must ask: what conclusion can we make about the population? how much evidence do we have?

First, consider the information given in our sample of GREEN. Our sample of 100 GREEN has 38% BEST SELLERS in it. What does this tell us about the GREEN population in general? We must assign a level of confidence, so let's use the .95 level, which is a common standard for science. Now, you might remember (or you might go back a couple of chapters and look up this information): in a representative sample of 100 individuals from a population, the margin of error for an observed frequency around 50% which gives a .95 level of confidence is ± .10. This means that the claim that is justified by our evidence (assuming a good sample), with .95 confidence, is that GREEN books in general contain 38% ± 10% BEST SELLERS. That is, we have adequate justification for the claim that among GREEN books, there are somewhere between 28% and 48% BEST SELLERS. Let's add this information to our picture. I'll draw the margin of error around the line representing the observed frequency in the bar for GREEN, and shade in the area representing our claim about the GREEN population as a whole.

What we can claim about the GREEN population as a whole is that the percentage of BEST SELLERS is somewhere—we can't say exactly where—in this shaded area.

Now, we'll do the same calculation for the evidence we have regarding the proportion of BEST SELLERS among OTHER COLOUR. We use the same level of confidence, .95. The sample of OTHER COLOUR is also 100, so the margin of error is again ± .10. The observed frequency is, in this case, 65%, so the claim we can make about the population of OTHER COLOUR is that the proportion of BEST SELLERS here is 65% ± 10%—in other words, somewhere between 75% and 55%.

I'll add this information to the picture:

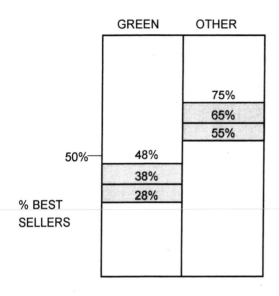

Now, remember that in order to claim that there's a negative correlation between GREEN and BEST SELLERS in the population of books as a whole, we have to be justified in claiming that the proportion of BEST SELLERS among GREEN in the real population (not just in the sample) is smaller than the proportion of BEST SELLERS among OTHER COLOUR. Can we claim this? We can't make any sufficiently justified claims about any exact proportions in the real population, but we can make sufficiently justified claims about ranges of proportions—maximum and minimum values. We can say that the proportion of BEST SELLERS among GREEN is somewhere between 28% and 48%, and that the proportion of BEST SELLERS among OTHER COLOUR is somewhere between 55% and 75%. But note that wherever in these ranges the two proportions are, the first will be smaller than the second. This is because the maximum value of the proportion of BEST SELLERS among GREEN (48%) is smaller than the minimum value of the proportion of BEST SELLERS among OTHER COLOUR (55%).

I'll put this point in terms of our pictures. The shaded range in the left-hand bar represents possible locations of the proportion of GREEN that are BEST SELLERS in the whole population. The shaded range in the right-hand bar represents possible locations of the proportion of OTHER COLOUR that are BEST SELLERS in the whole population. But every location within the left-hand bar is below every location in the right-hand bar. They don't overlap. Wherever the two are within their respective shaded regions, the one on the left must be below the one on the right.

Thus, we are justified in concluding that GREEN and BEST SELLERS are negatively correlated in the real population.

8.2 An Unjustified Conclusion About Green Books

But now let's imagine different results of our sample. Suppose instead that the number of BEST SELLERS among GREEN was a bit higher:

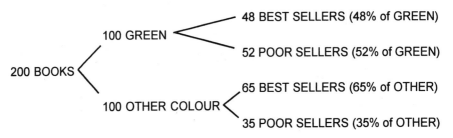

Here's the completed graph illustrating these numbers:

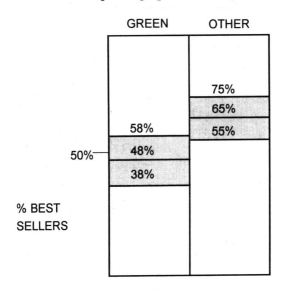

Now the shaded ranges overlap; that is, the maximum value, within its margin of error, for the proportion of BEST SELLERS among GREEN—the top of the shaded area of the left bar (58%)—is higher than the minimum value, within its margin of error, for the proportion of BEST SELLERS among OTHER (55%). For all we know, in the population the first proportion might be as high as 58%, and the second as low as 55%, in which case the first would be *higher* than the second. We're not permitted, given the level of certainty required, to claim that there is a negative correlation in the population of books as a whole. These figures do not justify the claim of a negative correlation.

8.3 Statistical Significance ████████

When the data in the sample do not justify a conclusion about a possible correlation in the population, the data are said not to be **STATISTICALLY SIGNIFICANT**. Statistically significant data do justify a conclusion about a correlation in the population. This technical term is a little misleading. Even though data that are not statistically significant don't justify a conclusion about a correlation, they are "significant" in the sense that we can derive valuable information from them with the requisite degree of confidence, as we shall see.

Now we can say that the first set of data would be statistically significant for showing a negative correlation, but the second set would not be statistically significant.

(A note on language: if you really want to impress people, use the word 'data' as a plural noun, which it is. For example, say "The data *are* statistically significant." The singular form of that word is 'datum'.)

8.4 Going Out on a Limb ████████

EXERCISE **?**
Suppose that you got the second set of data, and you had to guess, on the basis of these figures, whether there was a negative correlation or not. What's your best guess?

ANSWER **STOP!**
Your best guess would be that there was a negative correlation.

The overlap between the ranges of margin of error is quite small, after all, and it's likely that the proportion of GREEN that are BEST SELLERS in the population is, after all, smaller than the proportion of OTHERS that are. The figures we got do make it look somewhat likely that there is a negative correlation here. After all, it's not very likely, given the evidence of our sample, that the proportion in the population is actually very near the top of the left-hand bar: it's more likely to be somewhere near the middle of it, nearer the frequency observed in the sample. And the same thing for the proportion of BEST SELLERS among OTHERS in the population, which is most likely near the middle of the right-hand bar, close to the observed frequency in the sample. You might feel that it's reasonable, given these figures, to go out on a limb a little, and to make the claim that there is a negative correlation on the basis of these numbers.

But notice what this reasoning involves. Given the level of confidence we've been using, .95, the conclusion that there's a negative correlation is unjustified. To claim that there is one would give less than a 95% chance you're right. Of course, you might not feel that such a high level of confidence is necessary for your claims: you might not mind having a greater danger of being mistaken; you might think, what the hell, I'll go out on a limb a little. Maybe, then, you'd prefer to use a lower level of certainty—for example, the one represented by 1 standard deviation, or a .67 level of certainty.

We've already seen the sorts of calculations we need to use with this lower level of certainty. It turns out that a .67 level of confidence, given a representative sample of 100, means a margin of error of .± .05. Let's redraw the last graph, incorporating the narrower margin of error that corresponds to this lower level of confidence:

On this picture, incorporating the narrower margins of error, the shaded areas no longer overlap; we're justified now in saying that there is a negative correlation between the properties. Given the lower level of confidence required, the same data become statistically significant. We should bear in mind, however, that we're not quite so confident that this claim is true.

8.5 Different Sample Sizes

Suppose that instead of including 100 GREEN and 100 OTHER books in our sample we took much larger samples: 1000 each. As you should remember, a larger sample size, keeping the level of confidence constant, means a smaller margin of error. If the sample size is 1000, and the confidence level still .95, then the margin of error is about ± .03.

EXERCISE
Draw a graph, illustrating this bunch of data, assuming a confidence level of .95.

2000 BOOKS
1000 GREEN
480 BEST SELLERS (48% of GREEN)
520 POOR SELLERS (52% of GREEN)
1000 OTHER COLOUR
650 BEST SELLERS (65% of OTHER)
350 POOR SELLERS (35% of OTHER)

Notice that these observed frequencies, in terms of percentage, are identical to the ones in the cases we've just been considering. These observed frequencies did not justify the claim that there was a negative correlation when the confidence level was .95, and the samples were of 100 books of each sort. At the same confidence level, do the same observed frequencies from a sample of 1000 of each sort of book justify that conclusion?

ANSWER

GREEN   OTHER

% BEST
SELLERS

50%—
68%
65%
51%
48%
62%
45%

Notice that, given the smaller margins of error produced by the larger samples, the shaded regions do not overlap, and now the conclusion is justified. The data are statistically significant.

8.6 A Positive Correlation

Now imagine that we got these figures:

200 BOOKS
100 GREEN
49 BEST SELLERS (49% of GREEN)
51 POOR SELLERS (51% of GREEN)
100 OTHER COLOUR
28 BEST SELLERS (28% of OTHER)
72 POOR SELLERS (72% of OTHER)

Here's the graph for these new figures, assuming a confidence level, as before, of .95.

Because the shaded regions do not overlap, and because the possible values for the proportion of BEST SELLERS among GREEN are all *higher* than any possible values for the proportion of BEST SELLERS among OTHER COLOUR, the data are statistically significant, and we have sufficient evidence to claim that there is a positive correlation between GREEN and BEST SELLERS. This would mean that, contrary to the publisher's advice, it's actually more likely for a green-covered book to be a best seller than a book with another coloured cover.

8.7 Evidence for No Correlation

When the two shaded regions in our graph overlap, then it's possible that there is no correlation. But could there be sufficient evidence to claim that there is no correlation? The surprising answer is no.

Here's why not. When the observed frequencies for the two groups are different, then that makes it likely, to some degree, that there's a correlation. (When the shaded areas overlap, as we've seen, the evidence is not, however, strong enough.) But now consider a case in which the observed frequencies are identical, for example:

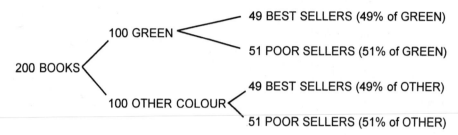

Doesn't this give evidence that there's no correlation? Well, it gives some evidence, but not sufficient evidence. Here's the graph for this:

What this graph shows is *that it's possible* that there is no correlation between these properties in the population— it's possible, that is, that the proportion of BEST SELLERS among the GREEN books in the population is exactly the same as the proportion of BEST SELLERS among the OTHER COLOUR. But we can't claim that there is no correlation, because the proportions in the population might be anywhere within the shaded areas. One might, as far as we are able to claim with 95% confidence, be above or below the other.

Well, what would happen if we were using a higher or lower confidence level? A higher or lower confidence level would change the size of the margin of error. A lower confidence level would make for a smaller margin of error. But no matter what confidence level we picked, there would always be *some* margin of error surrounding the two observed frequencies. As long as there is some margin of error, no matter how small, we're still not allowed to claim that the proportions in the population are exactly equal.

Similarly, we might make the margins of error smaller by using a large sample. But no matter what size sample (with replacement!) we're using, identical observed frequencies will not sufficiently justify the claim that there's no correlation in the population. There will always be *some* margin of error surrounding the two observed frequencies, so we'll still be unable to claim (no matter what certainty level we choose) that there is no correlation.

The strange but true result of this reasoning is that no sample can justify the claim that there's no correlation between two properties in the population.

SOME MORE EXERCISES
In all these exercises, a confidence level of .95 is assumed. In each case:
  (1) draw a tree chart illustrating the data
  (2) draw a graph showing the data, with margins of error
  (3) do the data have statistical significance?
  (4) on the basis of your graph, state whether there's sufficient evidence to claim that there's a positive correlation, a negative correlation, or no correlation between the relevant properties.
To do these exercises, you'll need to know what the (approximate) margins of error are, given a .95 confidence level, for various sample sizes. Here's a chart giving these values:

Sample Size	Margin of Error
10	± .30
50	± .14
200	± .07
500	± .04
1000	± .03

A. Imagine that a pollster is investigating voting preferences in Québec. She interviews 1000 Québecois altogether, 500 francophones (people whose first language is French) and 500 Others (people whose first language is not French). Of the francophones interviewed, 220 indicate they prefer the Liberal candidate. Of the others, 290 indicate they prefer the Liberal candidate. Consider what this pollster can claim regarding the possible correlation of being a Francophone and preferring the Liberal candidate.

B. It's conventional wisdom that Fords manufactured on Mondays are more likely to have defects than those manufactured on other days. Imagine that Henry Ford hears about this, so he hires a Quality Control Engineer to test whether there's a correlation between being manufactured on Monday and having significant defects. Ford provides the engineer with 10 cars manufactured on Monday, and 10 each manufactured on Tuesday, Wednesday, Thursday, Friday, and Saturday. (In those days, Saturday was not a day off.) Among the Monday cars, the engineer finds four with significant defects. Among all the rest of the cars, 16 are found with significant defects. What should the engineer tell Henry Ford regarding the possible correlation between being a significantly defective car and being manufactured on Monday?

C. (REAL CASE) Researchers in Lithuania gave health questionnaires to 202 drivers whose cars had been struck from behind one to three years earlier. The drivers were asked about symptoms, and their answers were compared with those of a second group, made up of the same number of people of similar ages and from the same town who had not been in a car accident. (C1) Thirty-five percent of the accident victims reported neck pain, but so did 33 per cent of the no-accident group. (C2) 53 per cent who had been in accidents had headaches, but so did 50 per cent of the no-accident group.

D. A researcher interviews 1000 men, 450 of whom have ever seen the TV show "America's Tackiest Videos", and 500 women, 220 of whom have ever seen it. What should the interviewer claim on the basis of these interviews about a possible correlation?

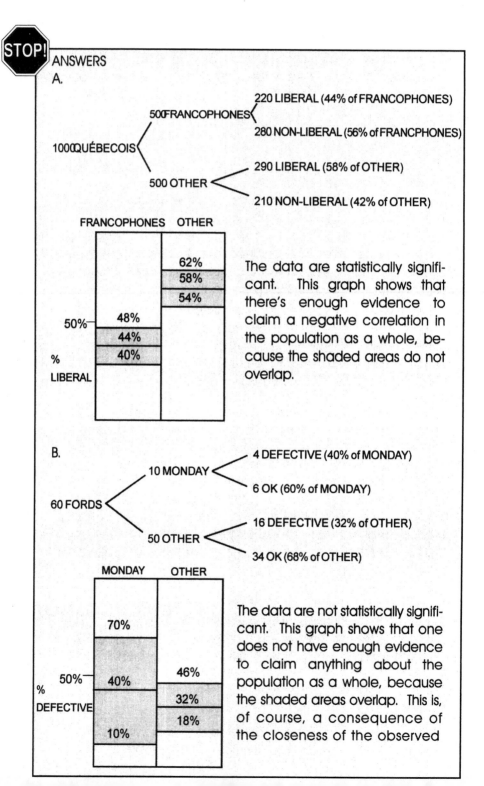

STOP! ANSWERS

A.

220 LIBERAL (44% of FRANCOPHONES)

500 FRANCOPHONES

280 NON-LIBERAL (56% of FRANCPHONES)

1000 QUÉBECOIS

290 LIBERAL (58% of OTHER)

500 OTHER

210 NON-LIBERAL (42% of OTHER)

FRANCOPHONES   OTHER

62%
58%
54%

50%   48%
44%
40%

% LIBERAL

The data are statistically signifi-cant. This graph shows that there's enough evidence to claim a negative correlation in the population as a whole, be-cause the shaded areas do not overlap.

B.

4 DEFECTIVE (40% of MONDAY)

10 MONDAY

6 OK (60% of MONDAY)

60 FORDS

16 DEFECTIVE (32% of OTHER)

50 OTHER

34 OK (68% of OTHER)

MONDAY   OTHER

70%

50%   40%   46%

% DEFECTIVE

32%

18%

10%

The data are not statistically signifi-cant. This graph shows that one does not have enough evidence to claim anything about the population as a whole, because the shaded areas overlap. This is, of course, a consequence of the closeness of the observed frequencies, and of the huge size of the margin of error—the result of the small samples. Henry Ford's Quality Control Engineer hasn't done a good job on this sampling test: the samples are too small for reliable information. It's also clear that Henry himself also isn't doing such a hot job at building cars. Even this comparatively uninformative data show us that *at minimum*, 10% of Monday's cars are defective, and 18% of the rest. Thus, even though we say that the data are not statistically significant, some "significant" information can be extracted from it.

C(1).

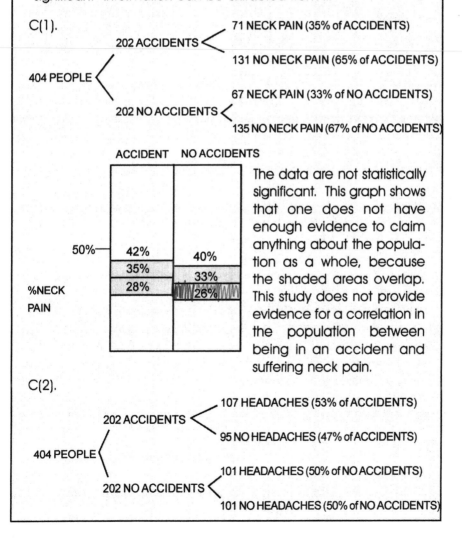

404 PEOPLE

202 ACCIDENTS
- 71 NECK PAIN (35% of ACCIDENTS)
- 131 NO NECK PAIN (65% of ACCIDENTS)

202 NO ACCIDENTS
- 67 NECK PAIN (33% of NO ACCIDENTS)
- 135 NO NECK PAIN (67% of NO ACCIDENTS)

ACCIDENT   NO ACCIDENTS

%NECK PAIN

50%—

42%
35%
28%

40%
33%
26%

The data are not statistically significant. This graph shows that one does not have enough evidence to claim anything about the population as a whole, because the shaded areas overlap. This study does not provide evidence for a correlation in the population between being in an accident and suffering neck pain.

C(2).

404 PEOPLE

202 ACCIDENTS
- 107 HEADACHES (53% of ACCIDENTS)
- 95 NO HEADACHES (47% of ACCIDENTS)

202 NO ACCIDENTS
- 101 HEADACHES (50% of NO ACCIDENTS)
- 101 NO HEADACHES (50% of NO ACCIDENTS)

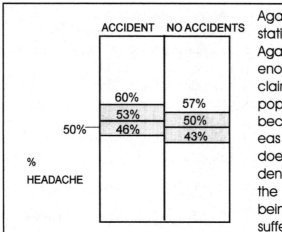

Again, the data are not statistically significant. Again, one does not have enough evidence to claim anything about the population as a whole, because the shaded areas overlap. This study does not provide evidence for a correlation in the population between being in an accident and suffering headaches.

Note carefully just how little information we have extracted so far from this study on accidents, neck pain, and headaches. All we have discovered is that the study does not provide evidence for a correlation in the population. It's important for you to understand that we have not shown that there is no correlation. Read over the beginning of this section again if you don't understand what the difference is between not showing that there is a correlation, and showing that there is not a correlation, or if you don't see why this sample doesn't give sufficient evidence that there is no correlation, and why no sample could give sufficient evidence for this.

But this is not to say that nothing at all, of any interest, can be concluded on the basis of this sample. In the next section we'll see what of interest can be concluded.

You can probably guess that this study was intended to cast light on the question whether car accidents *cause* neck pain or headaches. As we'll see later, *cause* is quite a different matter from *correlation*. What if any conclusions we can draw about the causal relation between car accidents, neck pains, and headaches, is a matter we'll deal with much later, beginning in Chapter 19.

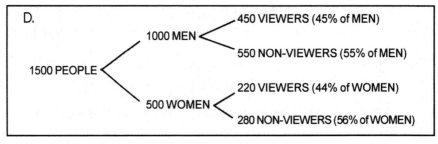

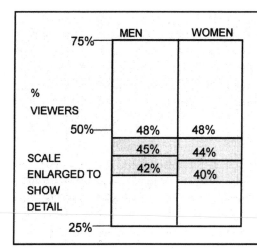

Note that the vertical scale has been enlarged on this graph. Again, the shaded areas overlap, this time because the difference in observed frequencies is so small.

8.8 Strength of Correlation

In the population as a whole, 84% of children love Chocko-yums, while 38% of adults love them. How do I know this? I couldn't have found out information this exact by induction from a sample; there's no margin of error. I could have found this out only by ascertaining the feelings about Chocko-yums of every single person. Obviously, I just made this information up. Well, anyway, let's imagine it's true. It shows that there's a positive correlation between being a child and loving Chocko-yums, and it's a pretty strong positive correlation too: the percentage of children who love Chocko-yums is much larger than the percentage of adults who do. We can get a very rough estimate of the strength of this correlation by subtracting the second percentage from the first. (This is only a rough way of doing it: real statisticians have more complicated and better ways to calculate strengths of correlation; but it will do for our purposes.) So we can say that the strength of the correlation is 84% - 38% = 46%. If, instead, 81% of adults loved Choco-Yums, then there would still be a positive correlation between being a child and loving Choco-Yums, as shown by the fact that the percentage of children who do is larger than the percentage of others (adults); the strength is estimated by the same sort of subtraction: 84% - 81% = 3%. This is a much weaker positive correlation.

Suppose that during the past decade it rained on 54% of the weekdays in my city, but that 59% of the weekend days are rainy. This means that during this period there was a negative correlation between being a weekday and being rainy in my city. The strength of this correlation is given in the same way, by subtracting the second number from the first: 54% - 59% = -5%. The negative result of this subtraction shows that this is a negative correlation. This is not a very strong negative correlation: only -5%. If it were, say, -20%, then this would be a much larger negative correlation.

Suppose that 7% of adults have colds right now, and 7% of children. To calculate the strength of the correlation between being an adult right now and having a cold, we take the percent of adults who have a cold right now (7%), and subtract the percent of non-adults who have colds right now (7%): 7% - 7% = 0%. Saying that a correlation has a strength of 0% is the same thing as saying that there's no correlation.

Now consider the sort of case in which we don't know the exact proportions in the real population but are able to estimate them, with a margin of error, on the basis of a sample. Here's a graph for an imagined set of sample data about the selling power of green books:

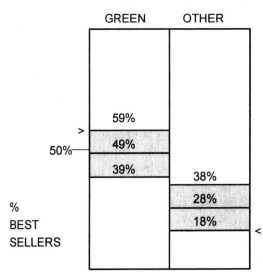

It's clear that we have sufficient evidence for a positive correlation between GREEN and BEST SELLER here, but how strong is it? We can't say exactly what the relevant proportions in the population are, but we can say some things about the strength of this positive correlation.

Look for the little '>' mark on the left edge: this marks the *maximum* size we can justifiably claim the proportion of BEST SELLERS among GREEN has: 59%. Look for the little '<' on the right edge. This marks the *minimum* size we can justifiably claim the proportion of BEST SELLERS among OTHER has: 18%. Subtracting the second number from the first gives us the maximum strength for this positive correlation: 59% - 18% = 41%.

Now look at this graph for the same data:

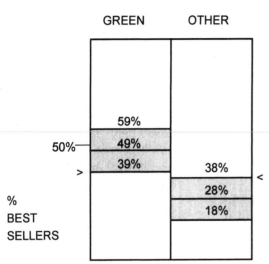

This is the same graph, but I've moved the little marks. Look for the little '>' mark on the left edge: this marks the *minimum* strength we can justifiably claim the proportion of BEST SELLERS among GREEN has: 39%. Look for the little '<' on the right edge. This marks the *maximum* size we can justifiably claim the proportion of BEST SELLERS among OTHER has: 38%. Subtracting the second number from the first gives us the *minimum* strength this positive correlation could be: 39% - 38% = 1%.

In sum, then, in this case, we can estimate the maximum and minimum strengths for this correlation: between 41% and 1%. The fact that all the magnitudes in this range are positive shows, of course, that what we have here is a positive correlation.

Now let's do the same thing for a negative correlation:

We calculate the strength of this correlation in much the same way. Its lowest possible value is 28% - 75% = -47%. Its highest possible value is 48% - 55% = -7%. The range of strength of correlation here is from -47% to -7%. It might be anywhere between a fairly strong negative correlation (-47%) to a fairly weak one (-7%). In any case, it's a negative correlation.

Now consider a case in which we're unable to say whether there's a positive or negative correlation in the population:

Calculating things the same way, we can say that the possible ranges for correlation strength here are between 58% - 55% = 3%, and 38% - 75% = - 37%. This gives important information: that *if* there's a positive correlation in the population, it's a very small one, with a maximum strength of 3%. But there might also be a negative correlation, and a whopping one at that—it might have a strength of up to -37%.

What this means is that despite the fact that the data represented in this graph don't justify saying that there's a positive or negative correlation. Nevertheless we can say that if there's a positive correlation, there's only a very weak one; but there might be quite a strong negative correlation. This is some information, after all, and might be quite valuable to us. So even though this is a case where we say the data have 'no statistical significance', we can make some claims with "significant" informative value, and with the required high degree of confidence.

Finally, consider again a case where the observed frequencies are identical:

GREEN   OTHER

	GREEN	OTHER
50%	59%	59%
	49%	49%
	39%	39%

% BEST
SELLERS

As I hope you remember, neither this nor any other set of data can justify the claim that there's no correlation. But applying the same sort of calculations for magnitude of possible correlations, what we can say here with sufficient justification is that there might be a positive correlation with a strength of up to 59% - 39% = 20%, or that there might be a negative correlation with a strength of up to 39% - 59% = (-20%). So although we can't say that there's a correlation, and we can't say that there's no correlation, we can give the information that if there's a correlation, it's not a really strong one; that there isn't any sort of strong positive or negative correlation in the population represented here. This is worth saying: it gives useful information.

Both of the last two graphs represented data which was not statistically significant: neither justifies the claim that there's any sort of correlation. Nevertheless, some important information can be gleaned from both, in terms of the possible strength of correlations there might be in the real population.

EXERCISES

Now go back to the exercises you did in part 8.7 and calculate the range of strength of each possible correlation.

ANSWERS

A. The correlation ranges between (48% - 54%) = -6% and (40% - 62%) = -22%. There's a negative correlation here, and it might be a weak one, as small as -6%, or a moderately strong one, as large as -22%.

B. The correlation ranges between (70% - 18%) = 52% and (10% - 46%) = -36%. In other words, we can say that in the population of cars as a whole, there might be anywhere between a +52% correlation and a -36% correlation. So there might be, in the population as a whole, a large or small positive or a negative correlation, or no correlation at all. This is precious little information, and shows why this study is not much good.

C(a) We can conclude that the population has a correlation between (42% - 26%) = 16% and (28% - 40%) = -12%. Thus there might be a positive correlation, up to +16% (fairly weak at best), no correlation, or a negative one, up to -12% (fairly weak at best). As mentioned earlier, we can't conclude that there is no correlation in the population. We can, however, conclude that if there's a correlation, it's not a very strong one.

C(b) We can conclude that the population has a correlation between (60% - 43%) = 17% and (46% - 57%) = -11%. Again, there might be a positive correlation, up to +17% (fairly weak at best), or no correlation, or a negative one, up to -11% (fairly weak at best). We can't conclude that there is no correlation in the population. We can, however, conclude that if there's a correlation, it's not a very strong one.

Compare this study with the one imagined in (B) above. Neither tells us whether there's a positive or negative correlation, or no correlation; but (C) does give us information that (B) does not: if there's any sort of correlation, it's a fairly weak one. (C) is a more informative study than (B).

D. The correlation ranges between (48% - 40%) = 8% and (42% - 48%) = -6%. In other words, we can say that there may be no correlation, or a positive or negative correlation in the population as a whole; but if there is a positive or negative correlation, it isn't a very strong one.

PART II

Explanations

CHAPTER 9

Explantions Explained

9.1 Smithian Science Again

Mrs. Smith thought that collecting facts was the main scientific task, although she was, no doubt, aware of other things science does. The facts she urged us to begin gathering were just naked brute facts: facts about particular things, at particular times and places. Here are some samples of the sorts of questions that she took to be paradigm scientific questions:

- What colour is that bird?
- What is it eating?
- When, exactly, do the leaves start to fall off the tree in your back yard?
- How long does that bee spend inside the flower?
- What's it doing in there?
- The next time it snows and then thaws, which melts faster: the snow on your lawn or on your sidewalk?
- On a partly cloudy day, are the clouds all moving in the same direction?
- What colour do you get when you mix this yellow paint with that blue paint?
- Try mixing this baking powder with water. Exactly what happens?

Mrs. Smith was in love with facts about the natural world. They're so wonderful! They're all over the place! All you have to do is begin looking carefully! She urged us to become aware of them, to remember them or write them down, to accumulate bigger and bigger piles of them.

Nobody can deny that fact-piles have a certain charm, and that there's an enjoyment that comes from awareness of them, and from collecting them. Some of us in the class who usually spent our time either in a daze, or in a frenzy of involvement with ourselves or with other people, discovered that it was fun to walk around the world alert to our environment. It was a relief and a pleasure to take a close look at a bird or a bug instead. When we did, we thought we were well on the way to becoming scientists.

But in the last few chapters, we have been looking into a different sort of scientific activity. As we've seen, this goes beyond mere observation, though it starts from there. The kind of facts it aims at accumulating are facts about groups of things: about "populations," where some of the members are unobserved. When you hang around the mall asking passers-by how they might vote, you're not doing this just for its own sake. You're doing this because you're really interested in how *all the voters in Québec* are going to vote, and you're using the particular facts you pile up as evidence for this more general conclusion. The negative correlation of green cover and good book sales is a more complicated sort of general fact: it's about all books, and the relation one particular property that they may have has to another.

This non-Smithian sort of scientific investigation does not, however, exhaust the field, as you won't be surprised to learn, given that there's much of this book left. Another kind of scientific activity, perhaps more important in certain ways than this, is **EXPLANATION**.

9.2 What is an Explanation?

This is a difficult question to give a really adequate answer to, and I'm not going to try. Here's an easy if not particularly enlightening account of what an explanation is: it's what answers a "why" question.

Notice, first of all, that none of the Smithian questions listed at the beginning of this chapter are "why" questions. Most of them are "what" or "when" or "which" questions. None of these questions asks for an *explanation*. Of course, once any of these bare naked facts becomes known, then it might be time to seek an explanation (*Why* does the snow melt first on the sidewalk?); and surely some bare naked facts will figure in an explanation of others. Bare fact collection is important not only in itself, but insofar as it is an essential part of finding the things that need explanation and explaining them. But answering a bare fact question like those above is not the same as providing an explanation.

EXERCISE

Make a list of a dozen or so questions someone might be interested in answering. (They don't have to be scientific questions, or questions you don't know the answer to, or questions that anyone would particularly be interested in answering.) Now look over the list. I'll bet that most of the questions are about bare naked facts. How many of them are like this? Are there any general questions, about groups of things? Are there any "why" questions? See if there are any questions that are in none of these three categories. If so, how would you characterize them? Are there any that you're pretty sure go into one or the other of two of the above categories, but you're not sure which?

9.3 The Distinction Between Factual and Explanation Questions

The clarity of this distinction is marred somewhat by the fact that essentially the same question can be asked in "why" and in "what" form:

- What's responsible for the disappearance of the cod from the Atlantic?
- Why did the cod disappear from the Atlantic?

Like any "what" question, both of these questions can be answered by stating a fact. In this case the answer is (maybe) given by the fact that seals are eating the cod. Nevertheless, both of these questions ask for *explanation*.

Typically, questions that use the word "what" but which are actually requests for explanation of a fact will use phrases such as:

- What is the explanation for F?
- What brings about F?
- What is responsible F?
- What is the cause of F?
- What is the reason for F?

where 'F' names the fact in question.

EXERCISES

A. Take a look at the list of questions you constructed to answer the question in the exercise assigned in part 9.2. Are there any questions in there which you initially construed as requests for brute fact information which are requests for an explanation?

B. Construct a list of a few questions which call for explanation. Try to make them different, in significant ways, from the examples I've given.

9.4 Explanation and Truth

A bit of technical jargon that will be useful to us: philosophers call the fact that is to be explained the **EXPLANANDUM**. What is provided as explanation of this fact is the **EXPLANANS**. (Despite having an 's' on the end, this word is singular.)

Why was there such a good crop of rhubarb this spring? The explanans is: there was a very mild and wet winter.

Note the obvious fact that one condition for a good explanation here is that the explanans ("There was a very mild and wet winter") has to be true. If the winter wasn't very mild and wet, then this can't explain the rhubarb bonanza.

Somebody who already knew that the winter was mild and wet might still wonder about the explanation of the good rhubarb crop, maybe because they don't know that mild wet winters produce good rhubarb crops in the spring, or maybe because they did know this but just didn't make the connection.

9.5 Explanation and Deduction

The next condition for explanation is that the explanandum, logically speaking, *follows from* the explanans. That is to say, if the explanans were true, then the explanandum would also be true. Consider this explanation: your car stalled in the middle of the street because it ran out of gas. It seems to follow from the fact that a car ran out of gas that it would stop.

You can see the motivation for this condition by comparing another candidate for explanation. Suppose I try to explain the fact that it's raining today by pointing out that it's Thursday. Suppose this satisfies the condition that the proposed explanans is true: it really is Thursday. Why is this not an explanation? Well, clearly my attempted explanation fails because the fact that it's Thursday appears to be completely irrelevant to the fact that it's raining. It can perfectly well be Thursday but not be raining. What we want here is for it to be the case that that the truth of the explanans would make the explanandum true: that the explanandum would follow from the explanans.

But let us be a bit more careful here. We can understand what's meant by one statement "following from" another in terms of a valid deductive argument. Statement C follows from Statement P when P is the premise, and C the conclusion of a valid deductive argument. (This may be a good time for you to re-read part 2.4, to remind yourself of what a valid deductive argument is.)

EXERCISE

Is this argument a valid deductive argument?

> Your car ran out of gas just now.
> Therefore your car stopped.

ANSWER

No. It's possible that the premise is true and the conclusion is false.

Remember that deductive validity is a very strict matter. In the real world, of course, cars don't keep going if they run out of gas. But this general rule is not stated in the argument above. Unless we state that general rule, the argument is invalid.

But consider this argument:

> Your car ran out of gas just now.
> Whenever a car runs out of gas it stops.
> Therefore your car stopped.

This is a valid deductive argument. And, it seems, this argument spells out in full what was really assumed when the explanation was provided for why your car stopped. What was said didn't include the other premise, and didn't need to, because it was so obvious that it was implied.

Let's say, then, that for an explanation to be a good one, the explanandum has to follow deductively from the fully spelled out explanans, including the parts that were unstated but assumed.

9.6 The Deductive-Nomological Model

In a hugely influential paper written in 1948, Carl Hempel and Paul Oppenheim presented what they called the Deductive-Nomological Model of scientific explanation.* The "Deductive-Nomological Model" is the account of explanation we've been looking at. Because that name is such a mouthful, we'll call it the D-N Model. Hempel and Oppenheim's paper presents and defends the D-N Model with enormous detail and precision; but we're going to deal with it only in rough outline (you'll be relieved to hear). Since the publication of this paper, there has been a noisy and prolonged philosophical controversy over it: many philosophers have raised objections, and many others have tried to make small fixes to the D-N Model to make it work. We'll go on to consider some of the first steps in this debate in the next chapter, but again we can't go into things very deeply. You should be aware that there's a lot more to be said about it than we will here.

We've already been talking about one of the two basic features of the Deductive-Nomological Model—the part indicated by the word "Deductive" in its title. This is that the Model specifies as a necessary condition for any successful explanation that the explanandum follow deductively from a bunch of true premises, and that these premises constitute the (full) explanans.

---

* Carl G. Hempel and Paul Oppenheim, "Studies in the Logic of Explanation," *Philosophy of Science* 15, pp. 135-175. Reprinted in Hempel, *Aspects of Scientific Explanation and Other Essays in the Philosophy of Science* (New York: The Free Press, 1965), which also contains another long and detailed article by Hempel on the subject: "Aspects of Scientific Explanation." The Hempel/Oppenheim article is also reprinted in Joseph C. Pitt (ed.), *Theories of Explanation* (New York: Oxford University Press. If you want an introductory but still complicated discussion of the Hempel/Oppenheim position and its problems, you should look at an article by Wesley C. Salmon called "Scientific Explanation". It's Chapter 1 of *Introduction to the Philosophy of Science*, by Merrilee H. Salmon et. al. (Englewood Cliffs, NJ: Prentice Hall, 1992).

A second necessary condition, not yet explicitly mentioned, is indicated by the "Nomological" part of the title. **NOMOLOGICAL** means *having to do with general laws of nature*. The idea here is that at least one of these premises must be what we might loosely call a "general rule". The general rule, the law of nature, in the car explanation was "Whenever a car runs out of gas it stops."

There's much more to be said about what a "general law of nature" is. Not every general statement, it appears, is a law of nature. Which ones are? and why? This is a question we'll get to in Chapter 16. For the moment, however, let's just wonder whether the D-N Model is correct in thinking that at least one general-law statement is really necessary (if only implicit and unstated) in every adequate explanation.

Consider this attempt at explanation:

Why do you have a black eye?
Because I have a black eye and my feet hurt.

EXERCISE
State this attempt at explanation in premise-conclusion form. Is it deductively valid?

ANSWER

> PREMISE: I have a black eye and my feet hurt.
> CONCLUSION: I have a black eye.

Yes, it's deductively valid. It's impossible that the premise be true while the conclusion is false.

This attempt does not provide an explanation, despite the fact that the explanandum follows deductively from the explanans. What's gone wrong here is that no general law has been mentioned in the explanans. Consider, by contrast, this attempt at an explanation:

Why do you have a black eye?
Because Irving slugged me hard in the eye last night, and when someone slugs you hard in the eye, a black eye results.

Now it appears we have a genuine explanation. We can display it as an argument with two premises:

PREMISE 1: Irving slugged me hard in the eye last night

PREMISE 2: When someone slugs you hard in the eye, a black eye results.

CONCLUSION: Therefore I have a black eye.

This is a deductively valid argument. Premise 2 is a general law. If we assume that both premises are true, then all the conditions specified by the D-N Model are satisfied, and it appears that we in fact have a good explanation here.

9.7 The Mysterious Whistle

Consider this example.

You and your sister are sitting in the kitchen, and you hear a loud whistle. What's going on? "I'll go check on that," says your sister, and she rushes off. She returns in a minute and says it was nothing. "Why was there that high-pitched whistle?" you ask, requesting an explanation. "Well, Uncle Fred was in the hall, smoking a cigar," she says.

According to the D-N Model of explanations, explanations are premises which together deductively imply the explanandum. We just have one statement here in the explanans. Here's the explanation expressed as an argument:

PREMISE: Uncle Fred was in the hall, smoking a cigar.

CONCLUSION: There was a high-pitched whistle.

This argument is not deductively valid. Again, we might treat what is actually said here as a short form for a longer argument in which some other premises are left unsaid; when we add all the unspoken premises, we get the full form of the argument which would be deductively valid. What these other premises are depends on the particular context, but let's try to imagine what they might be. Here's a plausible try:

When somebody is smoking a cigar in a small room with poor ventilation, the room becomes very smoky.

The hall is a small room with poor ventilation

Uncle Fred was smoking a cigar in the hall.

Whenever there's a working smoke alarm in a very smoky room, the
   smoke alarm will go off.
There's a smoke alarm in the hall.
The smoke alarm was working.
When smoke alarms go off, they produce a high-pitched whistle.
Therefore there was a high-pitched whistle.

Notice that there are three "general rules"—laws of nature, perhaps—in this
fuller explanation. The rest of the premises state the **FACTUAL CONDITIONS**—
the facts that make the laws apply.

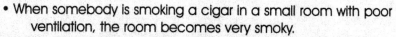

EXERCISE
Look through this fuller explanation and identify the three "general
rules".

ANSWER
They are:
- When somebody is smoking a cigar in a small room with poor
   ventilation, the room becomes very smoky.
- Whenever there's a working smoke alarm in a very smoky
   room, the smoke alarm will go off.
- When smoke alarms go off, they produce a high-pitched whistle.

   The explanation we've arrived at has six premises; these together constitute the explanans. But your sister can't be faulted for having stated only one
of these six premises, when she might have stated all of them: she did, after
all, know all the other five, and know that they were relevant, and so did you.
Ordinary talk is usually acceptably shorthand, leaving a lot out. Only philosophers insist on spelling everything out, and as you've noticed, having
read the earlier parts of this book, this can get very tedious.

9.8 Which Premise Gives *the* Explanation?

   Why did she pick the particular premise she did to mention? Suppose
she had stated another one of them instead; what if she had stated one of the
other factual conditions, for example, "The hall is a small room with poor
ventilation?" Or one of the laws, for example, "Whenever there's a working

smoke alarm in a very smoky room, the smoke alarm will go off." Your re-
action would have been puzzlement: you might reply, to either of these statements, "That's not the explanation." We regard the statement she did make,
about Uncle Fred and his cigar, as *the* explanation. Why?

It's a rule of general conversation that the obvious need not be stated,
and these other premises state the obvious—or at least, what would be obvious under the conditions we imagine. You can already be expected to know
that they were true. The only one of these premises you didn't already know
was (we suppose) the one about Uncle Fred and his cigar. Putting this new
information together with what you already know gives you the full explanation.

Under other circumstances, you might not know about one of the other
premises. For example, if this is not your house you're sitting in, you might
not be aware that the hall is a small room with poor ventilation, but maybe
you did know that Uncle Fred was in there smoking a cigar. In this case the
information that the hall was small and poorly ventilated is what you need,
and you'd count this as *the* explanation.

In this case, as in many other cases, the factual condition that is mentioned as "the" explanation is the one that's new or slightly unusual. Let's
call this the **RECENT FACTUAL CONDITION**, meaning that this is the one that has
become true the most recently. The other factual conditions have been true
longer. Let's call them **STANDING FACTUAL CONDITIONS**. The hall has always
been small and poorly ventilated. There's been a smoke alarm in the hall for
a long time. The premises which state general laws in the full explanation
have also been true for a long time. Smoke alarms normally work that way.
People smoking cigars in small poorly ventilated rooms invariably fill them
with smoke. Perhaps it's not unusual for Uncle Fred to smoke a cigar, or to
be sitting in the hall, but this is the one premise in the full explanation that is
not true all the time, or for a long time until now. Because it's the one that
hasn't been true for a long time, it may be the one you're unaware of; it
would be the one that would provide you, when added to what you already
know, with the full explanation.

But it's not always the case that we take the recent factual condition to
give *the* explanation. We can imagine circumstances when a standing factual
condition, or a general law, would provide you with the explanation, because
this was what you didn't know.

Sometimes, of course, more than one of the premises is unknown. Then
more than one of them needs to be presented in giving an explanation.

9.9 Emphasis and Explanation

There's a feature of requests for explanation, and of what counts as giving the explanation that is worthy of attention here. Suppose someone asks "Why was your cat chasing that mouse?" Just these words alone don't tell us what sort of information the questioner might be after. Clues about this might be given by the context of asking, or by the emphasis the speaker placed on different parts of the sentence. For example, suppose that the cat is in the midst of lots of mice; perhaps the question really is "Why was your cat chasing *that* mouse, as opposed to any of the other mice?" Or suppose that there are lots of cats, but only yours goes after the mouse. Then perhaps the question really is "Why was *your* cat, as opposed to any of the other cats, chasing that mouse?" Or perhaps the questioner knows that cats sometimes chase mice, and sometimes ignore them. In that case, the question really is "Why was your cat *chasing* the mouse, as opposed to ignoring it?" Each of these questions calls for a different answer, making something different count as *the* explanation.

I hope that the D-N Model—or the very simple version of it I've presented—seems to you to have some plausibility as an account of what an explanation is. In the next chapter, however, we'll see that it needs a good deal of qualification and discussion.

CHAPTER 10

Problems with the D-N Model

10.1 Explanations in History

In this chapter we'll discuss various problems with the D-N Model of explanation. The first one, which we've already briefly considered, is that in many sorts of ordinary explanation, laws don't seem to be mentioned at all.

One area in which the law-requirement stipulated by the D-N Model has come in for a good deal of criticism is in considering the sorts of things historians do. If you look in history books, you'll find very few (if any) general laws mentioned. All there seems to be is stories of what happened.

Some historians—not very many—flatly deny that it is any part of their job to discover and produce general laws, because they also think that it's not part of their job to produce explanations. They think that their only job is to tell us brute facts about the past—the story of what happened. If they don't know and don't care about general laws of history, then they can't offer us D-N style explanations. "Fine!" reply some of these historians. Maybe they don't think there are any general laws in history. But they don't care. "We don't explain; we just tell true stories. We're not scientists—we're historians!"

I found most of my history classes in high school very boring and useless. In these classes we encountered nothing but long lists of facts about the past. You know the kind of thing:

- Millard Fillmore was the thirteenth President of the United States.
- The War of the Spanish Succession was fought by Austria, England, the Netherlands, and Prussia against France and Spain.
- Berlin used to be the capital of Germany before the country was divided into East and West Germany.

And so on.

Who cares? I muttered to myself. Well, my history teacher cared. He was a Mrs. Smithian about history. He loved facts and wanted us to love them too. He urged us to accumulate more and more of them in our memories. I hated this.

Some people, of course, love facts, and there's nothing wrong with that. But most people want more than just facts out of history. They want explanations: I would have been (slightly) more interested in my high school history class if it tried to deal with questions like this:

- Why was Millard Fillmore elected thirteenth President of the United States?
- What was the reason Austria, England, the Netherlands, and Prussia fought against France and Spain?
- Why did they move the capital of Germany out of Berlin?

Most historians do want to produce explanations, and you'll typically find things like this in history books:

Because Delft was a walled city, it was chosen by William the Silent, Prince of Orange, as his residence during the Dutch revolt against Spanish control. *

This is clearly intended to be an explanation. The problem is that no law is mentioned here. As before, we might want to interpret this as a short-form explanation, one that presupposes obvious and umentioned general laws (and other obvious premises) which together do form the premises of a deductive argument for the explanandum. But what laws, exactly? We might try to come up with some candidates, but they look pretty silly:

- William the Silent always chose a walled city to live in whenever the Dutch revolted against Spanish Control.
- Princes of Orange choose walled cities for their residence during revolts.
- Rulers choose protected locations for their residence during times of trouble.

---

* In case you care, this is from *Vermeer & the Art of Painting* by Arthur K. Wheelock (New Haven: Yale University Press, 1995), p. 2.

Some of these "laws" are silly because they're so particular: there couldn't have been more than a very few instances of the events mentioned throughout history, so it's stupid to think of them as "laws of history" at all. Others of them are more general—have more instances—but they don't seem to be really true, at least, not without exception. (Shortly, we'll take an extended look at the problem of finding true laws.)

Maybe we're just making a mistake in thinking about historical explanations in terms of the D-N Model in the first place.

10.2 An Alternative View of Explanation

Here's another way of seeing explanation in history.

What we're talking about here, it seems, is a particular event—one that is very unlikely to be repeated. How can there be any general laws about it? All we can do is to point out the surrounding facts, and make it somehow make sense. The idea here may be that when we tell the facts and put them into historical context, we can understand the motivations of the people involved—we can see why they did what they did.

Perhaps what we're after in this kind of explanation is a sort of empathetic understanding of the actions of the people involved. A successful historical explanation tells us the relevant facts about a particular circumstance, and we're able to understand how the people involved acted when we think about how *we* would have acted under those circumstances—how it would have seemed reasonable to act, given the circumstances and personalities involved.

There's a larger issue here than just explanation in history. Very often we're interested in explaining human actions, and there's a good deal of controversy about whether the sort of explanation involving general laws is appropriate here. Think of normal everyday explanations you give of your actions, or of the actions of others. Are there any real general laws here? Or is it merely a matter of making things seem reasonable under the circumstances?

Or maybe, despite the difficulty of specifying exactly what the laws are, there really are general unspoken laws in the explanation of human actions.

10.3 The Prevalence of True-ish Laws

We're not going to say the last word about the problem of explanation of human actions here, so let's just let it sit there, and we will move on to a different problem.

You may have noticed that some of the examples of fuller explanations give laws that are *sort of* true: true most of the time, by and large, with some exceptions, under normal circumstances. In fact, it's quite difficult to give laws that are absolutely true without exception. Consider the request for an explanation in a very simple case, where it's clear what's going on: why did that match light? We're tempted to say that the match lit because it was struck. But the argument

> The match was struck
> Therefore the match is lit

isn't deductively valid. It would be deductively valid if we added the premise

> Matches light whenever they're struck

but this premise isn't, strictly speaking, universally true. Matches that are soaking wet don't light when struck. The explanans has to be true. So let's revise it to

> Dry matches light when struck

and add the fact that this match was dry. Now we have the argument

> The match was dry.
> The match was struck.
> Dry matches light when struck.
> Therefore this match lit.

This is better, in that the premises of the argument present a fuller explanation. It's deductively valid: if the premises are true, then the conclusion must be true. It makes the general-rule premise more accurate, and it more explicitly spells out the initial conditions which together were responsible for the match's lighting.

But as long as we've decided to speak strictly, we must notice that the general-rule premise is still not exactly true. Dry matches don't always light when struck. Striking a dry match very lightly will fail to light it. So we need to change that general rule to

> Dry matches light when struck hard

and add the fact that this match was struck hard. Well, even dry matches struck hard don't light when they're not in the presence of oxygen. (They will flare up—they contain some oxidant in their heads—but then they'll quickly die out.) And there are lots of other things we must add to get an argument which is deductively valid and in which all the premises are, strictly speaking, true. Even a dry match struck hard in the presence of oxygen won't be lit if somebody blows hard on it, or if it's very windy.

> Dry matches light when struck hard, in the presence of oxygen, and when there's not much wind.

But probably this isn't strictly speaking true either. Perhaps even in the lack of wind, a dry match (etc.) wouldn't light if the air temperature were really low, around absolute zero. Probably there are some cases in which dry matches, struck hard in the presence of oxygen, within the normal range of temperature, and in the absence of wind, don't light. It's difficult to see how to fill this "law" out fully, so that it's true without exception.

Take a look at the other "laws" we've mentioned: if you know enough about the phenomena we're talking about and think about things for a while, you'll realise that none of these are true without exception. All of them are true-ish. That is, all of them are true for the most part, under normal circumstances.

Very few of the laws scientists cite when they fill out explanations are strictly universally true. If they seem to say something about *every* case of a certain sort, they are almost always true "on the whole"—by and large, normally, in the usual cases, in the majority of cases, or everything else being equal. Take a look at any sample of "laws" of science, and you'll see that this is the case. Here's a fairly random sample of such "laws":

- Water freezes at 0° C. (Not really. Most samples of water we actually have contain a variety of concentrations of various dissolved substances, and this alters the freezing temperature somewhat.)

- The price of an item increases in proportion to the increase in demand
  and decreases in proportion to the increase in supply. (It doesn't
  always. Sometimes demand remains constant, supply increases,
  and the price remains constant.)
- All beavers build dams. (Beavers in zoos don't, if they're not
  provided with the opportunity. Baby beavers in the wild don't.)
- Eating lots of eggs increases the cholesterol in your blood. (Maybe it
  usually does, but sometimes it doesn't.)
- Doubling the pressure of an enclosed gas at a constant temperature
  will halve the volume. (Not precisely; this fails to take into account
  the volume of the gas's atoms.)
- Planets travel in ellipses around the sun. (They don't: small
  gravitational effects on each other, and other factors, make their
  paths diverge from perfect ellipses.)
- All insects have six legs. (Most do, but there are rare mutations with
  more or less. And if you pull some legs off an insect, it will have
  fewer than six.)
- $v = gt$. This is Galileo's law of falling bodies, and it doesn't exactly
  describe them. The force of gravity changes slightly as something
  gets closer to the centre of the earth; and, of course, this "law"
  doesn't take into account wind resistance, which all falling bodies
  suffer to varying degrees.

And so on.

There are a few laws of science which are claimed to be true without
exception. We could reformulate Galileo's law, for example, to:

- $v = gt$ for objects falling in a vacuum

and get it closer to being true, but the problem is now that this will not describe very many real falling objects. Actual falling objects (around here)
are almost never found in vacuums. But here's a more serious reason why
this law isn't exactly true. It contains 'g', the so-called gravitational constant, which is a measure of the downward force of gravity. But this isn't a
constant: it varies at different places on earth and at different heights above
sea-level. Any object that falls will get closer to the centre of the earth,
changing the value of g a little. It's such a tiny bit that we can ignore it, but
strictly speaking, Galileo's law, even fixed up to include air resistance, ap-
plies to no real objects. "Well!" you reply, "let's just fix up Galileo's law to

include this." Okay, but then there's the matter of minute gravitational pulls from things other than the Earth. There's *always* something more. We hope that these additional factors will make such a small difference that we can ignore them, and often they do. But the point here is a logical one: strictly speaking, we haven't got a true law of falling bodies.

The law I mentioned above about enclosed gasses is sometimes stated in the form of an "idealized" gas law, which is supposed to apply only to gasses with zero-volume atoms. Stated this way, it is precisely true, without exception; the problem is, there are no such ideal gasses. If there were another premise in the argument which stated that some enclosed space contained a fixed quantity of gas which had zero-volume atoms, it would be false.

We could turn all the true-ish statements into true ones by inserting a word in each like "usually" or "probably" or "by-and-large," or something like that.

The trouble with this is that it would make any arguments in which they appear as premises no longer valid deductive arguments. These would turn into inductive arguments.

EXERCISE

Stop now and make sure you understand why any argument modified to put "probably" or something like that into its law-premises would be inductive.

These new inductive arguments would be strong, so why is there a problem? Don't we still have an explanation if the premises constitute a strong inductive reason for the truth of the conclusion?

Maybe; maybe not. We'll take a brief excursion into some considerations along these lines.

10.4 Deductive-Nomological Vs. Statistical Explanation

Hempel and Oppenheim noticed the fact that the laws we spell out when trying to provide full explanations are only true-ish—that they're only true by and large, usually. The approach to this problem that they decided to take was to turn them into genuine, fully true laws by inserting words like "probably" or "usually" or "normally" into them. As we've seen, this would make the arguments no longer deductively valid; it would make them (strong) inductive arguments instead. Accordingly, they distinguished two patterns of explanation: the D-N pattern we've been considering, and the **STATISTICAL** pattern. In the statistical pattern, the laws are of this "probably" or "usually" kind: that is, they state that under certain conditions, something happens *most of the time*. Sometimes, in fact, scientists can be more specific, giving actual numbers—statistics—for the proportion mentioned. This is why this pattern is called 'statistical'.

There are lots of problems in explaining exactly how statistical explanations work. These are complex and confusing, and you'll be happy to learn that we're not going to go into these matters. We'll avoid these problems by sticking to one pattern of explanation, the D-N one. However, you should recognize that there is widespread doubt that the D-N pattern, at least in the basic version we've been examining, can be made adequate.

10.5 Statistical Explanations Might Really Be Short-Form Deductive Ones

Consider the following explanation of why Fred's headache went away at 12:15: he took two aspirins at 12:00. In the usual way, we might try to make the argument here more complete:

> Fred had a headache at 12:00.
> Fred took two aspirins at 12:00.
> When people with headaches take two aspirins, the headache goes away
>   fifteen minutes later.
> Therefore Fred's headache went away at 12:15.

As usual, the general law here is not exactly true. Let's imagine that scientific investigation of the effects of aspirin concludes that taking two aspirins makes headaches go away in 85% of the cases. So let's change the argument to make the premise true:

> Fred had a headache at 12:00.
> Fred took two aspirins at 12:00.
> When people with headaches take two aspirins, the headache goes away
>   fifteen minutes later, 85% of the time.
> Therefore Fred's headache went away at 12:15.

This is no longer a deductively valid argument, but it is fairly inductively strong. The 85% figure gives us an idea of just how strong it is. Now we have an argument that fits the statistical pattern.

But can we understand what's going on here also under the D-N model? I think, and probably you do too, that this argument doesn't give the whole story. Imagine that there are two kinds of headaches, call them α-headaches and β-headaches. α-headaches respond every time, in 15 minutes, to two aspirins; β-headaches don't respond at all. Because 85% of headaches are α-headaches, this explains why headaches in general are cured by two aspirins in 15 minutes only 85% of the time. The full explanation, then, would be:

Fred had a headache at 12:00.
Fred's headache was an α-headache.
Fred took two aspirins at 12:00.
When people with α-headaches take two aspirins, the headache goes
    away fifteen minutes later.
Therefore Fred's headache went away at 12:15.

You'll notice that this argument is deductively valid, and (we assume) its law is true, not just true-ish. What we have here is no longer statistical or inductive. It's a standard nomological-deductive explanation.

Now, this business about α- and β-headaches isn't real scientific fact: I just made it up. The important thing here is that, even though this particular full explanation isn't the real one, we all suspect strongly that there is some real full explanation, even if we (and headache-scientists) don't know what it is. After all, there must be some difference between headaches that aspirin cures and headaches that aspirin doesn't cure. So there must be some full explanation possible. If we don't know what the full explanation is, the best we can do is to speak statistically. But our strong suspicion, that there is a full explanation involving a law which is not merely true-ish, or merely statistical, leads us to think that the explanation given, that Fred's headache went away at 12:15 because he took two aspirins at 12:00, is right—because the explanans is one premise of a full *deductive* argument implying the explanandum.

In other words, whenever the best we can do is to give a statistical (inductive) argument, we feel that there nevertheless is a non-statistical (deductive) argument we can't produce, which is the full story. The idea here, then, is that whenever we're stuck with an argument which has only statistically true laws in it, and is thus only an inductive argument, we can see it as an incomplete version of a full deductive argument with non-statistical, fully true (not just true-ish) premises. This means that we can continue to regard all explanations as really showing the D-N pattern. This is what I'll do.

But is it right to think that in back of every merely statistical law, there is some non-statistical law, one which is part of the full explanation? It seems right. We can't help thinking, in the case of the headache example, that there must be some exceptionless generalizations that we don't know about—that there must be some difference between headaches that aspirin cures and those it doesn't. I'll have more to say about this position later on in this book, when we get to the discussion of causes in Chapter 17. (One of the things I'll touch on is the surprising claim that in certain areas of science, it's often claimed that statistical laws are the final truth: there can't be any "fuller" explanation.)

10.6 Explanation and Relevance

We've been claiming that "the explanation" of an explanandum is the premise, unknown to the asker, of a of a valid deductive argument with true premises which has the explanandum as conclusion.

Here's an objection to that position. Consider this argument:

Muffins turn out tough if you stir the batter a lot.
You stirred the batter for these a lot.
The imperial residence during the Northern Sung dynasty (960-1127
    A.D.) was Shangkiu.
Therefore these muffins turned out tough.

This is a valid deductive argument. All its premises are true. I'll bet you didn't know that fact about the imperial residence during the Northern Sung dynasty (A.D. 960-1127). So it follows from our account of explanation that this fact needs to be included to explain the conclusion to you. But this is obviously a mistake. That fact is no part of a correct explanation of the conclusion. Our account of explanation has to be mistaken.

But this is easy to fix. We just need to modify our account slightly, to specify that the premises of the deductive argument in question have to be all essential ones: that is, for each of them, the argument would no longer validly imply that conclusion if it were left out. Of course, the argument above would still validly imply its conclusion if that premise about the imperial residence were left out.

Remember the exercise in Chapter 2, in which we were presented with a valid deductive argument including the irrelevant premise about Asunción? (See part 2.4 if you've forgotten.) We've just seen the relevance of this point to explanation.

10.7 Screening Off

Here, however, is an objection to our account of explanation which is harder to deal with.

Consider your friend Fred. On the basis of some crackpot medical advice he once got from his holistic healer, he's been taking female birth-control pills for years. Of course, over that stretch of years, he has not become pregnant either. (Fred's a *man.*) Now consider this obviously mistaken explanation of why Fred hasn't become pregnant:

Fred has been taking birth-control pills over the last few years.
Nobody who takes birth-control pills over a stretch of time becomes pregnant then.
So Fred hasn't become pregnant over the last few years.

Nobody thinks that this is a good explanation of why Fred hasn't become pregnant. The problem here is that this example appears to fit the D-N model for explanation.

EXERCISE
It will serve as a good review of the D-N account of explanation if you try to remember right now what its requirements for a good explanation are, and apply them to the Case of Fred.

ANSWER
This is a valid deductive argument, with the explanandum as conclusion. The first premise is a law of nature, and is true (or at least close enough). None of the premises could be left out without making the argument invalid.

So this argument passes the test proposed by the D-N account for a good explanation, except it obviously isn't. Something is wrong with the D-N account.

An attempt to deal with this objection and others like it would take us into deep waters, where things get technical and complicated,* and is far beyond the scope of this book. I'll just give you a hint of what might be done here.

Of course it's true that if a man takes birth control pills, the probability he'll get pregnant is zero. But never mind whether a man takes birth control pills or not: the probability that any man gets pregnant is zero. In other words, the probability that a person will get pregnant given that that person is a man equals the probability that a person will get pregnant given that that person is a man and takes birth control pills. Philosophers say that the property taking birth control pills is "screened off" by the property being a man. If you're a man, in other words, taking birth control pills is irrelevant to whether you'll become pregnant: it doesn't change the probability (which is zero whether you do or don't).

Here's another example of the same thing. Suppose you stir a teaspoon of sugar into a cup of hot tea while chanting the magic incantation, "Ala peanut butter sandwiches!" The sugar dissolves! But, of course, the magic incantation doesn't have any part in an explanation of why the sugar dissolved; the sugar stands the same chance of dissolving when stirred into hot tea whether the magic incantation is chanted or not. It's screened off by the other circumstances. It appears that we must specify that a genuinely explanatory property not be "screened off."

Giving a full account of explanation is a very complicated and controversial task, and we've just scratched the surface in this book. We'll come back (briefly) to "screening off" in Chapter 18, when we talk about *causal* explanation.

---

* One good place to look for a much fuller version of the account of how this sort of difficulty might be dealt with is Wesley C. Salmon's book *Statistical Explanation and Statistical Relevance* (Pittsburgh: University of Pittsburgh Press, 1971); see his article in this book called "Statistical Explanation."

CHAPTER 11

Hypotheses and Explanations

11.1   Explanation and Hypotheses ████████

Now that we have seen, to some extent, what an explanation involves, it's time to turn to procedures for providing a good explanation.

Recall the sample explanation we were looking at in the last chapter. You and your sister hear the whistle; what's the explanation of this? Here's the (fairly full) version of the explanation we finally arrived at:

> When somebody is smoking a cigar in a small room with poor ventilation, the room becomes very smoky.
> The hall is a small room with poor ventilation.
> Uncle Fred was smoking a cigar in the hall.
> Whenever there's a working smoke alarm in a very smoky room, the smoke alarm will go off.
> There's a smoke alarm in the hall.
> The smoke alarm was working.
> When smoke alarms go off, they produce a high-pitched whistle.
> Therefore there was a high-pitched whistle.

Well, at the point when neither of you knows what the explanation is, at least one of the premises here is not known to be true. Let's assume that we both already know the general laws on this list:

- When somebody is smoking a cigar in a small room with poor ventilation, the room becomes very smoky.
- Whenever there's a working smoke alarm in a very smoky room, the smoke alarm will go off.
- When smoke alarms go off, they produce a high-pitched whistle.

And some of the initial conditions:

- There's a smoke alarm in the hall.
- The hall is a small room with poor ventilation.

Suppose, however, that we don't know yet whether or not this whistle is a smoke alarm going off. If it is, there are smoke alarms in other rooms than the hall too, so we don't know which room's smoke alarm is going off; we also don't know yet what's going on that would make that smoke alarm go off. Here are some other things we know (some particular facts, and some general laws):

- There's a smoke alarm upstairs.
- There's a smoke alarm in the basement.
- There's a furnace in the basement.
- A fire in the house would make a smoke alarm nearby go off.
- A steamy atmosphere will make a smoke alarm go off.
- There's a radiator in the hall.
- Leaky radiators fill the surrounding room with steam.
- When furnaces malfunction in a certain way, they produce a lot of smoke.
- Smoke alarms which are broken in a certain way go off despite nothing unusual in the air.
- When the oil-delivery man pumps oil into the tank out back it produces a high-pitched whistle.

Accordingly, there are various **HYPOTHESES** we could consider here, in addition to the one which turns out to provide the correct explanation. 'Hypotheses' are conjectures that might account for some fact. The word is plural. Its singular is **HYPOTHESIS**.

Here's a partial list of alternative hypotheses:

- The smoke alarm in the basement is going off; the basement has become filled with smoke produced by a malfunction in the furnace.
- The smoke alarm in the hall is going off; it's broken. (Smoke alarms sometimes break in such a way that they go off despite nothing in the air to make them go off.)
- The smoke alarm upstairs is going off; there's a fire in the bedroom.

- The smoke alarm in the hall is going off; the radiator has sprung a leak there, and has filled the room with steam (a very steamy atmosphere makes working smoke alarms go off).
- Oil is being pumped into the tank out back.

and so on.

Note that these hypotheses represent alternative possible explanations for the whistle; they're short form versions of explicit arguments whose premises would deductively imply that there's a high-pitched whistle.

Perhaps some of these don't even occur to us as we sit in the kitchen hearing the whistle. We haven't yet decided which of the ones that do occur to us to believe.

11.2 The Necessity of Hypotheses

Mrs. Smith, you might recall, gave the following advice to junior scientists: observation is everything. But here we are, just sitting around in the kitchen entertaining hypotheses (philosophers speak of **ENTERTAINING** a hypothesis, meaning considering it without necessarily believing it). We're making things up, guessing about what the explanation of that whistling noise is. Why are we doing this? Why don't we just go take a look? Why are hypotheses necessary at all?

Here's why. Without hypotheses, we wouldn't even know how to begin looking. Imagine you hear a whistling noise while in the kitchen; now just go take a look, with a mind completely empty of any hypotheses. Where to look? Smithian observation, remember, is completely random: you just look at anything. Okay: take a look in the oven, inside your left shoe, in the trunk of your car; hop into a plane and go check out what's happening in the tallest skyscraper in Buenos Aires. This is ridiculous. A really random search is obviously practically guaranteed to be completely useless. On the other hand, a list of working hypotheses tells us how to carry out a search with a better chance of coming up with something. Our list of hypotheses suggests that we go look out back, to see if oil is being pumped into the oil tank, and that we go look in the three rooms in the house where there are smoke detectors.

Now wait a minute, you're saying. What's all this business about creating hypotheses? This is all stupid. If you hear whistling, why not just go see what's making that whistle?

Well, of course you're going to have to go and see, but where? It's not apparent what direction that high-pitched whistle is coming from. You might walk in some direction to see if it gets louder, but which direction? So you think: maybe it's coming from the back yard; you poke your head out the back door to see if it's much louder there. If it isn't, then you say: maybe it's in the front of the house, so you walk that way. It seems like any of your actions have to be based on a hypothesis.

I've been claiming that coming up with hypotheses is an important step when trying to answer questions about explanation—"Why?" questions. The implication is that this step is more important than when trying to answer questions about bare facts—"What?" questions. Is this really the case? If so, how come?

EXERCISES

Question 1. Is it always necessary to create hypotheses as a first step in answering an explanation-question? Are there some explanation questions for which this step is unnecessary? Try to find a plausible example of one.

Question 2. Is it never a good idea to begin answering bare-fact questions by creating a list of hypotheses? Are there some bare-fact questions for which this preliminary step would be a good idea? Try to find a plausible example of one.

ANSWERS

1. No, it's not always necessary to create hypotheses as a first step in answering an explanation-question. Here's an example. When you put on your coat, you feel a bulge in one of the pockets. Why is there this bulge? You might begin the process of answering this explanation-question by coming up with various hypotheses about what's in your pocket making this bulge, but this is unnecessary. You can instead eliminate this step, and just put your hand into the pocket to find out what's in there.

2. It's sometimes a good idea to begin answering bare-fact questions by creating a list of hypotheses. Here's an example. Suppose you're leaving the house in the morning, and you discover that your keys aren't on the dresser where you usually leave them.

Where are they? You might jump right into investigation by wandering around the house looking at random. But this is a bad strategy. Looking inside the unopened can of cat food in the back of the cupboard would be a useless waste of time, for example, because your keys clearly aren't there. The best strategy is to stop first and create a list of hypotheses: where is it plausible to expect that you might have left your keys?

Okay, it seems that hypothesis formation isn't always necessary in answering "Why?" questions, and isn't always unnecessary in answering bare-fact questions. But I implied that hypothesis is more important in answering "Why?" questions. Why is this the case? What is it about "Why" questions that makes hypothesis formation more usually necessary?

Bare-fact questions often—typically—ask for a characteristic of a particular thing or group of things.

- What colour is that bird?
- What is it eating?
- When, exactly, do the leaves start to fall off the tree in your back yard?
- How long does that bee spend inside the flower?
- What's it doing in there?
- The next time it snows and then thaws, which melts faster: the snow on your lawn or on your sidewalk?
- On a partly cloudy day, are the clouds all moving in the same direction?
- What colour do you get when you mix this yellow paint with that blue paint?
- Try mixing this baking powder with water. Exactly what happens?

These questions direct us toward the correct strategy for answering them. They tell us where to look: look at the thing in question, and see what its characteristics are.

Requests for explanation, however, are typically answered not by giving a characteristic of the thing already mentioned, but by discovering a fact about something else altogether. Think about possible answers to these questions:

- Why is my shirt missing from the closet?

- Why have codfish stocks diminished in the North Atlantic in recent years?
- What's responsible for that whistling noise?
- How do butterflies find their way thousands of miles to their nesting grounds?
- What causes leaves to turn colour in the fall?
- Why wouldn't my car start this morning?

Of course, facts about the thing mentioned (my shirt, codfish, the noise, butterflies, leaves, my car) will figure relevantly in the correct explanation, but other facts, about other things entirely, will also be relevant. My shirt is missing because my roommate borrowed it. That whistling noise is caused by a smoke alarm going off. And so on. Because facts about other sorts of things are normally relevant here, the question itself doesn't tell us where to start looking. We have to take some guesses about what the explanation is— create some hypotheses—before we can begin a sensible investigation.

11.3 The Fallibility of Hypothesis Formation

Investigation based on our hypotheses doesn't guarantee success for two reasons.

First of all, if we haven't come up with the right hypotheses among the list of those which we entertain and which guide our investigation, then we might not look in the right place. Suppose for example that it didn't occur to us that the whistle might be coming from a smoke detector; we look out back to see whether the oil tank is being filled, and it isn't. Now we're at a loss. Or suppose that we don't think of that smoke detector in the hall, and check out only other smoke detectors in the house. Failure again.

Secondly, even if we do get the right hypothesis on our list, and go check this one out, it isn't guaranteed that we'll find out the correct information when we do take a look.

Well, as usual, it isn't guaranteed that science will succeed, even when using the right method. This method is the right one because it stands a much better chance of success than the alternatives. Clearly, a well-done process of thinking up hypotheses, followed by investigation of each of them, stands a far better chance of success at determining real explanations than a random set of Smithian observations.

11.4 Bathtubs and Dreams ██████████

Where do we get hypotheses?

You may have heard this old story. Archimedes was given the task of finding out whether a crown was actually made of solid gold. He reasoned that gold was denser than other metals, so all he had to do was to find out the density of the crown; he could weigh it, but how to find out its volume? One day he was splashing around in the bathtub, and suddenly a hypothesis occurred to him: all he needed to do was to immerse the crown in a full container of water, and measure the volume of water that spilled out. "Eureka!" he screamed (which is Greek for "By cracky! That's it!"), hopped out of the bath and ran around town dripping wet and stark naked. Although this story is no doubt one of those mostly-false picturesque myths, nevertheless we can take it as an illustration of the fortuitous, accidental sources of hypotheses.

Here's another story of hypothesis formation. This one is weirder, but it's more likely to be true. August Kekulé, a Nineteenth Century German chemist, was responsible for a couple of major discoveries in organic chemistry: the chain-structure of many organic molecules, and the ring-structure of benzene. These served enormously to explain many hitherto puzzling facts about the composition and behaviour of benzene and other organic compounds. Where did he get these hypotheses? Here's an account of the processes which led him to entertain these hypotheses, in his own words:

One fine summer evening I was returning by the last bus.... I fell into a reverie, and lo, the atoms were gamboling before my eyes! Whenever, hitherto, these diminutive beings had appeared to me, they had always been in motion; but up to that time I had never been able to discern the nature of their motion. Now, however, I saw how...the larger [groups] formed a chain, dragging the smaller ones after them but only at the ends of the chain. The cry of the conductor: "Clapham Road," awakened me from my dreaming; but I spent a part of the night in putting on paper at least sketches of these dream forms. This was the origin of the "Structural Theory."

Something similar happened with the benzene theory.... I was sitting writing at my textbook but the work did not progress; my thoughts were elsewhere. I turned my chair to the fire and dozed. Again the atoms were gamboling before my eyes. This time the smaller groups kept modestly in the background. My mental eye...could now distinguish larger structures of manifold conformation:

long rows, sometimes more closely fitted together all twining and twisting in snake-like motion. But look! What was that? One of the snakes had seized hold of its own tail, and the form whirled mockingly before my eyes. As if by a flash of lightning I awoke; and this time I spent the rest of the night in working out the consequences of the hypothesis.

Let us learn to dream, gentlemen, then perhaps we shall find the truth.

For good measure, Kekulé throws in a little poem:

> And to those who don't think
> The truth will be given.
> They'll have it without effort. *

Well, that's where he got his hypotheses: from dreams about atoms arranging themselves into molecules. The second dream (he isn't quite clear) may even have been about snakes.

Now, of course, having a dream isn't enough. A dream about a snake biting its own tail wouldn't have helped Kekulé come up with the hypothesis that benzene has a ring structure if he hadn't already known a great deal about benzene already, and hadn't seen clearly what the problem was. If you don't know anything about chemistry, then you can dream about snakes biting their tails from now until Christmas, and you still won't come up with any hypotheses about the structure of benzene that are worth anything. Kekulé already had a thorough background in chemistry, and had thought about the problems consciously a great deal. This obviously provided the psychological conditions for this mysterious act of dreaming the hypotheses. Without this background, his dreams wouldn't have occurred. Even if they had, their applicability to the problems at hand wouldn't have been recognized. It takes a thorough grounding in chemistry to recognize the analogy between the "atoms gamboling" in his dreams and forming into chains or rings, and the real-life problems about the structures of organic molecules. The analogy between the snake biting its tail and the ring of six carbon atoms which form the core of the benzene molecule is far-fetched, and would never have occurred to anyone but a thoroughly trained chemist.

---

* All quotes from a speech given in the Berlin City Hall, 1890. Translated by O. Theodor Benfey, *Journal of Chemical Education*, 35: 21-30.

Remember that (we have been supposing) to count as an explanation-candidate at all, and thus to be worth considering, a hypothesis has to be (part of) a deductive argument whose premises imply the explanandum (or explananda [plural]). In this case, it turned out that the ring structure did (together with other things already known in chemistry) imply that benzene had properties and behaviours already known to chemists. So if you don't know a lot of chemistry already, you won't know that a ring structure would do the explanatory jobs—implying the explananda—that an explanation has to do, because you won't know what these explananda are. Even if you did know what the explananda are, you wouldn't know whether a ring structure would imply them.

Kekulé is obviously modestly exaggerating things a little when he quotes this poem which states that the truth will be given to those who don't think, without effort. A tremendous amount of effort was obviously necessary to prepare him psychologically to have these dreams, and to recognize their significance as possible explananda when they occurred.

11.5 Another Source for Hypotheses: Analogy

It's of course not very common in science that hypotheses are suggested by dreams. Often, hypotheses are suggested by analogies from some other field. For example, in 1911 Rutherford suggested the hypothesis that the atom was composed of electrons circling around a central nucleus, just like the planets circle around the sun. The solar system's structure might actually have suggested this hypothesis to him. Seeing this analogy was a creative, imaginative act; the facts about the solar system's structure have little relevance to the structure of the atom.

Another example: before his travel to the Galápagos Archipelago in 1835, Charles Darwin had accepted without question the then standard view that species were created all at once, as recounted in the Bible, and that they remained fixed. Doubts arose when he observed plants and animals on his travels: the species on adjacent islands showed only small differences from each other, but those further away showed larger differences. This seemed to show that there was once a uniform population. However, as bits of it separated off, moving further and further away, it gradually changed, so that the furthest-removed species, which had separated off longest ago, had changed the most. But he was at a loss to explain how and why these changes might have taken place. One day in 1838, he just happened to come across and read

Essay on Population by the political economist Malthus. In this book, Malthus theorizes about the dynamics of population size, the effects of scarcity of resources, and the mathematics of reproduction: food supply increases more slowly than population, resulting in a bitter struggle for existence. This suggested to Darwin his hypothesis that a similar struggle for existence among all life forms might result in the survival of only the fittest among the random variations in a species; this "natural selection" was thus responsible for gradual change. Darwin said that his hypothesis was simply "the doctrine of Malthus applied with manifold force to the whole animal and vegetable kingdom," but he was being a bit modest. Malthus's ideas were only analogies to what Darwin came up with. Some fairly substantial changes and additions to Malthusian theory about human population and economics had to be made to apply it to animals and vegetables. It took a fairly substantial creative leap of imagination to see that Malthus's theory, substantially extended and adapted, could be applied to questions in a completely different area.

Besides the dreams, there are several other items in Kekulé's past which might have suggested in some distant analogous way his hypotheses for chemical structures. Early in his life he showed an aptitude in both mathematics and drawing, and by consequence became an architecture student when he went to university; there, he tells us, he studied "descriptive geometry, perspective, shadow theory, stonecutting, and other interesting subjects." No doubt this prepared him for thinking about solving problems in terms of imaginative structural combinations. Perhaps he had analogous structures from some of these areas in mind. He was, at one point, involved in a court case: someone had stolen some jewelry including two rings in the form of a snake biting its tail. The image of a snake biting its tail is a familiar one in Indian mythology, and has rich symbolic content. This image showed up in his dream as an analogy to the benzene structure he was seeking.

We have seen cases of hypotheses suggested by analogy and by dreams. There are many other cases, however, in which they just seem to come out of the blue. Their discoverer thinks about a problem for a long time, and then one day, for no particular reason, a hypothesis just pops into his or her head. Most often, however, hypotheses don't come completely out of the blue. Darwin never claimed to have invented the idea of natural evolution; there were several prior influential thinkers who had suggested ideas rather like his. He did, however, fill in many gaps in these earlier hypotheses, and produce a version of these ideas that was worked out in much greater detail, and thus was more clearly directly applicable to natural phenomena. We have to recognize *both* that these "new" hypotheses have their roots in earlier thought, and that they add a significant new element, an imaginative breakthrough.

11.6 Is There a Logic of Hypothesis Formation?

Compare the problem of hypothesis formation to an arithmetic problem, for example, of adding up a column of figures. You all know how to do the addition: there are techniques that we've all learned that guarantee you'll get the answer if you put in sufficient effort and follow the rules correctly. (This is not to say that everyone will always get the right answer, as abundantly demonstrated whenever I try to balance my chequebook.) But the production of hypotheses is a far different kind of procedure. Hypotheses can come from anywhere—or apparently from nowhere at all. There aren't any rules which guarantee, if you use them correctly, that you'll come up with a good hypothesis. It seems to be a matter of inspiration, of creativity, rather than of method. It's more like painting a picture than like solving an arithmetic problem: you can't give rules which will get it done right, and often people don't know exactly how they do it.

The analogy of painting a picture is instructive in another way. Painting often involves some sort of mysterious inspiration and creativity, but it doesn't follow that there's nothing you can do—no method to follow—to increase the chances that you'll be a good painter. There are all sorts of techniques you can learn in art classes; you can get all sorts of guidance by watching someone else do it, or by getting advice; it takes hard work and concentration. (None of this guarantees, however, the inspiration necessary for a really good painting.)

Similarly, there are some very good techniques to follow if you want to produce a good crop of hypotheses. Thorough background and training in the field are of course necessary—but not sufficient—for coming up with interesting new hypotheses worth pursuing. Kekulé says that "germs of ideas, like spores, fill the atmosphere," but these can develop only in the person who is alert to them. Being alert to possible analogies, and being prepared to think of how they might apply to the problem at hand, are also important. Whatever can foster your creativity and imagination is a good idea; habits can be fostered which will lead to increased imagination. Pay more attention to your dreams. But this isn't all there is to it. Remember Edison's famous quote: "Genius is one per cent inspiration and ninety-nine per cent perspiration." *

---

* This quote comes from his book modestly called *Life*, where he also said "There is no substitute for hard work."

CHAPTER 12

Two Strategies for Hypothesizing

12.1 More Imaginative Whistle-Hypotheses ███████

In the last chapter, I was stressing the part that imagination, creativity, and even dreaming play in hypothesis formation—how this is not a matter of rational calculation.

Well, let's return to the example of the high-pitched whistle and apply this lesson. You and your sister are sitting in the kitchen; you hear the whistle. You've already got a short list of hypotheses:

- It's a smoke alarm going off
- It's the noise of the oil tank being filled

and even these two take a bit of imagination to think of. But this is certainly a stodgy, boring, uncreative list. Be creative! Let your minds go wild! Dream up some hypotheses—maybe even literally *dream* them up.

There are, of course, some other hypotheses which might be among the premises of other deductive arguments that imply the conclusion that there is a high-pitched whistle. A fertile imagination can produce an endless list of them. Here are some really bizarre ones:

- A rare tropical whistling parrot has flown down your chimney
- Your cousin from Moose Jaw has unexpectedly arrived; she's recently taken up the clarinet, and has decided to practice it in your living room
- Your cat is exploding, with a whistling noise
- Martians have landed in your back yard, and the whistle is how they talk to each other

- There's a snake biting its tail, whirling around at a great speed in your bathroom, making this whistling sound

and so on.

 EXERCISE
Use your imagination: make up an additional four or five equally stupid hypotheses.

12.2 Open-Mindedness About Hypotheses

Any of these just *might* be true. They are hugely implausible, but Mrs. Smith told us to be open-minded, so maybe we should entertain all of these too? No.

Why not? The answer is that they're all completely implausible. None of them is utterly impossible perhaps, but they're all very unlikely, to the degree that they're not worth considering, especially because there are already some stodgy unimaginative hypotheses on your list that stand a much better chance of being true.

Remember what this list of hypotheses is for. Considerations arising from the reasons to create this list give us rather contradictory advice on whether to include implausible hypotheses.

(A) The list is created with the hope of including the correct explanation somewhere in the list. In order to stand a chance of getting the right answer on your list, you should include all the hypotheses you can think of which stand a fairly good chance of being true; you'll make this judgment based on what you already believe. But it's also worthwhile to include hypotheses which your existing beliefs make less likely. It just might turn out that a less likely hypothesis is the true one. You want to have a list including the real explanation; so you ought to include less likely hypotheses too. Many of the real breakthroughs in science, after all, were accomplished by imaginative scientists who thought up and entertained hypotheses that everyone thought were highly implausible.

EXERCISE
Imagine that you are in this situation. Your sister, an imaginative dreamer, suggest that you go look up the chimney for rare parrots, and check the bathtub for circular snakes; she agrees that these are implausible hypotheses, but reminds you that they're possible, and that in the interests of finding out the truth, you should open-mindedly include even implausible hypotheses to check out. Do you agree? What would you really say? Come on now, be sensible. I realise that many people think that philosophy is done by forgetting all about the real world, and letting your reasoning lead you to conclusions and advice which nobody in the real world would give a second thought to. This is wrong. Get real.

ANSWER
These hypotheses are too implausible.

(B) On the other hand, your list of hypotheses is going to govern your investigation. It's going to guide you in your search for the real explanation, by limiting the sorts of things you'll do when you start looking. The longer the list is, the less limited a search you're going to have to do. If you have a really long list, then you'll have to spend a great deal of effort checking out every hypothesis, and it just might not be worth all this trouble to find out the real explanation. Remember what was wrong with Mrs. Smith's advice that we should look without any prior hypotheses at all: this would entail a completely random search, extremely unlikely to turn up anything relevant. Searching on the basis of a really long list that included hypotheses which you've already decided are highly unlikely wouldn't be much better. If you search on the basis of this list, you will probably waste a lot of time and effort checking the highly unlikely ones out, and finding out that they're false—something you already suspected. Searching sometimes costs money, and you shouldn't waste funds looking for things you're almost positive aren't there. In this case, it might even be dangerous to take the very unlikely fanciful possibilities seriously. It's fairly likely that that noise is a smoke alarm, and it could be that while you're looking up the chimney for rare parrots, or checking in the bathtub for snakes, your house is starting to burn down.

Considerations (A) and (B) then give us contradictory advice. (A) tells us to include implausible hypotheses, and (B) tells us to exclude them. What to do?

12.3 Solving the Impasse

We can raise considerations here to help us solve the contradictory advice given to us by (A) and (B).

Clearly, there's a tradeoff between the motives of having a really inclusive list of hypotheses and having a practical guide to efficient investigation. You want a list long enough to make it likely to include the true explanation, which means that you should include some relatively less likely items; but you don't want to make it too long because you've included imaginative but extremely unlikely hypotheses. There's a median point, a compromise, somewhere in between: a list which is of the right size. Finding this compromise-point is a hallmark of well-done science. It's a matter of judgment and good sense. Here again, there aren't any particular rules or calculations which will guarantee the right results.

EXERCISE

Imagine that you're a scientist who has been hired to explain why Canadian fishermen in the North Atlantic have been catching drastically reduced numbers of codfish during recent years. To guide your investigation, you need a list of hypotheses. Spend a few minutes and construct a list of maybe a dozen hypotheses. Include some really imaginative (and implausible) hypotheses in your list. (It might help you to get some really bizarre hypotheses if you take a nap first. Maybe you'll have a dream.)

Once you have a list, look through it and try to assess the relative plausibility of the hypotheses on this list. Now, remembering that this list will guide your investigations, cut it down to the ones worth investigating. Where would it be sensible to draw the line? Why did you draw the line where you did?

STOP! ANSWER

Here are some sample hypotheses. First, the more plausible ones:

• After Brigette Bardot was photographed cuddling those cute baby seals, seal-hunting was banned; now those seals are eating up all the cod.

- Some oceanographer friends tell you that they think that the water in the North Atlantic has been getting warmer. Maybe cod don't reproduce as fast in warmer water.
- Fishermen have just taken too many codfish out of the North Atlantic.
- Whatever codfish like to eat has become much more rare in that area.
- There's an epidemic of some codfish disease that's killing them off.
- Fishermen have been spending less time than they used to fishing.

So far, we have a pretty good list of hypotheses: all are fairly plausible, given what we know. Are there some fairly probable hypotheses on your list which I've left out?

Here are some less plausible ones, in (more or less) the order of their plausibility, ranging all the way down to the ridiculous.

- Codfish are migratory, and once in a while they head off for somewhere else for no particular reason.
- Nuclear waste being dumped into the ocean is killing them off.
- The boats fishermen use nowadays are noisier, and that's scaring the cod away.
- Evil Eastern-European and Portuguese rival fishermen have been stealing the cod out of the Canadian fishermen's nets when nobody was looking.
- The fish have learned how to avoid getting caught.
- There's a huge sea-monster unknown to science living down there, eating all the cod.
- Aliens from another galaxy are kidnapping all the codfish to perform strange sexual experiments on them in their flying saucers.

Based on what I know about fish (admittedly not much), I'd say that the first six hypotheses are plausible enough to form our working list. They're all fairly likely, and this list of six, I would guess, is likely enough to contain the true explanation. My limited research budget is sufficient to investigate these six, but no more. Investigating them will take effort and money, but this is likely to pay off.

> The next six (post-nap) hypotheses aren't worth considering. One of them just might be the real explanation, but they're too implausible to make them worth investigating, given my research budget and the energy I'm willing to put in.

12.4 The Argument for a "Mixed Strategy"

Different people will have different estimations of the initial plausibility of a hypothesis. This is inevitable, and it means that different scientists, all following acceptable method, will construct different lists of plausible hypotheses. Putting the matter another way: the fact that there is no way exactly to determine the initial plausibility of any hypothesis means that there will inevitably be disagreement about what method to use in providing an explanation.

An example of this might be provided by the case of E.S.P. E.S.P. stands for Extra Sensory Perception: the alleged ability to find out facts at a distance, without using your ordinary senses. Most scientists find this idea so absurd that they think it's not worth spending money on investigations. Others think that the possibility that this exists is somewhat higher, and think that it at least bears investigation. This sort of disagreement is inevitable, and does not (necessarily) show that some scientists are failing to follow good scientific method. This sort of disagreement is typical of good science in action. I think that E.S.P. is so implausible that it doesn't warrant investigation. But the point is that it's a good thing that there are people who take it seriously enough to investigate this possibly crackpot notion, and people who don't.

A second source of disagreement among scientists is not over exactly how plausible a hypothesis is, but rather over how plausible it has to be to merit investigation. Conservative scientists will require a fairly high degree of initial plausibility in order to include a suggestion as a genuine hypothesis. Others will go ahead and investigate what they agree is a very unlikely supposition. There isn't any way to figure out exactly how plausible a hypothesis must be before it merits consideration. So science should tolerate this sort of disagreement also.

It's a good thing that scientists with different temperaments will judge the initial plausibility of a single hypothesis differently, and will require different levels of initial plausibility to justify inclusion on a list of working hypotheses. Both of these disagreements will result in a variety of scientific practice within the scientific community; and this variety is healthy. It wouldn't be a good idea if everyone agreed and did exactly the same thing. You wouldn't want a scientific community in which everyone was the same. You need some ultra-conservatives who resist new ideas; after all, the old ideas have been pretty good, and new ones might not work. You also need some radical crackpots; they make for progress (sometimes). Crackpots sometimes are right after all. The best sort of science, in the long run, is provided by a scientific community with a wide mixture of strategies.

Notice, by the way, how Mrs. Smith was off-base here again. We've seen several points at which scientists' own judgments, tastes, personalities, and values are and must be relevant to the observations they make.

12.5 Were Darwin and Galileo Crackpots?

As I mentioned earlier, Darwin himself—as well as most other scientists and lay-people—initially found the evolutionary hypothesis most implausible and not even worth thinking about. Darwin changed his mind, but many other people didn't. They found the idea that species evolve—especially with its implication that humans might have evolved from something ape-like—so implausible that it wasn't even worth investigating. They thought that Darwin was a crackpot. We judge the initial plausibility of any hypothesis on the basis of what we already believe; this is correct scientific procedure, as I've been emphasizing. In this sense, Darwin's critics were using good scientific procedure. Does this mean that Darwin—who after all, turned out to be right—did so despite using *bad* scientific procedure?

The same phenomenon can be seen in the story of Galileo, which I recounted in Chapter 1. Galileo's hypothesis was that there were moons going around Jupiter. According to the story, Galileo's critics refused to look through his telescope, saying, in effect: "I don't care what those spots of light are doing. There just can't be moons going around Jupiter, because Jupiter, as we all know, is imbedded on a crystal glass sphere, and moons couldn't get through it. It's common knowledge that everything circles around the Earth, so there couldn't be things circling around Jupiter. Whatever's going on up there with those spots, they can't be moons. It's not worth the trouble to investigate your hypothesis, because it's so implausible." Again, this seems right, given what we've said. You rule out very implausible hypotheses from the start. Given the standard beliefs at Galileo's time, it seems that they were justified in thinking that he was a crackpot and in rejecting his hypothesis out of hand, even without looking. These critics turned out to be wrong, and Galileo's very surprising hypothesis turned out right; but this isn't exactly the point here. The point is that in a sense Galileo's critics were following the right scientific method.

Were Darwin and Galileo, then, unscientific crackpots who irrationally rejected conventional wisdom and accidentally blundered onto what turned out, in the long run, to be true? Not exactly.

In both cases, observation had turned up evidence to show that the accepted views were unsatisfactory. In Galileo's case, it seemed to him that nothing in the accepted view could explain the movement of these dots. Whatever the dots were, it seemed that they were inconsistent with the crystal-sphere Earth-centred picture of the universe. The reason he had to come up with an alternative hypothesis wasn't just that he was a crackpot dreamer. The reason was that the accepted views of the time had turned out to be inadequate.

The situation is similar in Darwin's case. While sailing around in the Galápagos Islands and elsewhere in South America, he noticed the peculiar fact that neighbouring areas, comparatively isolated from each other, contained species which were different in only small ways, and that these differences increased with increasing distance. This fact turned up again and again. What in the accepted view—that each species was created at once, and remained forever exactly as it was created—could explain this regularity? Conventional science had a problem. It didn't seem to Darwin that it could be fixed up to account for these newly discovered facts.

According to this way of interpreting the two stories, neither Darwin nor Galileo should be seen as a crackpot. They had both discovered previously unknown facts which, they judged correctly, the views of the time couldn't explain reasonably. The old explanations just wouldn't do. Under these circumstances, it becomes unreasonable to hold on to the old views; something different has to be tried. Any alternative to the views widely accepted at the time would be thought an implausible view; but given the new discoveries, the old views should have been rejected, and new hypotheses which were previously thought implausible must be entertained. However, it doesn't follow merely from this that the new views proposed by Darwin and Galileo were the right explanation. All that follows is that, under the circumstances, it was time to try to dream up some new hypotheses.

A second feature that distinguishes the work of Darwin and Galileo from the wild musings of crackpots is that neither of them stopped once they had dreamed up an alternative hypothesis consistent with what they had observed. This is the point where much of the work of science begins. Now they had to show that their new hypotheses were true. We'll talk about this second stage in the next chapter.

CHAPTER 13

Disconfirming Hypotheses

13.1 Not the End of the Explanation Story

Well, time is wasting while we're sitting around in the kitchen listening to that whistle and making up hypotheses. We'd better get busy finding out which of these hypotheses actually provides the real explanation of that whistle, especially since it might mean that the house is about to burn down. When you come up with a list containing more than one plausible hypothesis, and have made sure that each of these hypotheses actually does deductively imply the explanandum (perhaps together with some assumed other general laws and factual conditions), then you (usually) have to do some more work to try to find out which hypothesis actually does explain what you need to explain.

This was probably what Kekulé meant when, after he recited that little poem about getting the truth without effort, he added: "But let us beware of publishing our dreams till they have been tested by the waking understanding."

13.2 Reasoning to the Best Explanation

But suppose you can only come up with one hypothesis that implies the explanandum and has enough plausibility even to be considered. That's the end of the story: no further work need be done. Let's imagine a case of this.

Suppose you've moved into a new apartment, and the second day you're there, you get a letter in the mail with your name and brand new address on it. What explains this? Who could have mailed this letter that arrived today? You're going to try to reason the matter out scientifically. Various hypotheses come to mind:

- Sally has sent you a letter.
- Fred has sent you a letter.
- Arnold has sent you a letter.

These are your three best friends, the only friends who might write you a letter. No: all of these hypotheses are too implausible even to consider. You haven't told your address to any of them yet. It's remotely possible that someone, through some devious means, has found out your new address anyway; but this is extremely unlikely. Who else might write to you?

- The telephone company has sent you a bill.
- Your bank has sent you a statement.
- Your dentist has sent you a reminder of your regular checkup.

No, these and similar hypotheses are implausible for the same reason: you haven't given any of these your address either.

- It's from your mom.

You did tell her your address. So far so good, but let's fill in the whole story here. You gave her your new address two days ago. She lives in Moose Jaw. It takes several days for mail to get here from Moose Jaw. Once we've filled in this information, it turns out that this hypothesis doesn't imply the explanandum, that the letter arrived, addressed to you, today. No, given what else you know, this is implausible too.

Aha! Maybe

- It's a junk mail advertising circular, delivered by the postal carrier to everyone on the route.

Oops, no, this wouldn't explain what needs to be explained. The letter has your name and new address written on it, and junk mail is unaddressed, or addressed to "RESIDENT".

It doesn't even pay to worry about other hypotheses, evidently utterly implausible, such as

- You mailed this letter to yourself.
- It's a letter from the Nobel Prize Commission telling you that you've won.

So far, no hypothesis is worthy of consideration. You're puzzled. Suddenly another hypothesis occurs to you:

- Your new landlord has sent you a letter.

Your new landlord, of course, knows your address. He's known it for days, long enough for this letter to reach you. This is a hypothesis, at last, which has some probability of truth. How probable is it that your new landlord has sent you a letter? Well, you don't know, exactly, but you do know that this hypothesis does have some probability of truth which is much higher than that of any of the other hypotheses you've considered; all the rest are way too improbable to be considered. It doesn't matter that you can't estimate very precisely what the initial probability of your new landlord's writing to you is. The fact is, it's the only hypothesis you can think of which implies the explanandum, and is not ruled out as far too implausible by your other information. So you're entitled to reach the conclusion that your new landlord has sent you a letter. You don't even have to check out your conclusion by opening the letter. You can start believing it right now.

The moral is: when there's only one hypothesis which both implies the explanandum and it is plausible enough to merit consideration, then you can stop there: that's what you should believe is true, and that is the explanation. This process is called **REASONING TO THE BEST EXPLANATION**. The fact that one explanation is much more plausible than any other you can think of constitutes, all by itself, some degree of confirmation for that hypothesis. (Do you remember what 'confirmation' and 'disconfirmation' mean? If not, look back now to sections 2.9 and 2.10.)

In this case, there's only one hypothesis you can think of that implies the explanandum and which has any plausibility at all.

13.3 How Trustworthy Is Reasoning to the Best Explanation?

It works fine in the case we've imagined. You've done a good job of dreaming up hypotheses, and of rejecting ones that are wholly implausible or which don't imply the explanandum. It's of course possible that a mistake has been made in this reasoning, however. For each hypothesis you dream up, you must decide whether, given your background information, this hypothesis has plausibility, and whether it in fact implies the explanandum.

You may be mistaken in any of these reasoning steps. There may be some relevant information you've ignored, or the relevance of which you've miscalculated. You may be unaware of some relevant information.

But another source of possible error is that there are some plausible hypotheses which you haven't even thought of. This source of error is interesting because there's no methodology for ensuring that you've thought up all the possibly relevant hypotheses. As we've seen in the last chapter, although there are ways of increasing your hypothesis-generating capacity, hypothesis generation is just something that happens to you: it's not something you can do better by following a set of rules. Trying harder—thinking longer and deeper—might get you a more complete set of hypotheses, and it might not. Real scientists sometimes get caught in this sort of mistaken reasoning despite their good training and best efforts, simply because a plausible hypothesis has not occurred to them.

13.4 Checking Up on Hypotheses

Now remember the letter you received in your new apartment. Of course, it's no trouble to check out who wrote it: just open it and take a look. Because of the inherent problems and fallibilities of reasoning to the best explanation, checking up on the conclusion when possible, even when you think it's the only plausible hypothesis, is often a good idea. When it's easy enough to check up on the only plausible hypothesis in this sort of way, then it's not clear why you went through this line of reasoning in the first place. (Just *why* were you fooling around with all this reasoning, when you simply might have opened the letter?)

In many cases, however, the process of reasoning to the best (only plausible) explanation won't be possible, because there's more than one plausible hypothesis which implies the conclusion. In this case, what we have to do is to check up on all the plausible hypotheses.

There are two ways of checking up on a hypothesis. We can simply look and see whether it's true or false, or we can begin to accumulate indirect evidence for or against it.

When there is more than one hypothesis under investigation, finding out that one of them is true is not good enough. This is a very important point. I'll explain, and you should make sure you understand the explanation.

We'll begin with an example. Imagine that you see Fred in the library. You know that Fred goes to the library if the pub is closed. Why is he in the library today? Suppose that these are the only hypotheses that (under the circumstances) you find plausible:

- The pub is closed.
- Fred has a big test tomorrow.

The first hypothesis is relevant because Fred goes to the library if the pub is closed. So if the pub were closed, that would explain why he's in the library. The second hypothesis is relevant because Fred always studies in the library the day before he has a big test. So if he had a big test tomorrow, that would explain why he's in the library.

Now it's time to begin checking up on these hypotheses. You decide to check up on the first one first. You go to the pub and take a look: sure enough, it's closed. Can you conclude that this explains why Fred is in the library? The answer is No.

(?)

EXERCISE
See if you can explain why not.

STOP!

ANSWER
The reason is that both of these hypotheses may be true, and yet only one of them is the real reason why Fred is in the library. Suppose that Fred actually does have a big test tomorrow, and that this is why he's in the library. He doesn't even know that the pub is closed.

13.5 Disconfirming Hypotheses

When you have a list of more than one plausible hypothesis, what you have to do to show that one hypothesis actually does explain the explanandum is not to show that it's true, but rather to show that *all* the other ones are false. If you can do this, then you have reduced the number of plausible hypotheses to one, and now you're back to the situation we have described earlier. You can now conclude that the only remaining hypothesis is the explanation.

What this means is that, in theory, you don't have to consider the remaining hypothesis at all. Let's see how this can work in our example involving Fred's location. You started with two hypotheses:

- The pub is closed.
- Fred has a big test tomorrow.

If you can show one of them is false, then you have reason to conclude that the remaining one is the explanation. Suppose you went to the pub and find out that it is open. You would have disconfirmed one of the hypotheses directly, by just taking a look. That would reduce the number of plausible hypotheses to one: that Fred has a big test tomorrow. That would have to be the explanation of why he's in the library.

So, off to the pub to take a look at whether it's open or closed. When you get there, you see that it's closed. You've confirmed that hypothesis directly, by just taking a look. But that doesn't help with the process of finding an explanation. The fact that the pub is closed doesn't mean that that's why Fred's in the library. He might be in the library because he has a big test tomorrow. You want disconfirmation of a hypothesis, not confirmation. Now what you have to do is to try to disconfirm the other hypothesis.

How could you disconfirm that Fred has a big test tomorrow? You can't do it directly, by just going and taking a look. (At least, you can't do that today.) Well, it's possible to disconfirm this indirectly. You know that whenever Fred has a test the next day, then Sally (who is in Fred's class) is in the library studying too. If Fred has a test tomorrow, then Sally is in the library. Okay, off to the library, where you take a look around to see if Sally is there. She isn't. Now you know that it's false that Fred has a test tomorrow. The only remaining hypothesis why Fred is in the library is that the pub is closed. So that must be the explanation.

13.6 A Summary

We've set up quite a complicated structure for finding an explanation, and it will help to summarize it. Suppose that we want to find an explanation for phenomenon P. Suppose (for comparative simplicity) that we can only dream up two plausible hypotheses which would explain P; call them H1 and H2. In order to explain P, both H1 and H2 would have to be premises in deductively sound arguments with P as the conclusion. (Do you remember what "deductively sound" means? It means that the argument is valid and the premises are true.) At least one premise in each argument will be a law; the others (subsidiary information) may be laws or factual conditions. We'll abbreviate laws by 'L' plus a number, and factual conditions by 'F' plus a number. In a simple case, the situation may look like this:

H1	H2
L1	L2
F1	F2
P	P

Of course, there may be more than two plausible hypotheses, and each hypothesis may be a premise of a much longer and more complicated argument involving several other laws and factual statements. We're just looking at a simple case.

We must be satisfied that the premises of both arguments are true. Usually the laws (L1 and L2) and the other factual conditions (F1 and F2) are things we already assume, so no new confirmation process is necessary; but there has to have been some confirmation process for these somewhere along the line. (In the next chapter, we'll consider special circumstances surrounding the confirmation of laws.)

As we have seen, there's no point in confirming H1 or H2. What we want to do is to disconfirm one of them.

Suppose H1 can be disconfirmed (if false, or confirmed if true) directly, simply by taking a look. Well, take a look then. Suppose that H1 turns out to be confirmed (or at least, not disconfirmed). Okay; now we must try to disconfirm H2. Suppose that H2 cannot be disconfirmed simply by taking a look. In order to disconfirm H2 then we'd have to do it indirectly, on the basis of evidence that H2 is false. This requires construction of another different deductive argument with H2 as a premise, and suppose it looks like this:

$$H2$$
$$\underline{L3}$$
$$S$$

Again we've shown only a very simple argument; more premises may be necessary, including other laws, and subsidiary factual statements.

S is a statement we can determine is false (perhaps by merely taking a look this time), and we do. The argument is deductively valid, so at least one of its premises is false. We assume (on the basis of previous knowledge, probably) that L3 is true. So it must be that H2 is false.

Now that we know that H2 is false, we can conclude that H1 is the real explanation for P.

EXERCISE

Now go through the account of explaining why Fred's in the library, and determine which statements in this account are abbreviated just above by P, H1, L1, F1, H2, L2, F2, L3, and S.

ANSWER

P: Fred is in the library.
H1: The pub is closed.
L1: If the pub is closed, Fred goes to the library.
F1: The pub is closed.
H2: Fred has a big test tomorrow.
L2: If Fred has a big test tomorrow, Fred goes to the library.
L3: If Fred has a big test tomorrow, Sally is in the library.
S: Sally is in the library.

13.7 But What If...?

Let's roll back the Story of Fred tape a bit, and look at some other possibilities.

Suppose that you come up with these two hypotheses, and you begin by going to the pub to check out whether or not the pub is closed, as above, but you find out (contrary to the story we told above) that the pub is *not* closed. It's open. Now that you know that one of the hypotheses is false, you can conclude your investigation. You have now shown that the explanation of why Fred is in the library must be that he has a big test tomorrow.

Why don't you need to check out whether or not it's true that Fred has a big test tomorrow? If you were right to start off with in thinking that these are the *only* plausible hypotheses, then the fact that one of them is false must mean that the other one is true. It might reassure you a bit to check out, in addition, whether in fact Fred has a big test tomorrow. Suppose you do, and it turns out that he does. What difference would that make? It would show that this is the explanation of why he's in the library only if there were no other (third, fourth, etc.) hypotheses which were plausible. You've already ruled this out, and finding out that he did have a big test tomorrow wouldn't help decide whether there were any other plausible hypotheses; so it wouldn't do any good to check.

But suppose that you check and find out that he actually *doesn't* have a big test tomorrow. You have now found out that both hypotheses are false; so what now? Now it's back to the drawing board. Now you have no idea what explains the fact that he's in the library. You need to think of other hypotheses worth considering; it shows that you've made a mistake in the first step, hypothesis formation. This is something valuable to learn, and for this reason it's worthwhile checking. But on the assumption that your two hypotheses really were the only ones which had any possibility of explaining his presence in the library, then this wouldn't happen.

Suppose, on the other hand, that you check first on the hypothesis that the pub is closed, and find out that that's true. Of course, this doesn't justify the conclusion that this hypothesis explains why Fred's in the library. Now you need to check on the second hypothesis, that he has a big test tomorrow. Suppose this turns out to be true too. This doesn't justify the conclusion that his presence in the library is explained by the fact that he has a big test tomorrow. You've found out that he has a test, and that the pub is closed; but you're still in the dark about which one really explains the fact that he's in the library. What do you do now? Again, it's back to the drawing board. We'll take a look at what to do in this sort of situation in a moment.

EXERCISE

To make sure you've got all this, let's look at some general possibilities. See if you can say what conclusion (if any) can be drawn from the following circumstances:

(a) All but one of your plausible hypotheses are disconfirmed.

(b) You've confirmed one of them. (The rest haven't been confirmed or disconfirmed.)

(c) You fail to disconfirm two of them.

(d) All of your plausible hypotheses are disconfirmed.

(e) You confirm all but one of them. The remaining one is neither confirmed nor disconfirmed.

ANSWERS

(a) This is the fortunate situation: you can conclude that the remaining one (which has not been disconfirmed) is the explanation.

(b) The one you've confirmed might be the explanation, but so might any of the others on the list. Now you have to try to disconfirm all the rest. Right now, you can't conclude anything.

(c) The two you've failed to disconfirm are both candidates for the explanation, but you can't say which. You have to reformulate things to try to narrow the possibilities down (see next section).

(d) This means that you didn't have the explanation on your list of plausible hypotheses. Something you didn't think of at all, or something you thought of and rejected as implausible must be the explanation. Go make a new list.

(e) The remaining hypothesis might be the explanation, but so might any of the others you have already confirmed. As in (c), you need to reformulate your hypotheses to narrow things down.

13.8 When You Can't Disconfirm All But One

Suppose now that, try as you might, you can't disconfirm all but one of your hypotheses. Perhaps you can't find out anything about two or more of them. Or perhaps two or more of them are confirmed. What then?

What you need to do now is to reconsider your set of hypotheses: to reformulate what you have, perhaps with more detail, so that it might be possible to find out that one of the new set is false. Let's go back to the Story of Fred to see an example. Suppose that both of the hypotheses on your list of plausible explanations have turned out to be true: the pub is closed, and Fred has a big test tomorrow. Which is the reason he's in the library? What you should do is to formulate a new, more detailed, list of hypotheses, hoping that you can disconfirm all but one on this new list. Here's a sample new list:

- Fred wanted to go the pub, and went there first; it was closed; then he went to the library.
- Fred didn't go to the pub first; he has a big test tomorrow, and went straight to the library.

These hypotheses spell out the possible explanations in more detail, so they give you more possible grounds for finding out that one of them is false. Note that the information that you found out while checking out the first hypothesis set doesn't show that either of these new ones is false. You found out, we imagine, that Fred does have a big test tomorrow. That's consistent, of course, with the second new hypothesis, but it's also consistent with the first. You also found out that the pub was closed, and that's consistent with the first new hypothesis, but it's also consistent with the second.

But now you can do some more checking, suggested by this new hypothesis set. You can try to find out where Fred went first that morning. For example, you already know that when Fred goes to the pub first, he always walks there directly, and that the direct route to the pub involves turning left out of Fred's house. So you can check with people who might have seen Fred leaving his house that morning. If someone saw Fred leave his house and turn right, then you have good reason to think that the first new hypothesis is false; so you can conclude that the second one must explain his presence in the library.

13.9 Or Else...

Or else, instead of going through this whole to-do, you could just ask Fred why he's in the library. Well, this is obviously the best thing to do; why did we just go through this long story involving hypotheses and everything? Because just asking is a way of finding out explanations only when the sort of explanation we're looking for is someone's reasons for doing something. (Sometimes you can't even find out someone's real reasons by asking.)

13.10 Are We Then Only Interested in Showing Statements False?

What I've been claiming is that our most direct concern in explanation is disconfirmation of hypotheses, not confirmation. We can't show that a candidate hypothesis really explains the explanandum by confirming it—by getting evidence that it's true. The only way we can show that a candidate hypothesis really explains the explanandum is by disconfirming alternative hypotheses—by getting evidence that every other plausible hypothesis is false.

But disconfirmation is not the only thing necessary in the whole process of finding an explanation. As I've been stressing, when it comes to the matter of choosing the explanation from among the other hypotheses, you must disconfirm all but one of them. But at several points in the process of providing an explanation, confirmation of statements is of central importance, because it's important that these other statements are true.

Remember first that a good deal of background information is necessary, on the basis of which you judge that some hypotheses are plausible enough to warrant consideration. Next, each hypothesis you have on the list of plausible ones has to be a premise of an argument which deductively implies the explanandum. The other premises—laws and facts—have to be independently confirmed.

13.11 Explanations and Mrs. Smith

Notice again how different the complex process of explanation is from empty-minded Smithian observational science. We pointed out in the last chapter how the process of hypothesis formation, and of choice of the plausible hypotheses to investigate, is surely not mere Smithian observation: in order to do it, you need to have a good deal of background knowledge, and need to exercise some degree of inventive creativity; values are also relevant. We can add now some additional non-Smithian characteristics. Some hypotheses can be disconfirmed by mere looking, but others need to be ruled out indirectly. We've seen that subsidiary information must be presupposed for indirect disconfirmation of a hypothesis. An empty-minded scientist would be forbidden from assuming any subsidiary information, and thus would be incapable of finding explanations in many cases.

EXERCISE

Try imagining a fairly real-life example of finding an explanation which shows the features we've been looking at. Indicate: (1) a few plausible hypotheses, and a few that are implausible. (2) For each plausible hypothesis, what other premises are in the argument that deductively imply the explanandum? (3) Which of the hypotheses you can check out directly, by just looking? (4) which of the hypotheses you can check out indirectly? And for each of these (5) the deductive argument for which the falsity of the conclusion will disconfirm that hypothesis.

You should imagine a sucessful explanation— that is, a case in which you're able to disconfirm all plausible hypotheses but one.

As we've seen, you need to have background knowledge of an area to find an explanation for a phenomenon in that area. So you should pick an area you have some knowledge of to do this exercise. Here are some suggestions for explanation-questions for this exercise:

(a) Why is your dog limping?

(b) Why did those cookies you just baked burn at the bottom?

(c) Why is your favourite shirt missing from your closet?

(d) What explains that terrible smell in your basement?

(e) Why is there a brown patch in the middle of your lawn?

CHAPTER 14

Empiricism Revisited

14.1 Illusions and Hallucinations ▐▬▬▬

We've already seen several ways in which the simple empiricist view of science is wrong. In this chapter we're going to explore some more complicated subtle ways.

One way in which science goes beyond simple observation—a way we've been stressing a good deal in the book so far—is that science uses induction. The conclusion of an inductive argument goes beyond what was observed. Whenever science accepts indirect evidence for something, it's going beyond simple observation. But this picture still leaves a good deal of room for a simple empiricism in science. On this picture, there are two sharply distinguished ways we find things out. One way is by simple looking and seeing—direct confirmation or disconfirmation—the kind of thing that Mrs. Smith stressed. She insisted that this procedure, in order to give objective and trustworthy knowledge about the world, should be done without any preconceptions on the part of the observers. The observers should be passive and empty-minded, letting nature impose herself on them. (Remember the contrast between Galileo and the others in Brecht's play.) We have been accepting this Smithian view, more or less, as the account of how we get the basic data. What we have added to it is that these data can be used in induction to confirm things not apparent to the senses. Smithian raw perceptual data form the premises for inductive arguments which tell us more than we find out by simple looking and seeing.

This view accommodates going beyond simple looking and seeing in science, but it's still basically an empiricist view, in that it makes the information we get by simple perception basic—the foundation of our scientific knowledge. It's firm and indubitable. Probabilities and the possibility of mistake come in when we use this firm and indubitable data in induction, which goes beyond perception, and so offers the possibility of mistake.

But many philosophers in this century have come to doubt that there is a simple distinction between the data, firm and certain, gotten by naïve presupposition-free passive observation, and what we infer from it with increasing degrees of dubitability. There are several reasons they have for thinking that this view is not exactly right.

Here's the first: perception is sometimes mistaken. On the following diagram, visually compare the lengths of lines AB and CD:

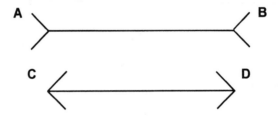

Despite the way they look, AB and CD are the same length. You can find this out by measuring them.

Here's another illusion, this one not optical but tactile, and a little less familiar and more interesting. Cross your index and middle fingers. Now position your hand so that the tips of both of these fingers are resting against the edge of something with a sharp corner, like the edge of your desk or the edge of this book. Move your hand up and down the edge, changing the angle of your hand a little. If you get the angle right, you get a really vivid feeling that there are two separate edges you're feeling.

An illusion philosophers like to use as an example is that a straight stick looks bent from a certain angle when it's half-immersed in water.

These are all illusions—cases in which the senses present things that are really there in deceptive ways. There are also delusions—hallucinations—in which the senses present what isn't there at all. Those green snakes you saw running up and down the wall after you drank 38 beers last weekend are an example of this.

People are rarely fooled by any of these, and even if you are fooled by an occasional illusion or hallucination, you're usually able to correct the initially misleading impression. If you were fooled by that diagram with the two lines above, for example, you might have taken a ruler to measure the two lines. Using a ruler to determine the relative length of two lines is using an indirect way of finding things out; that relies on certain obviously true generalizations you already know, such as that rulers don't change length when moved from one place to another. What you're doing here, then, is using indirect confirmation methods to correct information you get immediately from just looking. What this example shows is that the information you get from just looking directly isn't always the most certain, the data on which we build all other beliefs. Sometimes it works the other way around: the information we get from the senses is less certain, and is corrected by indirect confirmation/disconfirmation.

On the very simple empiricist view, we passively and preferably open-mindedly get certain foundational knowledge from perception; this is used to build more complex and more dubitable knowledge by induction. But philosophers nowadays tend to have replaced this view with the idea that the process of getting knowledge goes in both directions: sometimes simple perception forms the basis for more complex and general beliefs based on induction. But sometimes things go in the other way round, as we've seen, and the more complex beliefs are the basis for what we think we perceive. The bent-stick-in-water case provides another example of this. We all have, by now, general knowledge of what happens to the way things look when they're half-immersed in water. It's this general complex knowledge that we use to form our beliefs about the way the stick really is, and to correct what simple perception misleadingly tells us.

Another way of putting this point is: accordng to the empiricist view, perception is the basis of all belief. Perception shapes our beliefs, and ought to. Beliefs don't (or at least shouldn't) shape our perceptions. The relation between perception and belief, on the empiricist view, should be one-way.

But we've seen examples in which the relation is, and should be, the other way around. When perception is unreliable (as in the cases of illusion and hallucination), our beliefs should shape our perceptions. Mrs. Smith insisted that when a perception didn't fit pre-existing beliefs, the perception was always right, and the pre-existing belief should be rejected. But clearly there are cases—like those above—when the right move is to reject the perception because of its conflict with pre-existing belief. Things don't always go this way either, of course. There are many occasions when a belief should be rejected because it conflicts with perception. And of course, many beliefs are gotten in the first place on the basis of perception. The relation between perception and belief isn't, and shouldn't be, one-way. It is and should be a complex back-and-forth.

14.2 Perception Is Coloured by Belief

Here's a second, more complicated, subtler, and more controversial criticism of Smithian empiricism.

Imagine what it was like to look through a telescope when Galileo saw the moons of Jupiter in around 1610. Remember that the telescope had just been invented. Nobody knew the scientific explanation of what the telescope did, and they wouldn't know for several years, until the philosopher Descartes first explained it (in around 1635). When people look through telescopes then, what do they see? Is it real things far away, or just illusions produced by this strange object? Nowadays, nobody has any doubts about what's behind the images in a telescope, and we can imagine that we see things differently when we look through the instrument. Because of our different beliefs, *things look different to us* when we look into a telescope.

Pre-Galileo, most people thought that the Earth was stationary and the heavens circled around it. Now we know that it's the Earth that's rotating. In those days, as now, of course, everyone noticed the slow movements of the stars around the sky during the night; but then they saw it differently from the way we do. Try this: go out on a starry night, and look up at the sky. First, imagine yourself as stationary, with the stars wheeling very slowly around you. Next, imagine the stars as relatively stationary, with the earth turning around with you on it. You *see things differently* from each perspective.* We can imagine that as the old view was replaced by the new, people started to see the sky very differently.

You must have had the experience of coming across your own reflection, for example, in a shop window, and not realizing that it's you. All of a sudden you realise that it's you, and the reflection suddenly changes drastically in the way it looks.

---

* This is a favorite example of the philosopher Paul Churchland, told to me in conversation.

These are all cases in which the way something looks depends on our beliefs. Perhaps there are a lot more of these. Imagine how a person in the stone age saw a tree; compare this to how you see it, and how a trained botanist or biologist sees it.

Imagine now the different ways all three would describe the same tree. These differences in words perhaps reflect differences in the perceptions. And the different perceptions of each person are shaped by the drastically different beliefs and backgrounds they have.

The (controversial) moral of this is that there is no such thing as pure, objective, passive, empty-minded perception. All perception is influenced by the kinds of beliefs we have. The idea that we can shed all our background and perceive things passively—the way they "really are"—is an illusion.

Does all this mean that there is no such thing as scientific objectivity? That it's okay to let your pre-conceived beliefs, prejudices and desires determine what you say as a scientist, because it's inevitable? Not necessarily. We'll come back to this question.

14.3 Theories

In our discussion so far, we have encountered two sorts of objects of scientific inquiry and belief: particular factual statements and general laws. But this isn't all there is to science. Science also contains **THEORIES**.

People say things like, "Oh, that's only just a theory!" meaning it's a highly debatable belief or maybe just a wild guess. But as this word is used in science, it does not mean a hunch that's unsupported by evidence. What's called a 'scientific theory' is sometimes a very basic law, one from which a number of other more particular laws can be derived. Usually the word refers to a whole system of interrelated comprehensive basic and derived laws, plus definitions of concepts special to this system. Here are some examples of what scientists call 'theories' in this sense:

- Einstein's theory of relativity
- Darwin's theory of evolution
- Mendelian theory of genetics
- Keynesian theory in economics
- The "Big Bang" theory of cosmology
- Freudian psychoanalytic theory

Although some of these are controversial, none of them is a merely unsupported guess. Some of them are extremely strongly supported and accepted by just about all scientists. So when those neatly-dressed earnest people come to your door carrying religious pamphlets, and tell you that Darwin's Theory is called a 'Theory' because it's just a wild unsupported hunch, you can tell them that that's not what the word 'theory' means in this context. In fact, Darwin's theory is regarded by just about all biologists as, in its main details anyway, extremely well-supported by the evidence, and beyond doubt.

14.4 Revolutions in Science

Individual factual beliefs are often arrived at directly, just by looking, or else indirectly, by induction from other beliefs. Law generalisations are often arrived at inductively, on the basis of a number of individual factual beliefs which act as evidence for the general law. Both processes are consistent with the empiricist view that regards things as built up from the factual beliefs given by perception. But theories arise in a different fashion.

Here's a (simplified) story which gives the basic steps some philosophers think are involved in the formulation and confirmation of a new theory.

New theories characteristically arise when there are problems with old ones. Imagine a certain area of science, a bunch of related laws and particular facts which scientists believe and use to predict and explain phenomena in the world. Problems have arisen: some things this theory predicts have not come true. Some new observations have arisen that seem inconsistent with the theory, and it's not clear that the theory can be fixed up in any convenient way to make it consistent with these new observations. (These things are called **ANOMALOUS DATA.**) Some things in the area the theory's supposed to cover can't be explained by it.

Think, for example, of the Ptolemaic Theory (the Earth-centered theory) of the relations of the heavenly bodies. Even before Galileo discovered those moons, which put severe strain on the theory, there were other problems. It turned out, for example, that it was very difficult to use this theory to calculate the paths of the planets through the sky.

Now, old theories have stayed around because they work, more or less, and you're not going to throw them away until you have something better to replace them with. Attempts are made to fix up the old theory; anomalous data can be ignored for a while.

Well, sooner or later someone (or some group of people) comes up with a radically different way of looking at things: a replacement for the old theory which sees things in a radically different way. People are, of course, fairly conservative in their beliefs. They won't be eager to reject the old theory, which they see things in terms of, and to accept the new one, which seems absurd. But the new theory passes the tests for acceptability, perhaps with some modifications. It turns out to do a better job at explaining and predicting than the old one. Sometimes someone figures out a **CRUCIAL EXPERIMENT**: one that can turn out only in two ways, each of which will show one theory right and the other wrong. There is a "scientific revolution" and the scientific community swings over to the new view.

Now, what you should notice in this story is that observations and induction play some part in it, but they are not all there is. Anomalous data are observations that play a crucial part in this story of scientific revolution, but they don't (all by themselves) serve to force rejection of the old theory: sometimes the old theory can be patched up to accommodate them. Sometimes, as we've seen, they're simply rejected as illusions or hallucinations, or as mistakes somewhere in subsidiary beliefs, such as those about how the instrumentation is supposed to be working. Or they may be considered problems which remain to be solved.

Neither do observations add up to the new theory. The motivation for production of a new theory, of course, was the observations that were anomalous for the old one; and a new theory that fits these observations will be one that stands a chance of acceptance. The new theory, once it's invented, will have to stand the test of observations: the predictions it makes will have to be observed to be true. Where there is a crucial experiment, then observations made during this experiment may be very important in the rejection of one theory and the acceptance of the new. But the point is that creation of a new theory is, like creation of a hypothesis list for explanation, a work of imagination and creativity. In its first stages, a new theory is a conjecture, often a shot-in-the-dark, a wild guess (but an educated one: you need a great deal of facility with the science as it exists to revolutionize it).

All this sounds familiar, and it should. When we were discussing explanation a few chapters back, some of the explanations we were considering were theories, not simple facts or laws.

14.5 Theoretical Entities

So far, we've been thinking of indirect confirmation as something that may introduce doubt, but which is practically preferable in some circumstances, when it costs too much or it's too difficult to just look and see. Even in cases in which we called it "impossible" to look and see, this was really mostly just a matter of lack of technology or funds. For example, with no limits on technology or funds, we'd never need to reason about a population on the basis of only a sample. We'd be able to go out and look at the whole damn population.

But theories provide us with an additional, more interesting, reason why we sometimes rely on indirect confirmation/disconfirmation: there's a peculiar sort of thing that is impossible to observe directly. I don't mean merely impractical. Consider, for example, the electron. It's not merely the case that this thing is too small to see. If this were so, then the fact that nobody's ever seen one would be merely the result of how acute our eyes were. It would be similar to the moons of Jupiter, which are too small and far away for our eyes to see directly, or to a mountain on the side of the moon that always faces away from the Earth. Nobody's directly seen it because you can't see it from Earth, and astronauts haven't visited that part of the moon.

Perhaps we have all sorts of information about this mountain indirectly, through photographs taken by space vehicles, for example. But if someone were there, they would be able to see what that mountain looks like. If astronauts flew past Jupiter, they could see those moons directly. But no matter where we went or how acute our eyes were, we couldn't see electrons; the reason is that they don't look like anything, because light waves don't and can't bounce off them. It is not merely a matter of where we've been and how we're set up that nobody's seen one. They're the sort of thing which, although there's indirect evidence for them, by their nature nothing could count as seeing them.

Other things share this sort of unobservability. Consider the force of gravity: we can, of course, measure this by observing its effects on things— seeing what they weigh, how fast they accelerate, and so on; but we can't take a direct look at it. Nor can we feel it directly. You can, of course, feel the weight of something if you hold it in your hand: but this isn't feeling gravity—it's feeling an effect of gravity.

These things are called **THEORETICAL ENTITIES**. The only reason that people have for believing in these things is that the claim that they exist is part of the best theory around for explaining the data or predicting events in some area.

Consider, for example, the electron. Nobody's ever seen one, and nobody ever could. Why believe in them? The answer is that theories in physics and chemistry claim that these things exist, and these theories are remarkably successful science. It would be extremely surprising if there weren't any such things as electrons, given that these theories work so well. This is perhaps another example of reasoning to the best explanation (see section 13.2).

You can see, however, why theoretical entities are troubling for empiricists. A basic belief of empiricists is—put very simply—that everything you say about anything has to boil down, in the long run, to observations you make or could make. To talk about things that nobody can or could observe strikes some empiricists as nonsense, something to be avoided in science at all costs. Sometimes empiricists react to this problem of theoretical entities by suggesting that talking about them is just a sort of shorthand for talking about other things we really do or could observe. Perhaps they're just fictions we invent for the purpose of providing explanations and predictions.

The split here concerns whether or not such unobservable theoretical entities should be thought of as really existing. The philosophical position which holds that they do is called **THEORETICAL ENTITY REALISM**, and the one which holds that they don't (but are just shorthand or fictions) is called **THEORETICAL ENTITY ANTIREALISM**. The word 'realism' doesn't have its ordinary meaning (practicality, a down-to-earth approach); in philosophy, realism in general is the position that something exists independently of human minds, out there in the real world.

CHAPTER 15

Categories

15.1 Classification

Even the kinds of naked facts that Mrs. Smith told us about, and urged us to collect for ourselves, implied that scientists had more in their minds than *just* a pile of facts. For example, when we found out that a particular robin was eating a particular earthworm, we were *classifying* that object we were observing as a robin, and what it was eating as an earthworm. (And what it was doing as eating.) When you classify things, you need to be aware of these classifications: how things were organized into groups, and what made a particular thing count as a member of a particular group.

In my high school biology class, we spent practically no time at all finding out particular facts about particular objects, and a whole lot of time memorizing the names of the groups of living things, and the characteristics that made something a member of one group rather than another. Living things (we were told, approximately) are divided into two "Kingdoms": the animals and the plants. The animals were divided into those with and without backbones. The backboned animals were divided into fish, amphibians, reptiles, mammals, and birds. The birds were divided into a variety of orders, including the Passeriformes (the "sparrowlike" birds), which includes lots of kinds of birds including sparrows, crows, thrashers, wrens, and thrushes. The American robin is a kind of thrush.

We had to learn what distinguishes birds from other animals with backbones: roughly speaking, they have warm blood, wings and feathers.

Well, so what? (This is the question I often muttered to myself in high school.) I understood that scientists like to talk about what kind of object a particular thing is, and have developed elaborate and many-tiered systems of classification to stick each object into classifications. But it seemed to me that this was a useless sort of activity, designed mostly to satisfy the personality quirks of strange scientists who liked to sort things out into a hugely complex set of pigeonholes they had constructed, just for the sake of sorting. (And also for the sake of torturing the high-school students who had to memorize all these categories.) I thought that this whole classification business was hugely arbitrary (after all, you could sort things out any way you felt like, couldn't you?), and entirely unnecessary.

15.2 Is Classifying Necessary?

But it's easy to see why I was wrong about classification being unnecessary.

EXERCISE
Imagine that you see something—anything. Is there anything you can say about it without classifying it—assigning it to a category? Is there anything you can *think* about it without assigning it to a category?

I'm presenting this question as a puzzle for you to muse about, and I'm not going to give a definite answer. I'm just going to give you some more questions.

Suppose you see your friend Fred. Of course, if you say (or think) that he's a human, or a male, or a friend of yours, you're classifying him. How about: "It's Fred?" Is this categorizing him? Into what category? Into the Freds? (The position that this sort of statement, which merely identifies it by its proper name, categorizes it, is implausible. Imagine you know someone named Lakeside A. Schmidlap. You don't know anyone else by that name, and you suppose reasonably that there isn't anyone else in the world with this name. So there doesn't seem to be any category called the Lakeside A. Schmidlaps.)

Here's another question for you to consider:

EXERCISE
Suppose you see something, and say, "There it is!" What categories, if any, does this put it in?

In any case, it does seem clear that the sorts of individual facts that scientists accumulate—the ones they're interested in—do depend on the existence of categories. "It's Fred" and "There it is!" aren't the sort of thing that a scientist would count as giving information of any scientific value. It's clearer still that the general statements they make involve categorization. After all, what we've been calling a general statement is about a kind of thing, which needs to be identified when you make that statement, even if you don't name it. If you say, merely, "That kind of thing eats that sort of thing," you haven't identified exactly what kind of things you're talking about. But you do presuppose that there are classifications they fit into.

I haven't answered the question of whether there's any sort of thing you can say or think which doesn't classify. But these considerations do point to the fact that a very large percentage (if not all) of what we think and say involves classification. It's very hard to see how we could say or think anything without it.

15.3 Categories Make a Difference

Imagine that you wanted to predict how tall your favourite tree in your back yard was going to be. With this in mind, you measured the tree every year on July 1, for the past several years. Here are your figures:

1993	163 cm
1994	172 cm
1995	181 cm
1996	190 cm
1997	199 cm

Now, you decide to construct a law of your-tree-growth on the basis of this sample, to enable you to predict what it's going to do in the future. One characteristic you notice is true of your tree over the past several years is that it has grown 9 cm taller over the year just past. You formulate this law:

My tree has grown 9 cm every year

and deduce from this law that it's going to grow 9 cm between July 1 1997 and July 1, 1998. Your prediction is that it's going to be 208 cm tall then. Well, allowing for the small sample and the known variability of tree growth in general, and so on, this looks like a good prediction.

But now you notice that there's another characteristic true of your tree every time you measured it over the past few years. It has been under 200 cm tall every time. You formulate this law:

My tree is under 200 cm every year

and deduce from this law that it's going to be under 200 cm tall on July 1, 1998.

You now have two laws, both of which can't be true; and two predictions, both of which can't be true.

Now, it's perfectly obvious which prediction is the right one to make, given the evidence. (I'm not saying it's bound to be true; I'm saying it's the one which is justified, to some extent, by the evidence.)

My question is not which one is right, but why. Both of these processes of reasoning appear to do the same thing: they notice that all observed items in the sample have a certain characteristic, and they generalize to say that everything has that characteristic. (We're ignoring margin of error here.) It appears that one of these characteristics—being under 200 cm tall—is the wrong one to use in an inductive procedure of this sort.

An interesting question I'm not sure I can answer is: what's the rule here? When is a characteristic okay to use in an inductive procedure like this, and when isn't it okay? It appears that being under 200 cm tall is a perfectly okay characteristic to use in other inductions. For example, if 45% of the trees sampled in a forest are under 200 cm, then it's perfectly okay to conclude that 45% of all the trees in the forest (± M.E.) are under 200 cm. Why is it wrong here?

In any case, the moral we can draw from this example is that what characteristic you see something as having—what category you put it in—does make a difference. It may result in success or failure in induction and in prediction.

15.4 Are Categories Arbitrary?

Consider this philosophical position—the one I more or less believed in high school: categories are completely arbitrary. We could categorize things any old way we liked. Certain ways of categorizing things are normal and habitual, and are built into our language; but all sorts of other ways of categorizing things are possible. Our language might have cut things up differently. The way our language is at the moment reflects (determines?) the way we like to cut things up—the conventional categories. But it's easy to define other sorts of unconventional categories in terms of the conventional ones, and we can create new words to name these newly created unconventional categories. I'll do some of this right now. Here are some unconventional categories I've just made up:

- FIVER: A fiver is anyone who lives at a house whose street number has digits that average 5 or more. I'm not a fiver because my current street address is 1543, but I used to be when I lived at 6287.
- TOWERLINGS: Everything that's within a 100-metre radius of the Eiffel Tower.
- BOOKANINES: Everything that's either a book or a dog. What you're reading right now is a bookanine, and so is Fido over there.
- GRUE: If it's before January 1, 2050, something is grue at that time just in case it's green at that time. All the emeralds anyone has examined so far have been grue. The sky is blue today, so it's not grue today. Starting January 1, 2050, something is grue at that time just in case it's blue at that time. If the sky is blue on the morning of that date, then it will be grue then.*

I don't expect these words to become widely used, and neither do you.

EXERCISE
QUESTION A. Why do you think these words won't pass into the general vocabulary? I'm not looking for an insulting answer like nobody's going to read this book. Suppose, implausibly, that all the major English-language newspapers in the world simultaneously published a front page article defining these new words. We still wouldn't expect these words to become part of the language. Why not?

ANSWER to QUESTION A
Because people don't categorize things in any of these ways, and they won't start, whatever you say.

---

* I lied: I didn't just make this one up. This one was made up by the philosopher Nelson Goodman; he uses this unconventional category in posing some interesting philosophical questions, which we'll touch on a little later. You can read about what he says about 'grue' in his article "The New Riddle of Induction," in his book *Fact, Fiction and Forecast* (Indianapolis: Bobbs-Merrill, 1965).

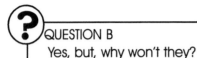

QUESTION B
Yes, but, why won't they?

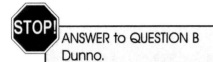

ANSWER to QUESTION B
Dunno.

Well, we'll think about QUESTION B some more.

15.5 Category Relativism

The examples I've been using—fivers, pocketcoins, towerlings, bookanines—are all categories I've made up, and there's something bizarre about all of them—something illegitimate. We wouldn't expect them to be used in any science that's any good. But according to the view that I had in high school, there's nothing particularly wrong with them; it's just that we don't happen to divide things that way. We could if we wanted to.

The view I've been talking about can be called **CATEGORY RELATIVISM**. 'Relativism' here means that there is no real truth of the matter, no real 'better' or 'worse' way of thinking about things. Category relativism claims that the scheme of dividing things up into kinds is arbitrary. According to this view, there are many ways—maybe even an infinite number of ways—things can be categorized. None of these ways is necessitated or even made preferable by the way the world is. The way we happen to categorize things is determined, entirely arbitrarily, by the vocabulary of whatever language we happen to have learned. Different languages can categorize things differently. Once we've learned a particular language, that way of categorizing things sticks with us.*

Do different linguistic groups in fact categorize things in substantially different ways? This is a scientific question, and it's not easy to answer. You may have heard that the Inuit have some large number of words referring to what English-speakers call by one word, 'snow'; but linguists nowadays believe that this is just false. In general, linguists tend to lean to the position that there is a good deal of universality of categorization-scheme in all human languages. Of course, they don't deny that there are *some* category-scheme differences; but they think that these happen in less "basic" areas of the language.

---

*In case you're interested, this widely discussed and (now) widely rejected position is known as the Sapir-Whorf hypothesis, credited to B. L. Whorf and his teacher E. Sapir. You can read Whorf's arguments in *Language, Thought and Reality* (Boston, MIT Press, 1969.)

Is the way we think totally determined by the arbitrary categories our language happens to have? The way we've answered the question in the last paragraph is relevant here. If there's a good deal of agreement in category-scheme among all languages, despite a good deal of diversity between languages in other ways, this may mean that the way we think is not wholly determined by the accidents of how our language happened to develop, or even by differences in our environment and interests. Rather, it is determined by more universal features in humans—for example, how our perceptual system is set up.

But these questions, however interesting, are somewhat beside the point. Even if there is a limited amount of variation between cultures in what categories they think or talk in terms of, and even if there are limits in the categories we can use based on the way language has evolved, or on human biology, nevertheless there surely is some free play within these limits. There surely are some differences in categorizations within cultures. And some changes within the history of our own culture in the way we categorize things.

A look at some of the changes in our own history may help clarify matters regarding the correctness of category relativism.

15.6 Witches and Whales

Once upon a time, whales were counted as a kind of fish. It wasn't because they didn't know that whales were warm-blooded, had lungs, breathed air, gave birth to live young whom they fed milk, and so on. It was because these facts weren't relevant to the classification FISH. To be counted as a fish, all it took was that something lived under water and had that sort of elongated tapered neckless shape. Well, they changed their mind. The classification now excludes whales. *Now* the facts that whales have lungs, are warm-blooded, breathe air, give birth to live young, and so on, definitely rule them out of the FISH category. It's important (for the purposes of our example—never mind the complexities of the actual historical story) to see this as a change in categorization, not as a growth in knowledge about whales or other sea-life. All they had to do was to decide to define 'fish' differently—that is, to use different characteristics in testing whether something was to count as a fish or not.

Compare this with what happened to the category WITCH. They used to divide people up into witches and non-witches, but it was gradually discovered that this sort of division did not form a part of good science. The word still hangs around, but most of us don't use it seriously. It's not just that we think that there don't happen to be any witches that exist. It's that we think that the categorization is illegitimate. This is an important point to understand. Compare the category GOLDEN MOUNTAIN. A golden mountain is a mountain made entirely of pure solid gold. We don't think that anything exists that falls into this category, but it's a genuine category: we have perfectly good ways of sorting things out into golden mountains and non-golden mountains. All the mountains we find just happen to go into the second category. There's nothing unscientific about the category GOLDEN MOUN-TAIN. It's just that there aren't any things that happen to fall into this category.

Different things, then, happened to the category FISH and the category WITCHES. The first one mutated—changed its meaning and the tests for counting as a member, with the result that animals that once belonged in the category didn't any more. The second one disappeared—it just dropped out of the categories used by sensible people in categorizing the world. Of course, at one time, certain people were judged to be witches, but nobody is any more. This is because the category is no longer used.

Both categories were replaced: the old category FISH was replaced by a new category with the same name, and with pretty much (but not exactly) the same membership; the old category WITCHES was dropped altogether, and the peculiar behaviour that some people performed, which was once relevant to classifying them as witches, was reinterpreted psychologically.

Now, the main reason scientists had for both of these category replacements is that the old categories didn't work very well in their science, and the new ones worked a lot better. In other words, they don't see this change as merely a substitution of one arbitrary way of cutting things up for another. They think of this as *progress*. They count the new categories as *better* ones.

15.7 Category Pragmatism

Category relativism claims that all categories are completely arbitrary, just an accident of culture; one system of categories is as good as another. But examination of the cases of WITCHES and WHALES suggests that this position is wrong: that the replacement of one system by another is actually scientific progress; that one system may work better than another. We'll call the claim that some categories are better than others because they allow better science **CATEGORY PRAGMATISM**. "Pragmatism" refers to a family of philosophical positions which stress practical usefulness as a test of acceptability.

There are several ways in which one system of categories might be more scientifically useful to us than others. We'll take a look at two:

(1) SHIFT OF INTEREST. In the old days, people were more interested in the outer shapes of animals and in where they lived than in anything else. These are the most obvious things you see, after all. As far as where they live and what they look like outside are concerned, whales resemble cod and mackerel much more than they resemble bears and elephants. But later on, scientists began to dissect things, and to pay more attention to the inside structures they found there. And internally, structurally, whales resemble mammals more.

To some extent, the disappearance of the category WITCHES may also be the result of a switch of interests. Classifying somebody as a witch interprets them in terms of old, sometimes even pre-Christian, religious beliefs— beliefs in demons and sorcery and black magic. During the last couple of centuries, religion receded from the absolutely central place it had played in peoples' lives, and people started finding other categories—for example, psychological ones—for interpreting things.

To some extent, this may imply a certain degree of what might be considered *relativism* about categories. According to the definition of category relativism we were using above, choice of categories is entirely arbitrary; but now we have seen a possible reason why some categories are better than others. But note that this is so only relative to the interests of the thinkers involved. A certain group of categories might suit the interests of one group of people just fine, but another one might suit another group of people (at a different place, or a different time) much better. For example, we wouldn't be surprised to find out that the Inuit of the far north use different categories in dealing with snow than the people who live in more southern locations. Snow is of course of much more interest, in different ways, to the Inuit. It might be appropriate for them to categorize it in different ways, to suit these different needs. It wouldn't be surprising; but, as I've already mentioned, it's probably not true! Nonetheless, in cases in which different groups have different needs and interests, different category-schemes are appropriate. So we wouldn't want to say that some schemes of classification are better than others, full stop. We'd want to say that this one is better, relative to this culture, and that one better relative to that one. But if there are some general human needs and interests that do not vary significantly from culture to culture, or from time to time, then this allows for the possibility that one classification-scheme might be better than another, full stop, that is, not relative to anything. It would be better if it suited these universal human needs and interests better.

Evaluations and moral concerns enter here, legitimately. If it's important to society that scientists investigate a certain area, then there's a reason why the categories appropriate to that area should be used in scientific thinking. Maybe the reverse is sometimes true: that it's morally important that scientific knowledge *not* be obtained in a certain area. This is a very controversial subject. Many scientists traditionally think that it's their job to find out truth, period, and that moral concerns ought not to enter. But there is another side to this issue. Is it a good idea for scientists to find out truths when those findings may be used to build more effective weapons? Some scientists are investigating possible IQ differences, on average, between races. Maybe it's not a good idea for us to know about this. Or maybe, if there are such differences, we'd be better off knowing about them.

(2) BETTER EXPLANATIONS. Some category-schemes, it turns out, are much better at producing explanations than others.

It should be clear why explaining something requires categorization of it. To explain something you have to stick it into a category. It might just be that the only way you can think or talk about something is to categorize it. In any event, the position I've been assuming in this book is that in order to explain something, you have to have a deductive argument (or at least think there is one) which includes at least one general law about that sort of thing. Even if you don't know exactly what this law is, and only have a true-ish law in mind, you do have to think that the thing belongs to a category which is subject to a general law.

Now a frequent reason for preferring one category-system to another is that explanation can be accomplished with one but not with the other, because laws can be found involving one sort of category but not the other. This can provide the motive either for abandoning one sort category altogether (as in the case of WITCHES), or for changing the way a category works (as in the case of FISH). We can't go into the historical details of either matter here, but you can imagine how this worked. You can see how there might not have been very many laws of fish that scientists could discover while whales were counted as fish. And witch-science never got very far in discovering laws of the behaviour of witches.

Note that this way of looking at the preferability of one method of classification to another makes it an absolute matter, not a relative one. That is, what would count as better doesn't depend on any particular facts about culture or environment. We could then say that the classification scheme that does without WITCHES, or the one that counts whales as non-fish, are objectively, really, non-relatively improvements over the ones they replaced.

We'll have much more to say later about why some categories are suitable for use in laws, and why some aren't.

15.8 Category Realism

Here's a question that might have occurred to you when you were reading about category pragmatism. Why is it that we can discover laws and produce explanations when we use certain systems of classification but not others?

One way of answering this question—a controversial way—is the following: the category-schemes which produce success in science are the ones which are really out there in nature. They're the ones which divide nature "at the joints"—which cut things up the way they really are cut up in reality. This is the position I'm going to call **CATEGORY REALISM**. There's that word 'realism' again which we encountered in the last chapter in connection with theoretical entities. Again, the word 'realism' doesn't have its ordinary meaning; this is the position that something—in this case, categories—exists independently of human minds, out there in the real world. The opponents of the category realists—category relativists or category pragmatists—are both **CATEGORY ANTIREALISTS**.

Is the world really objectively divided into real kinds of things, or is it just facts about us (our languages, our cultures, our interests, the ways our minds are set up) that make us tend to divide it in one way rather than in any other? This is a deep philosophical question. How we answer it has implications for how we view the job of science.

The main argument for category realism is this: it's a fact that some categories work—they allow explanation—and some don't work. The only possible explanation for this fact is that the categories that work are really out there—really features of the mind-independent universe. (This is very much like the argument to the best explanation used by theoretical entity realists, of course. It's the best argument realists have.)

This debate is an important part of the controversy between scientific realists and scientific anti-realists. There's a good deal of philosophical literature in this debate, but we're going to have to leave it here. Let's turn now to another historical example of debate over a system of classification. This example will illustrate a number of the concerns raised so far in this chapter.

15.9 Linnaeus and his Sexy Botany

Carl Linnaeus, the Eighteenth Century Swedish biologist, wrote in 1729:

> The flowers' leaves...serve as bridal beds which the Creator has so gloriously arranged, adorned with such noble bed curtains, and perfumed with so many soft scents that the bridegroom with his bride might there celebrate their nuptials with so much the greater solemnity. When now the bed is so prepared, it is time for the bridegroom to embrace his beloved bride and offer her his gifts... *

What's going on here? you might well wonder. Is this merely some sort of bad poetry? Is old Linnaeus not playing with a full deck? What's a supposedly great scientist doing carrying on like this?

Well, this turns out to be part of what actually was a hugely significant advance in the classification of plants, on the basis of sexual characteristics. Here's a translation of a chart he published, giving part of his classification scheme; take a look at what's going on here:**

---

* *Praeludia Sponsaliorum Plantarum.* quoted in "The Loves of the Plants" by Londa Schiebinger, *Scientific American* Vol. 274, No. 2 (February, 1996).

** Chart from *Systema Naturae* (1759 edition); translation from *A General System of Nature, Through the Three Grand Kingdoms*, by William Thurton (1802). Reprinted in Schiebinger's *Scientific American* article.

VEGETABLE KINGDOM
KEY OF THE SEXUAL SYSTEM

MARRIAGES OF PLANTS.
Florescence.
I. PUBLIC MARRIAGES
    Flowers visible to every one.
        A. In One Bed
                Husband and wife have the same bed.
                All the flowers hermaphrodite: stamens and pistils in the same flower.
                        i. Without Affinity
                        Husbands not related to each other.
                        Stamens not joined together in any part.
                                a. With Equality
                                All the males of equal rank.
                                Stamens have no determinate proportion of length.
                                    1. ONE MALE   7.   SEVEN MALES
                                    2. TWO MALES   8.   EIGHT MALES
                                    3. THREE MALES   9.   NINE MALES
                                    4. FOUR MALES   10. TEN MALES
                                    5. FIVE MALES   11. TWELVE MALES
                                    6. SIX MALES   12. TWENTY MALES
                                                          13. MANY MALES
                                b. With Subordination
                                Some males above others.
                                Two stamens are always lower than the others.
                                    14. TWO POWERS   15. FOUR POWERS
                        ii.   With Affinity
                        Husbands related to each other.
                        Stamens cohere with each other, or with the pistil
                            16. ONE BROTHERHOOD   19. CONFEDERATE MALES
                            17. TWO BROTHERHOODS 20. FEMININE MALES
                            18. MANY BROTHERHOODS
        B. In Two Beds
                Husband and wife have separate beds.
                Male flowers and female flowers in the same species.
                        21. ONE HOUSE   23. POLYGAMIES
                        22. TWO HOUSES
II. CLANDESTINE MARRIAGES.
    Flowers scarce visible to the naked eye.
        24. CLANDESTINE MARRIAGES.

It's clear that Linnaeus didn't take this business about beds and marriages too literally. He does give, in italics, some more literal interpretations in terms of stamens and pistils—parts of the flower.

What's interesting about Linnaeus's classification scheme is that it sorts out plants on the basis of sexual differences of the flowers. (It's also worth noting that the *main* divisions of plants, noted above, are made on the basis of characteristics of the *male* parts: these were then subdivided on the basis of the female parts.) Why did he do this? Was he a sex maniac? Well, no more than lots of people in those days, when human sexual and marital relations were of special interest. Revolutions proclaiming the equal rights of "men" (humans or males?) were in the air. People were wondering about the place of women in society, and many were eager to justify the subordinate place of women—and the importance of traditional marriage—on the basis of its universality throughout nature. Whatever their views about human relations, many people were starting to see gender-related matters as an important feature of nature. The strong analogy between the function of male and female sexual apparatus and the parts of the flower had just been discovered, in the early 1700s. It seemed appropriate to Linnaeus to divide up the "vegetable kingdom" according to gender relations.

EXERCISE

Which of the three theories of categorization above (category relativism, category pragmatism, category realism) is presupposed by this explanation of the preferability of Linnaeous's classification?

ANSWER

Category Pragmatism. Make sure you see why.

Linnaeus's system was widely adapted across Europe, but it was nevertheless from its creation a source of violent controversy. His system was widely attacked for being obscene. For example:

> What man, fumed Johann Siegesbeck, a professor in St. Petersburg, could believe that God Almighty would introduce such "loathsome harlotry" into the plant kingdom?*

---

* Schiebinger, p. 115

At first glance, Siegesbeck's objection may look like silly sexual prudishness, which has no place in real science. But perhaps from another point of view, it's not so silly at all. Siegesbeck, it seems, is arguing that a correct categorization of the plant world must be one that reflects the divisions really out there in nature: that is, the ones introduced by God Almighty. Of course, his reason to think that the plant world could not really be divided this way is that it's *dirty*—so "loathsome" and obscene. We're not inclined nowadays to reason quite this way: the fact that a distinction is loathsome doesn't exactly count as a reason to think that it's not really out in the world. But in a sense, Siegesbeck is doing something legitimate.

EXERCISE
When Siegesbeck objects that this could not be a division introduced by God, which account of categories is behind his evaluation?

ANSWER
category realism. He's offering (what he takes to be) a reason why this could not be the way nature is objectively divided at the joints.

Other sorts of criticisms of Linnaeus's system emerged too. Here's another, due to a man with the unfortunate name of William Smellie, the chief compiler of the first edition of the Encyclopaedia Britannica (1771):

> Smellie...maintained it did not hold up to facts of experience. Many animals (he mentioned polyps and millipedes) reproduced without sexual embraces, and if these were destitute of "all the endearments of love," what, he asked, should induce us to fancy that the oak or mushroom enjoyed these distinguished privileges?*

The Smellie reasoning here is perhaps this: if matters of "marital" relations were really a fundamental classificatory feature of the living world, we should expect to find it everywhere among life. But in the animal kingdom, where it's easier to recognize sexual relations where they happen, these classifications sometimes clearly do not apply. Therefore we can conclude that "marital" relations are not a fundamental feature of the biological world.

---

*Schiebinger, p. 115

EXERCISE
Which account of categories is behind Smellie's evaluation?

ANSWER
Category realism, maybe. He appears to be arguing to the conclusion that "marital" relations are an artificial classification; because they're not universally applicable in nature, they could not conform to the way the world is really divided. Or perhaps this argument presupposes a kind of category pragmatism. He may be interpreted as arguing that because "marital" relations are sometimes not applicable in nature, this category-scheme can be expected to have limited scientific value.

15.10 Sexy Botany Criticised

As time went on, it seemed to some scientists that dividing things this way would not provide the fundamental and clear divisions they needed. Although the names Linnaeus gave to plants on the basis of his categorization have stuck with them, this system of classifying plants has been rejected by botanists. Biologists now don't see matters of "marriage" as having fundamental classificatory relevance among plants, or among organisms in general.

What sorts of features of plants are likely to be connected up, in general, to their Linnaean "marital" characteristics—e.g., their number or arrangement of stamens; whether or not stamens and pistils are found on the same flower; whether or not there are separate male and female flowers? Perhaps there are a number of different generalisations we might discover which are of the form:

- All plants which have stamens cohering with each other, or with the pistil, are...
- All plants which have stamens and pistils in the same flower are...

And so on. This is something that can't be known in advance: we have to do some investigation to find out if there are any regularities of this sort. This sort of investigation might take place in something like the same way as the search for an explanation does. For example, a scientist might hypothesize that plants in which "husbands and wives have separate beds," that is, where a single species has separate male and female flowers, will usually have certain other characteristics—for example, will tend to have larger fruit, or will tend to occur in tropical climates, or will tend to be pollinated by wasps rather than bees. Of course, we then need empirical investigation to test these hypotheses.

This sort of evaluation of a classification scheme tests its scientific fruitfulness: how much in the way of laws and explanations will we get using these classifications? This sounds very much like an application of category pragmatism, although one can also interpret this sort of evaluation from a realist perspective. What we're interested in is which category scheme corresponds to the divisions in nature, and we can find this out by finding out which category scheme allows us to discover explanations of how things work by nature's laws.

But we don't merely evaluate a category scheme by the *quantity* of laws it allows us to discover, but also on the *use* of the discoveries it fosters. It seems clear that if the characteristics Linnaeus concentrated on show up in general laws at all, they're likely to show up to a large extent in matters connected with plant reproduction. That means that we can expect these laws to be centrally involved in explanations of reproductive features of plants (although they might be useful, for all we know, in explaining all sorts of other features of plants too). Clearly now we're testing the category scheme from a pragmatic perspective. Now, do the reproductive characteristics of plants figure importantly among the characteristics we're interested in explaining? Well, that depends. It depends not only on how much we're able to explain, but also on what we happen to be interested in explaining. In Linnaeus's time, these characteristics were perhaps more centrally important to (some) people than they are now.

Perhaps this might make the prudish reactions of some of Linnaeus's critics sound a bit more scientifically respectable, from a pragmatic perspective. We can interpret their criticisms as being, more or less, this: Linnaeus's system was based on the "marital" characteristics of plants. If categorizing plants according to these characteristics turns up any laws, they're likely to be the sorts of laws that explain plant reproduction (though other things may be explained too). Now, how vital, how central, is it to explain facts of plant reproduction, in particular? The only person who thinks that these facts constitute the majority of what's important to think about plantwise has an unhealthy fixation on sexual matters. There are plenty of other things that ought to concern us about plants.

Put that way, the "prudish" criticism of Linnaeus doesn't look quite so stupid.

EXERCISE

Cast your mind back again to Mrs. Smith's view of science. In what ways would the "empty-minded, value-free" young scientists she advised us to become be unable to produce a comparative evaluation of the relative merits of two classificatory systems, from the pragmatic perspective?

ANSWER

"Empty-minded" young scientists would be devoid of any other information which would help them estimate how many laws might be discovered involving the characteristics central to these systems of classification. (But then again, it might be that nobody would be able to estimate this. How fruitful a system of classification would be in discovering laws is often a question nobody can answer until they have tried.)

A Smithian scientist would also be unaware of what questions anyone might have— that is, of what facts people found in need of explanation at the time; neither would they have any value-judgments about what questions needed answering— that is, about what facts it's worth trying to find an explanation for.

Classification on the basis of characteristics of living things is still quite important. Some biologists find physical features like basic structure (not just sexual relations) important in determining the categories; others stress the importance of geographic and ecological distribution, or of similarity and difference in organisms' gene layout. Still others prefer classifications on the basis of evolutionary descent: groups are distinguished and related by their place on the tree of evolution. The battle over the "proper" way to classify living things continues.

15.11 Race: a Contemporary Example

Lest you think that argument over category schemes all happened in the past, here's an up-to-the-minute example. An article in the New York Times's Internet Version reports that many people are calling for abandonment of the traditional racial categories (white, black, Latino, etc.) which people often use to identify themselves and others, and which are officially recognized in the U.S. Census. Here's a quote from this article:

Increasingly, multiracial people are arguing—and many scientists agree—that race is a social construct, not a biological absolute. Many historians, said Steven Gregory, a professor of anthropology and Africana Studies at New York University, believe that the notion of race was largely invented as a way to assign social status and privilege. *

EXERCISE
Try to find hints of the various positions (category relativism, category pragmatism, category realism) in the above quote.

ANSWER
The division between "social construct" and "biological absolute" here shows that nobody seems to have category relativism in mind. (Category relativism views every category as a social construct.) Assigning social status and privilege, it's implied, is not a morally good thing; here we have a political/moral criticism of a categorization. Would race be okay as a category if it were a "biological absolute"? What would this mean? Perhaps the article is implying that racial categories might have some value if they were useful within the science of biology, but they're not. (The moral argument is a form of argument (1), and the use-in-science argument is a form of argument (2) within category pragmatism. Lastly, denying that race is a biological "absolute" might be a way of saying that it's not a real category out there in biological nature: it's only, instead, invented by humans.

---

* "Multiracial Americans Struggle to Redefine Racial Identity" by Michel Marriott. *TimesFax*, the New York Times World Wide Web Version, July 20, 1996, p. 6.

CHAPTER 16

Kinds and Laws

16.1 Natural Kinds

According to category realism, a good classification scheme is one that divides things up the way they really are divided in nature: it "cuts nature at her joints." People who believe category realism sometimes call the kinds of things which correspond to the natural divisions **NATURAL KINDS**. A natural kind is a categorization really found in nature. We can, of course, make up all sorts of other categorizations of things. No doubt a lot of categorizations we now have don't correspond to natural kinds. We can call these **NON-NATURAL KINDS**.

Now we should ask: why is this important for explanation? Why is it important that explanations categorize things according to natural kinds? Why should we take care to use distinctions that correspond to "nature's joints" when we're trying to explain something?

Well, one reason is that when we're trying to find an explanation for a particular fact, we need to think that there's a general truth from which it follows deductively. It's more likely that there is such a generalisation when the kind under which we consider the particular explanandum is a natural kind. Sometimes, anyway, there aren't any interesting regularities in non-natural kinds, so we can't discover any interesting general truths, and we can't give any explanations.

To see this, consider a transparently non-natural category: one which nobody has the slightest tendency to think would "cut nature at her joints". It's a category I made up earlier:

FIVER: Everyone whose street address has digits that average five or more is a fiver.

Do you think that there are any laws involving fivers? We can be pretty sure in advance that fivers aren't likely to be voting differently from non-fivers, or to have a higher or lower average income, or to be more likely to murder other people or less likely to own an electric toothbrush, etc. We can be pretty sure that this category occurs in no laws that give any useful explanations.

The idea here is that nature works regularly, and her natural kinds regularly show certain characteristics. When we think in terms of non-natural kinds, we're not likely to find any regularities.

16.2   The Total-Rating of New Cuyama

This is a real California road sign:

WELCOME TO NEW CUYAMA	
Population	562
Feet above sea level	2150
Established	1951
TOTAL	4663

There's a serious point to be made about this good joke. The point is that a "TOTAL-RATING" can be given for any town. People can figure out, and agree, on what that rating is. Independent adjudicators will agree on exactly what a town's TOTAL-RATING is. What's wrong with this categorization is not that it's not objective. What's wrong is that it's so completely scientifically useless.

16.3   Natural Kinds and Counterfactuals

But sometimes there are true general statements involving non-natural kinds.

Consider this example Right now, I have 10 coins in my pocket, and they all just happen to be silver-coloured (they're all quarters or dimes or nickels). Now, consider the category POCKETCOINS. I define this as coins in my pocket at 2:45 PM, January 27, 1996. The category POCKETCOINS I take to be another transparently non-natural kind.

EXERCISE
Are there any regularities involving POCKETCOINS?

ANSWER
Yes, there is one. Don't you know what it is? Weren't you paying attention? The regularity is:

All POCKETCOINS are silver-coloured.

This looks like a good regularity. It isn't even statistical or true-ish. It's one-hundred percent true. Just a moment ago, I said that we're unlikely to discover true generalizations involving non-natural kinds, but here's one. Doesn't this show that maybe non-natural kinds can show up in explanations perfectly well too?

The answer to this that we're urged to give by category realists is no, and here's why.

Let's notice first that this generalisation doesn't work as part of an explanation. Suppose I take a look at one of those POCKETCOINS and notice that it's silver. I ask for an explanation: why is this thing silver-coloured? You answer: because it's a POCKETCOIN, and all POCKETCOINS are silver-coloured. This clearly doesn't provide an explanation.

Do you remember how explanations work? If not, take a look back at the chapters on explanation, especially Section 9.6.

To have an explanation, we have to have a deductive argument with at least one general law as a premise, and the explanandum as a conclusion. In this case, we have:

PREMISES: All POCKETCOINS are silver.
                 This is a POCKETCOIN.
CONCLUSION: This is silver.

Well, what's wrong here? What's wrong is that that first premise is not a genuine law. It's a general statement and it's true, but it isn't a law. You might recall that in Section 9.6, I said that I'd have more to say about what makes something a real law. Well, here it comes now.

Why isn't this a real law? The reason is that there's nothing about being a POCKETCOIN that makes something silver-coloured. If I just happened to have some pennies in my pocket at the time I mentioned, they would be POCKETCOINS too, only they wouldn't be silver-coloured. It's just an accident that all the POCKETCOINS happened to be silver. That's why the generalisation about POCKETCOINS, even though completely true, doesn't explain why this thing is silver-coloured: it doesn't give a reason why this thing has to be silver-coloured.

Let's put the same thing another way. Now I hold a penny in my hand (obviously not a POCKETCOIN: I didn't get it out of my pocket, I found it on the floor). Now, imagine that this thing were a POCKETCOIN. (How could this be? Well, it would have been a POCKETCOIN if I had noticed it lying there earlier today, and if I had picked it up and put it into my pocket.)

EXERCISE
Now answer this question: if this penny were a POCKETCOIN, would it be silver-coloured?

ANSWER
Nope. It would have been copper-coloured.

Statements that start with "If this penny were a POCKETCOIN" are of the type called **COUNTERFACTUALS** (or **COUNTERFACTUAL CONDITIONALS**, or **CONTRARY TO FACT CONDITIONALS**: all three terms mean the same). A counterfactual conditional is a statement with a certain sort of structure. First, it's a conditional statement, meaning it's form is "IF ____THEN ____ ." Second, it's counterfactual, meaning that the first part, following the "IF" is contrary to fact—false. Thus, in the example in question, the coin isn't a pocketcoin; and the part following the "IF"—"it were a pocketcoin"—is false.

Notice carefully that the falsity of the first part of a counterfactual conditional doesn't necessarily make the whole thing false. Some counterfactuals are true, and some are false.

If apples were poisonous, I'd be dead right now

is a counterfactual conditional that is true.

EXERCISE

Are the following counterfactuals true or false? Some of them are difficult to decide for various reasons.

   (a) If elephants were bright blue, it would be easier to pick them out in the wild.

   (b) If you put your shoes in the bathtub, they would explode.

   (c) If you had thrown a brick really hard at that window, it would have shattered.

   (d) If Kennedy hadn't died in Dallas, he wouldn't have been so well-loved.

   (e) If Verdi (who was actually Italian) and Bizet (who was actually French) were fellow countrymen, they'd both have been Italian.

ANSWERS:

   (a) True.

   (b) False (unless they are very special shoes, or there's something funny about your bathtub).

   (c) True.

   (d) I think this is probably true, though it's open to debate. Maybe nobody can tell, really. Maybe nobody has enough information.

   (e) Do you think they'd both have been Italian? Do you think it's false, therefore, that they both would have been French? or Brazilian? This is a peculiar one. It's totally uncertain, but it's not debatable: it's hard to see what to debate about. It's not that we lack information either.

What makes some counterfactual conditionals true and others false is an interesting question we can't go into here. But everyone has a feeling, in some cases anyway, which counterfactuals are true and which are false.

The counterfactual "If this penny were a POCKETCOIN it would have been silver-coloured" is false. The counterfactual, "If this penny were a POCKETCOIN it would (still) have been copper-coloured" is true.

Now compare the situation involving counterfactuals related to genuine laws. Let's suppose that it's a genuine law of nature that silver conducts electricity. Now consider a particular hockey puck. Being made out of rubber, it doesn't conduct electricity. Now, consider these two counterfactuals:

1. If this hockey puck were silver, it would conduct electricity.
2. If this hockey puck were silver, it (still) wouldn't conduct electricity.

EXERCISE
Which one is true: 1 or 2?

ANSWER
1 is true; 2 is false.

If you think this is a reasonable answer, then you now can see the difference between a real law and a merely true generalisation: real laws *support their corresponding counterfactuals*; merely true generalisations do not.

What I mean by this is the following. Consider any general statement of the form "All As are Bs." A "corresponding counterfactual" associated with this statement is "If X were an A, then it would be a B." Now, if a statement is a genuine (and true) law, then it will "support its corresponding counterfactuals": that is, the truth of the statement will imply the truth of all of its corresponding counterfactuals. If it's not a genuine (and true) law, but merely a true generalisation, then it will not imply the truth of all its corresponding counterfactuals: that is, there will be some corresponding counterfactuals that are false. In the case at hand:

All things made of silver conduct electricity

is true, and a law, so it follows that

If this hockey puck were made of silver it would conduct electricity.

But

All POCKETCOINS are silver-coloured

is true, but not a law; accordingly it does not support its associated counterfactuals; so

If this penny were a POCKETCOIN, it would be silver-coloured

is not implied by the truth about all POCKETCOINS; in fact, it's false.

So there's one way of distinguishing real laws from merely true generalisations: laws support counterfactuals, but merely true generalisations don't.

Okay, but what does this have to do with natural kinds? The claim is that
real laws have to have natural kinds in them. If you have a generalisation
which is about a nonnatural kind, it won't support counterfactuals. If it's
true, it will be a merely true generalisation; it won't support counterfactuals;
it won't be a genuine law. It will just be **ACCIDENTALLY TRUE**—true by mere
chance or coincidence, not true because nature regularly makes it true. The
coins in my pocket just happened to be all silver.

The idea here is that there are certain things that *have* to be the way they
are, because that's the way that the external world works. The general rules
that express the ways the external world really works have to mention only
natural kinds, because only these kinds divide nature according to its real
divisions. Do you get the picture?

16.4 Laws and Mention of Particulars

Another characteristic of statements that is often supposed to be a necessary condition of being a genuine law is that the statement not make mention
of a particular event, object, person, time, or place. This would make a limit
on its complete generality; and laws are supposed to be completely general.
The reason for this is that it's thought that the regularities imposed by nature
do not vary from time to time, from place to place, from particular object to
particular object.

This is a further reason why we can rule out "All POCKETCOINS are
silver-coloured" as a genuine law. I defined 'POCKETCOINS' as coins that
are in my pocket *at 2:45 PM, January 27, 1996*. This mentions a particular
person (me) and a particular time, and is doubly disqualified.

Think about it and you'll see the connection of this requirement with the
others. If a statement names a particular individual or a particular time, it
limits the things that can be in a category to a particular few. This allows for
accidental universally true statements. Because POCKETCOINS were limited to those in my pocket at that particular time, it's possible for all of them,

just by accident, to have been silver-coloured. But compare open-ended classes of things, like lumps of copper. There are an indefinitely large group of things in this category. If all of them have some characteristic, it probably shows a regularity of the way nature works, not just a coincidence.

One problem with this suggestion is that it seems there are statements that violate this restriction but which nevertheless seem to be genuine laws—they provide explanation and they support counterfactuals. Consider, for example:

Everything in Calgary made of silver conducts electricity.

This does seem to support its associated counterfactual:

If this hockey puck were in Calgary, and made of silver, it would conduct electricity.

The way around this problem is perhaps to note that this generalisation is itself a special case of a genuine, general law:

Everything made of silver conducts electricity.

It can be derived deductively from this general law. So we can give an explanation of why a piece of silver in Calgary conducts electricity by pointing out:

This is made of silver (particular fact)
This is in Calgary (particular fact)
Everything in Calgary made of silver conducts electricity (derived law)
Therefore, this conducts electricity (explanandum, conclusion)

because we know that the next-to-last statement (which mentions an individual thing, Calgary) is derived from a general, genuine law, that all silver things conduct electricity. What this means is that there is a deductive argument involving the same particular fact plus the purely general law (the one that mentions no particulars) which deductively implies the conclusion:

This is made of silver (particular fact).
This is in Calgary (particular fact).
Everything made of silver conducts electricity (purely general law).
Therefore, this conducts electricity (explanandum, conclusion).

Note that in this version of the argument, the second premise is unnecessary. Remember that we insisted (in Section 10.6) that only necessary premises gave explanations. So the fact that this is in Calgary could not explain why it conducts electricity. This is as it should be.

Compare this "explanation," which does not manage to explain the fact that this thing weighs less than 1000 kg.:

This is made of silver (particular fact).
This is in Calgary (particular fact).
Everything in Calgary made of silver weighs less than 1000 kg.
Therefore, this thing weighs less than 1000 kg (conclusion).

The next-to-last statement here is true, and also mentions a particular thing (Calgary), but in this case it's not a derived law. There isn't any law of nature to the effect that all pieces of silver weigh less than 1000 kg. It's just a plain old "accidental" regularity. If you brought a 1001 kg silver thing to Calgary, it would still weigh 1001 kg. So this isn't an explanation.

EXERCISES

The following attempts at explanation use generalisations which mention particulars. Point out the particular mentioned in the generalization. Do you think that they are derived laws, and thus explain their explanandum? If you think so, try to say what regular (strictly general) laws they are derived from.

A. Explanandum: This maple tree's leaves are turning colour.
Explanation: It's fall now, and this fall every maple tree's leaves are turning colour.

B. Explanandum: This Kraft Dinner I've had in my fridge for two weeks is getting blue spots on it.
Explanans: Every food you keep in your fridge for a while gets blue spots on it.

C. Explanandum: Mildred is a nice person.
Explanation: Mildred is a friend of Shirley's, and all of Shirley's friends are nice.

D. Explanandum: Jean-Claude is wearing blue suspenders in this picture.
Explanation: It's a picture of him in his Sault Ste. Marie Slasher's uniform. Everyone on the Slashers has a uniform with blue suspenders.

STOP! ANSWERS

A. The particular mentioned in the generalisation is a particular time: this fall. This seems to be a derived law: it follows from the general law that all maple trees' leaves turn colour every fall.

B. The particular mentioned in the generalisation is your fridge. Of course, it's not a general law that every food anywhere gets blue spots on it after a while. But perhaps there is a law to the effect that foods of a certain sort, kept under certain conditions for a while, get blue spots on them.

C. The particular mentioned in the generalisation is Shirley. It's not clear whether this is a derived law or not. Is Shirley one of a sort of person who always has only nice friends? Perhaps there's some sort of a psychological law that we can derive this from. Or maybe Shirley just happens, purely by accident, to have a bunch of nice friends, and there's nothing about her that makes this a derived law.

D. The particular here is the Slashers team. It may be a rule of the team that they have to wear blue suspenders when in uniform, but it hardly seems to be derivable from a law of nature.

16.5 Explanations Other than Natural Ones

EXERCISE D raises a question for you to think about. I think it's pretty clear that the generalisation in the explanans isn't derivable from any law of nature, and that from our point of view, it's merely an "accidentally" true generalisation. Nevertheless, it does seem that this "explanation" really does explain things, and that the generalisation does support counterfactuals. For example:

> If Garth were a member of the Slashers, he'd be wearing blue suspenders when in uniform.

This generalisation is something a little stronger than a mere accident: it's a human rule. Of course, it's not a law of nature. But human rules can explain things too. I suppose what this shows is that the kind of explanation we're concentrating on is the kind that's provided by natural laws only, not by human rules. This is perhaps what distinguishes explanation in the natural sciences from (at least some) explanations in history, political science, sociology, and so on, where human rules are often invoked.

Here are some more generalisations which appear to support counterfactuals, and to provide explanations, although they too might not be considered to be natural laws, but rather human rules:

- Fords straight from the factory say FORD on the front.
- People stop their cars at red lights.

16.6   A Puzzle About Laws: Barney the Weird Beaver ▮▮▮▮▮▮

But there are mysteries here. It's not always quite clear what is a law and what isn't. Consider:

All beavers build dams.

A philosopher of science I know argues that this isn't a law because 'beavers' names a species, and species aren't natural kinds. This is surprising if true. How could we tell? Well, let's suppose that this thing is a law. In that case, it would support counterfactuals like:

If X were a beaver, then it would build dams.
If something didn't build dams, then it couldn't be a beaver.

If the statement "All beavers build dams" were a law, then these counterfactuals must be true. Are they true? My friend argues that they're not. For example, he argues, consider Barney. He's a beaver, and he builds dams. Now imagine that Barney didn't build dams. Could he still be a beaver?

If Barney didn't build dams, he wouldn't be a beaver.

My friend thinks this isn't true. If Barney didn't build dams, he could still be a beaver. He'd just be a peculiar beaver. So it isn't true that:

If something didn't build dams, then it couldn't be a beaver.

Therefore it isn't true that

All beavers build dams

is a law.

Is this right? Do you agree that if Barney didn't build dams, he could still be a beaver? It's hard to figure out what to say here. One problem is that our judgments about which counterfactuals are true and which aren't are shaky. We often don't know what to say. Of course, my friend's discussion of this matter has much more to say than I do here. Perhaps if you read it, you'd find his position more convincing. *

16.7 Another Puzzle About Laws: The Grue Emerald

Here's a second puzzle about laws you might enjoy musing about. You'll remember that one of the non-natural kinds I mentioned away back in this chapter is grue: if it's before January 1, 2050, something is grue at that time just in case it's green at that time. All the emeralds anyone has examined so far have been grue. The sky is blue today, so it's not grue today. Starting January 1, 2050, something is grue at that time just in case it's blue at that time. If the sky is blue on the morning of that date, then it will be grue then.

If you agree that green is a natural kind, but grue isn't, then you'll agree that

All emeralds are green

is a law of nature, but

All emeralds are grue

isn't.

Consider the first emerald observed on New Year's Day, January 1, 2050. Because we take it to be a law of nature that all emeralds are green, then we predict that this emerald will be green then. If we took it to be a law of nature that all emeralds are grue, then we'd predict that it would be grue then. But of course, if it were grue then, it wouldn't be green: it would be blue. No problem! "All emeralds are grue" has turned out to be true so far, but it isn't a law of nature, so we don't have any problem about which prediction about that emerald will be true.

---

* Section 7.5, pp. 201-203, of *The Structure of Biological Science*, by Alexander Rosenberg (Cambridge: Cambridge University Press, 1985).

Well, it seems clear that "All emeralds are grue" isn't a law, but what makes you so sure? Here's a suggested answer: remember that one test something has to pass in order to count as a law is that it doesn't mention a particular event, object, person, time, or place. Aha! Look at that definition of 'grue': it mentions a particular time, January 1, 2050. That's why "All emeralds are grue" isn't a law.

Not so fast. You (and I) define 'grue' in terms of 'green' (and 'blue') plus a time, but that's because we speak a language with 'green' (and 'blue') and not 'grue' in it to start off with. Now imagine someone—call him Nelson—who grows up with a language that has 'grue' and 'bleen' in it to start off with, but not 'green' and 'blue'. What's 'bleen' mean? Nelson helpfully explains, defining 'bleen' in terms we can understand:

> If it's before January 1, 2050, something is *bleen* at that time just in case it's *blue* at that time. Every clear day so far, the sky has been bleen. This emerald is green today, so it's not bleen today. Starting January 1, 2050, something is *bleen* at that time just in case it's *green* at that time. If this emerald is green on the morning of that date, then it will no longer be bleen then. It will have turned grue.

"Now look, Nelson," you object, "these words 'grue' and 'bleen' are weird. They aren't real colours, which we assume are natural kinds. They are defined in terms of real colours plus times."

But Nelson replies: "No, you've got it backwards; *you're* speaking the weird language. My language names the real colours. When I first heard you using those strange words 'green' and 'blue', I didn't understand. But later I realized that you were using words that I could define in terms of real colours. I figured out that 'green' applied to grue things before January 1, 2050, and to bleen things after. And that 'blue' applied to bleen things before January 1, 2050, and to grue things after. You, of course, are using words that don't name natural kinds. They are to be understood in terms of a particular time. So it follows that 'All emeralds are green' isn't a law at all, even though every emerald anyone's ever seen so far has been green. You have to admit that all those emeralds have been grue too. That's the real law."

You and Nelson aren't just arguing about words. You're making different predictions about what's going to happen. You think that emeralds will stay green after January 1, 2050 (i.e., they'll turn bleen), and he thinks they'll stay grue after that date (i.e., they'll turn blue). We'll all have to wait and see who's right.

The moral of this fable might be taken to be that what you take to be a genuine law depends on what you take to be a natural-kind word, and that depends on what language you start out speaking. It looks like we're back, in a way, to category relativism, the view that how you categorize things is just an arbitrary matter, an accident of culture or language.

PART III

Cause

Chapter 17

Seeing Causes

17.1 Can We Perceive Causes?

Let's take a look at a case of something causing something else, and consider exactly what we see.

Watch very carefully now. There goes a white billiard ball, heading down the billiard table. It's heading right for that red one, which is stationary in the middle of the table. There! It hit the red one, and now the red one is moving.

Obviously the white one hitting the red one caused the red one's motion. But what exactly did you see? Let's rewind the video tape and play that once more, slower this time. Now pay attention. First we see the white one moving, and the red one is still. The white one gets closer and closer to the red one, and then they're touching for an instant. Then the red one moves away.

Where is the *cause* in this? Did you see anything like that? No? Neither did I. All we saw was the second one starting to move after the first one touched it. Why do we think that the first one *caused* the second to move?

David Hume, the great Eighteenth Century Scottish empiricist philosopher, thought about this problem. Like Mrs. Smith, Hume thought that perception was the source of all knowledge, so this example troubled him. Here's what he had to say.

First, Hume argued, there's nothing that you see in this particular case all by itself to justify the conclusion that there's cause and effect here. All you see is one thing and then another. The idea that these two particular things are cause and effect depends on your believing that these two *sorts* of things *always* happen that way. That is to say: your belief that the white ball hitting the red ball *caused* the red one to begin to move involves the belief that one billiard ball's hitting a second stationary one is always followed by the second one's starting to move.

Hume thought that for a particular event *x* to be the cause of another particular event *y*, the following had to be true:

1. *x* comes before *y* ("Temporal priority")
2. *x* and *y* are right next to each other in space ("Spatial proximity")
3. *x*-type events always precede *y*-type events ("Constant conjunction")

The second condition doesn't interest us too much. Hume thought that events that took place at a distance from one another couldn't be related by cause and effect. Of course, there are some causes that occur far away from effects: for example, if I flip on the light switch on the wall (cause), the light goes on on the ceiling (effect); but we believe that there are a chain of events that take place between the light switch and the light, connecting them in space (though the connecting wire, of course). On the other hand, maybe there are some causes and effects which are at a distance from each other, but which aren't connected by things in between. For instance, when the moon is overhead, this causes a high tide in the ocean, because of the moon's gravity; but it isn't as though the gravity is a "thing" connecting the moon physically to the ocean. Well, never mind about this.

Should we agree that causes must come before their effects? Could you have causation that worked "backward in time," with the cause coming after the effect? Some philosophers think this makes no sense. More plausible, perhaps, is the objection that some causes and effects are simultaneous. For example, when you push down one side of a see-saw, this causes the other side to go up, simultaneously.

But the most interesting of the three conditions is "constant conjunction." This means that in order for it to be true that *x* caused *y*, it has to be true that *x*-type things are always associated with *y*-type things; that there is a general rule: Whenever *x*-type thing, then *y*-type thing. Together with the factual condition that something of type *x* happened, it will follow deductively that something of type *y* happened.

This is probably starting to look familiar to you. It is in fact what goes on when we have an explanation.

17.2 Causes and Explanations

What this boils down to is that we can say *x* caused *y* when we have a general law relating *x*-type things and *y*-type things: that is, when the fact that *x* happened explains the fact that *y* happened.

One difference between Hume's account and the account of explanations in this book is that he didn't think of general statements as laws, but merely as "constant conjunctions." In the last couple of chapters, we have been talking about how only some "constant conjunctions" will be laws.

It's clear that some explanations are causal explanations. Take a look at the past few chapters, and consider the examples of explanations we've been looking at. Which ones clearly indicate causal connections? In that case we spent so long on in Chapter 9, the Case of the Mysterious Whistle, it seems that the explanation also established a causal connection. The explanation for the whistle is that Uncle Fred was smoking a cigar in the little room with the smoke alarm in it; Uncle Fred's smoking the cigar *caused* the whistling sound. We can specify things in more detail by describing all the links of the causal chain between Fred's smoking the cigar to the whistling sound: Fred's smoking caused the air in the little room to become filled with smoke; this caused the smoke alarm to go off, and this caused the whistling sound to pervade the house.

Similarly, in Chapter 10, the fact that the match was lit was explained by the fact that it was struck (plus a lot of other conditions and general laws). Here also there is a causal relation: the striking of the match caused the match to light.

You might wonder whether all explanations reveal causes—whether all explanations are causal explanations. This is an interesting philosophical problem; some philosophers argue that they are. But we won't get into this here.

17.3 Does Everything Have a Cause?

EXERCISE
Imagine that your car is doing something peculiar. Often when you stop the car at a stoplight, it gives a shudder and a squeak, and stalls. You take the car in to the car-repair shop. When you return, Arnold the mechanic tells you, "I've taken things apart and had a look, and there's nothing inside which is causing that." You ask: "You mean, it's something I'm doing?" "No," says Arnold, "I drove it a little and that stalling happened, but I wasn't doing anything wrong." You say, "You mean, you couldn't find the cause of the stalling?" Arnold says, "No, I looked everywhere. If there were a cause, I would have found it. I mean there isn't any cause."
The question is: What time is it?

You're convinced that there is a cause and that Arnold hasn't found it. Maybe a new mechanic won't find the cause either, but there has to be one. Why are you convinced of this? You think, and I do too, that everything that happens in your car has a cause, including this peculiar shudder, squeak, and stall. We both think, in fact, that everything that happens in the world has a cause (maybe with certain kinds of exception which I'll mention in a moment). This is an interesting thing to think. It doesn't seem to be a fact that you've found out from experience; after all, there are things that nobody can find the cause of. It hasn't been a fact of your experience that you can find a cause of everything. Mrs. Smith told us to believe nothing except what you find out for yourself, by looking and seeing. You haven't seen that *everything* has a cause, and neither has anyone else. Why do you believe this? Do you have any reason to believe this?

This is a good question, and philosophers have tried to find an answer. It's of course related to the question of whether everything has an explanation.

The 19th century German philosopher Immanuel Kant agreed that our experience hasn't given us reason to believe that everything has a cause. He nevertheless thought that we all believe it, and that it was a justified belief. His reasons for this are complicated and a bit obscure, but they are roughly this: the assumption that everything has a cause is a precondition for rational thought altogether. If you didn't think this, you couldn't even begin to think rationally. That's why everyone rational must think that everything has a cause.

This is an interesting view, but it probably isn't right. As we'll see below, nowadays scientists in certain areas, for example quantum physics, insist that certain events don't have causes, and they seem to be capable of rational thought.

What we should note here, in any case, is that we expect scientists in most areas (e.g. car scientists: mechanics) to act as though everything had a cause, and to think that it's their job to find out what it is. Often enough they do find out what the cause of something is. If they didn't begin by thinking that everything had a cause, they wouldn't even look. Whether it's true or not that everything has a cause, it's still a good methodological principle to adopt. If you didn't think that everything has a cause, then you might give up looking, and then you wouldn't find the cause when there was one. Scientists (or car mechanics) who give up looking, who shrug and say that maybe there just isn't any cause, aren't doing their jobs.

17.4 Stochastic Causes

Okay, so you take your car into another auto-repair shop. When you return, their mechanic Marvin has better information for you. "Your carburetor is gummy. That's why the car sometimes stalls." This is progress, but you want to know more. "Look, Marvin, sometimes when I stop at a stoplight the car stalls, and sometimes it doesn't. Why does the car stall at those times and not at others?" "Well, I don't know," says Marvin. "That's just what happens when you have a gummy carburetor. It makes the car stall sometimes, and sometimes it doesn't."

Marvin's information is better than Arnold's. What he's told you is that a gummy carburetor makes a car stall when it's stopped at a stoplight *part* of the time. The proportion of times a car stalls at a stoplight when the carburetor *is* gummy is much larger than the proportion of times a car stalls at a stoplight when the carburetor *isn't* gummy. (That is, when everything else is working properly. If the idle is set too low, then your car will stall every time you stop at a stop light, whether or not your carburetor is gummy.)

At least now you know what's making your car stall. But Marvin's information is still incomplete. If you had the full story, you'd know more than this. There must be something else that combines with the gummy carburetor to make your car stall when it does, and that's missing when your car doesn't stall. Maybe for example, the gummy carburetor makes your car stall when the RPMs of your engine fall below a certain level, and when they stay above that level, the car doesn't stall. This would provide the full story. If you knew this, then you'd know exactly what makes your car stall: you'd know what conditions (gummy carburetor + low RPMs) will make your car stall every time. What Marvin told you is good enough; now you know that your car will stop stalling if you get your carburetor de-gummed. But he didn't tell you the full story.

What Marvin has given you is information about a factor that makes it much more likely that your car will stall at a stoplight, but it doesn't fully determine it. The cause that Marvin told you about is called a **STOCHASTIC CAUSE**. It doesn't fully determine its effect: it just makes it more probable.

The full story, you think, would tell you the **DETERMINISTIC CAUSE**. When the conditions listed in the deterministic cause are there, your car stalls every time you stop at a stoplight. When one or more of the conditions are absent (given that everything else is working) your car won't stall.

We've already noted your belief that everything has a cause. Well, Marvin has found the (stochastic) cause, so there's no problem with this belief in this case. But you also probably believe that everything has a deterministic cause: that there is a full story to be told here. Why do you think this? Another philosophical question we won't go into.

17.5 Non-Deterministic Science

We've already noted the fact that most scientific laws actually given by particular sciences as parts of explanation are not precisely true: they're true-ish. The case we're looking at here follows this rule. Most of what science tells us about cause is in stochastic form. Just as we expect that there's a full explanation of everything, we expect that the stochastic cause is just one factor entering into a situation; and that if we got the full story, we'd know exactly what determines that effect, not just part of the time. It's perhaps unthinkable to us that the stochastic cause is the whole story. When science gives us a stochastic story, this is valuable information; but we think that it must be only part of the full deterministic story.

This is a case of what we've looked at earlier, in Chapter 10, when we considered statistical explanations. We noticed that when an explanation contains premises that make the conclusion only probable, not necessary, that we haven't got the full story here. In the current case, it seems that although the gummy carburetor makes it probable that the car will stall, this is not the whole story. The whole story will tell you exactly when the car will stall and when it won't, without recourse to probabilities.

It's interesting, however, that in one area of science, it's claimed that stochastic causes *are* the full story: there are no deterministic causes. Let's take a quick look at an example.

The reason ordinary light bulbs give off light is that the electric current pushed through the filament gives a little extra energy to the atoms of the filament material, causing an outer electron to move further from its nucleus, to a higher energy state. This position is unstable, and after a little while, the electron will move back down to the lower energy state, sending out one photon of energy in the form of visible light. How long will it take the electron after it's been energized to drop back down? Scientists can tell you what the average length of time is. Suppose that the average is X seconds. (X is of course a very small number.) That means if you energize a large pile of atoms, after X seconds, about half of them will have sent out photons. But let's take a look at a particular atom: suppose it takes this one 2X seconds to send out a photon. Why did it take longer than average? Why did other atoms take less than the average time? The answer physicists give us is that *there is no reason*. It's not that there is a reason they haven't found out, or can't find out. The statistical—stochastic—law telling us how long on average these atoms take to release a photon after being energized is *the whole story*. There *aren't* any other factors entering in here that make one atom release a photon earlier than another. If you take two atoms *in exactly the same initial state, in every detail*, one of them will send out a photon after 2X seconds, and the other after only .5X seconds, and there's no reason why. That's just the way it happens. This is non-deterministic science.

Now, of course we can't go into their reasons for thinking that this is the whole story. Let's just note here that this shows that it's not literally unthinkable that a stochastic cause be all there is. This is shown by the fact that these scientists think it.

17.6 Causes and Human Actions ▮

We've noticed the almost irresistible tendency we have to think that every event has a cause, and that it must (if the full story were told) be a deterministic cause (except possibly in certain areas of physics). There's another exception (at least, according to a widespread view), this time in an area we all know something about. It's human action.

Imagine you see me walking into my university cafeteria. What am I going to order for lunch? Am I going to order the delicious sloppy joe sandwich, or the delightful chips with cheese curds and gravy? If you know that I hate chips with cheese curds and gravy, you'd be able to predict which one I'll order. But suppose you know that I like both of these things. Now it's totally my choice which to order, and you can't predict what I'll do. Why not? Is it because you don't know enough about the causal laws that govern my behaviour, and enough about what's happened to me in the past? One common philosophical position claims that this is *not* the reason you can't predict me. Even if you did know everything there is to know about me, you couldn't predict what I'm going to do, because my actions are *free*—I have *free will*. My decisions simply don't have causes.

Well, on some occasions this is perhaps a bit extreme. Suppose you know that I rather prefer chips with cheese curds and gravy to a sloppy joe sandwich, and that most of the time, faced with this choice, I'd choose the former. Now what you know about me is stochastic: given the initial conditions, I'll probably order chips with cheese curds, although sometimes I'll order the sloppy joe sandwich. Maybe you could find out that it's 85% probable that I'll order the chips, so the prediction that I'd order the chips is a pretty good one, though 15% of the time you'd be wrong. You can't be right every time. Clearly, at least sometimes, this probabilistic, stochastic sort of knowledge about humans is possible. Suppose that this is all that could possibly be known, even if you knew every fact there was to know about me. This is all there is to be known because humans are not deterministic machines.

Altogether, we have three possible positions:

- Human actions are deterministic, like (maybe) everything else.
- Human actions are sometimes completely free of cause altogether.
- Human actions, while subject to stochastic cause, are sometimes not subject to deterministic cause.

Which one of these positions is right? Again, there's a long philosophical debate we won't get into. Again, our experience of what science has already found out is inconclusive. The human sciences (psychology, sociology, maybe history, maybe political science) are notorious as being the least successful at finding causal regularities. In many cases, they're unable altogether to say anything about what causes human actions. This may be because they (like Arnold the mechanic) haven't looked long enough, or well enough; or it may be because there simply aren't any causes for free action. In other cases, human scientists have found some fairly reliable stochastic causes, but are nowhere near determining the full deterministic story. This may be because they (like Marvin the mechanic) haven't looked long enough, or well enough, to determine the whole story; or it may be because (as physicists think, in the case of the excited atoms) there isn't any deterministic story to be told.

CHAPTER 18

Causal Relations

18.1 Causes and Explanations

A **CAUSAL**[*] **EXPLANATION** is an explanation which explains the explanandum by giving its causes. As in all cases of explanation, we assume that the full explanans states the initial conditions plus some general laws; in this case, the laws will be causal laws, stating what events will have what effects.

Almost invariably, the full causal explanation of an event will name a variety of initial conditions. For example, a specification of what's responsible for that pain in your feet might include the tightness of your shoes, the length of the walk you had to take yesterday, the fact that this walk was mostly on hard concrete, and the weakness of your arches. All of these things conspired to produce the effect: if any one of them hadn't been there, then the effect wouldn't have happened.

So here's a typical picture of the full causal structure of events:

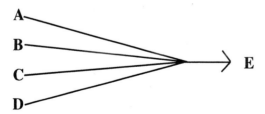

In this picture, the lines represent causal connections, with the arrow pointing from the conspiring causes A, B, C, and D to the effect E.

---

*You will send your teacher into a screaming fit if you spell that word CASUAL. Do you see the difference between CAUSAL and CASUAL? The first word means having to do with cause. The second word means informal or relaxed.

Another reason that there is a multiplicity of things that we might consider among the causes of something is that the most immediate causes themselves have causes, and these have causes too, and so on back.

$$\cdots\textbf{D}\longrightarrow\textbf{C}\longrightarrow\textbf{B}\longrightarrow\textbf{A}\longrightarrow\textbf{E}$$

Among the causes of your having taken that long walk yesterday was the fact that your car was broken down; so we might want to include that among the causes of the pains in your feet. And your car's being broken down itself has a cause, and so on, back further and further, maybe even to the beginning of the universe!

18.2 *The* Cause

But often we pick one of the multiplicity of conditions causally responsible for an event and call it **THE CAUSE** of your sore feet. An example of this we've considered earlier, at length, involves the explanation of the lighting of a match. The striking of the match is not alone responsible for its lighting: other relevant conditions were the presence of an oxidant, the dryness of the match, and so on. These are all part of the full (causal) explanation. But we're likely to single out the striking of the match as *the* cause of its lighting. Why?

Causal explanations are a kind of explanation. When we explain something, we often single out only one of the many conditions that conspired to produce what we're explaining. Do you remember this discussion? If not, review Sections 9.8 and 9.9. The following is a review of the considerations mentioned there, as they apply to causal explanations.

The choice of which one of the many relevant conditions to single out as *the* cause depends on various things. One of them is that changes that happened shortly before the event to be explained, as opposed to standing conditions that were constant for a longer period, tend to be picked out as *the* cause. Another one is the assumptions and beliefs of the person who is looking for an explanation. If a fire breaks out in your basement, you'll wonder about what caused it. One of the multiple conditions which were responsible for that event was the presence of oxygen there, but everyone assumes that this is the case: this is no news. The fact that there was a short-circuit in the wiring would probably be the condition we'd mention.

Note that the unknown condition of interest is not necessarily the most recent change. The person who asked you why your feet hurt might already know about your long walk over concrete yesterday and your tight shoes, and need to be informed about the standing condition (pardon the pun) that your feet are flat.

It's clear that your long walk was not *alone* responsible for your painful feet, and this might make you reluctant to call it *the* cause. There's nothing particularly wrong with speaking this way: it's an ordinary way of speaking which everyone will understand. But in order to prevent any confusions, we can speak instead of this "cause" as a **CAUSAL FACTOR**, implying that this may be one among several causal factors which together were responsible for the effect.

Let's add another bit of jargon which will make what we say a bit more precise. Suppose that if you put those pads inside your shoes, they prevent your feet from getting sore after a long walk, or make it less likely that you'll get sore feet, or more likely that you'll get less sore. In any of these cases, we can speak of putting those pads in as a **NEGATIVE CAUSAL FACTOR** for your feet getting sore: it prevents the effect from happening. Taking a long walk is thus called a **POSITIVE CAUSAL FACTOR**.

Well, in order to give causal explanations then, we need to know causal laws. These will be laws involving positive and negative causal factors.

18.3 Causes and Correlations

We've already spent a good deal of time talking about how we can confirm that a population contains a positive or a negative correlation. It appears that many positive correlations go with positive causal connections (and negative correlations with negative causal connections; and lack of correlations with lack of causal connection).

Some examples:

- There's a strong positive correlation between matches that are struck and matches that light (because, large samples show us, in the general population of matches, the ones that have been struck contain a much higher proportion of lit matches than the ones that haven't been struck). (As we've seen, of course, striking is only one of the causal factors.)

- Seeing the ad for Yummie Cheezelike Goodies is positively correlated with buying the stuff, and we'd probably think that seeing the ad is a positive causal factor for buying it.
- Having a green cover is negatively correlated with sales of the book, and it seems likely that it's a negative causal factor for sales.
- Prayer is uncorrelated with holding a winning lottery ticket. That is: the lottery tickets held by people who pray a lot are about equally likely to be winners as the lottery tickets held by people who don't pray a lot. Prayer is not a causal factor in making your lottery ticket win. It's causally irrelevant.

All these examples are cases in which a correlation (positive, negative, or zero) goes with a causal connection (positive, negative, or zero). But a very important thing for you to realise is that reasoning from the existence of a correlation to some sort of causal connection is a mistake. A positive correlation between A and B doesn't show that A is a positive causal factor for B. Similarly, a negative correlation doesn't show a negative causal factor; no correlation doesn't show no causal relation.

Why not? Well, to show that this is not the case, we could examine some cases in which cause and correlation *don't* go together.

18.4 Correlation Without Cause: Symmetry and Non-Symmetry

There is, of course, a very strong positive correlation among the population of matches between those that are struck and those that light. The proportion of matches that light among those that are struck is very high; the proportion of matches that light among those that are not struck is very low. Striking a match is a positive causal factor for its lighting. But I hope you remember that every positive correlation can be expressed "the other way around." (If you don't know what I'm talking about, reread Section 7.6.) In this case, it follows that there's a very strong positive correlation among the population of matches between those that light and those that are struck. The proportion of matches that are struck among those that light is very high; the proportion of matches that are struck among those that don't light is very low. Is this confusing? Put it this way: striking is positively correlated with lighting; and lighting is positively correlated with striking. Striking causes lighting, but lighting does not cause striking.

We can say that correlation is a **SYMMETRICAL RELATION** —that is, whenever it's the case that A is positively correlated with B, then B is positively correlated with A. But the causal relation is not symmetrical: it's often (not always, as we'll see) the case that A causes B, but B does not cause A.

This guarantees that there are cases of positive correlation that are not cases of cause. Typically, an effect will be positively correlated with its cause, but the effect is not the cause of its cause.

The same thing holds true for negative correlation. When A and B are negatively correlated, then it's automatically the case that B and A are negatively correlated. This might be the result of the fact that A is a negative causal factor for B; but it doesn't automatically follow that B is a negative causal factor for A.

To sum this up: correlation is always symmetrical, but causation isn't.

EXERCISE
Produce two plausible examples (different from the ones I've already given) of each of the following:
(1) A is a positive causal factor for B, but B is not a positive causal factor for A.
(2) A is a negative causal factor for B, but B is not a negative causal factor for A.
(3) A is causally irrelevant for B, but B is not causally irrelevant for A.

ANSWER
You've produced your own examples, but here are some more:
(1) Turning on the light switch is a positive causal factor for the light going on, but the light going on is not a positive causal factor for turning on the light switch.

Getting kicked in your shin is a positive causal factor for having a bruise on your shin, but having a bruise on your shin is not a positive causal factor for getting kicked there.

---

(2) Driving carefully is a negative causal factor for being involved in a car accident, but being involved in a car accident is not a negative causal factor for driving carefully. (In fact, being involved in a car accident might even tend to make people more careful drivers in the future, in which case it's a positive causal factor.)

Eating a hamburger is a negative causal factor for being hungry, but being hungry is not a negative causal factor for eating a hamburger. (Quite the reverse, again.)

(3) The fact that there's a cooked potato in the oven is causally irrelevant to the oven being turned on. (That is to say: it's neither a positive causal factor—it does not tend to turn the oven on—nor a negative causal factor—it does not tend to prevent the oven from being turned on.) But the oven's being turned on is not causally irrelevant to there being a cooked potato inside: it tends to make the potato cooked, so it's a positive causal factor.

The fact that the grass is nice and green is causally irrelevant to the fact that there's a dry spring. (That is to say, it's not a positive causal factor—it does not tend to produce a dry spring, or to prevent it.) But a dry spring is not causally irrelevant to having nice green grass: it's a negative causal factor.

18.5 Mutual Causation

In the examples of positive correlation we've been looking at, the causal relation works only one way: that is, A causes B, but B doesn't cause A. These will be cases in which B is positively correlated with A, but in which B doesn't cause A. So we can't conclude from the positive correlation of B and A that B causes A.

I suggested that this is sometimes the case, though not invariably. Sometimes there's a situation in which A is a positive causal factor for B and B is a positive causal factor for A.

Here's an example. Suppose there's a hilly area with a lot of topsoil and a thick growth of plants. A big rainstorm comes along and washes away some of the topsoil. This results in the death of some of the plants. The roots of the plants help keep the topsoil in place, and the death of some of them results in a greater tendency to soil erosion, so the next time it rains, more soil washes away, resulting in still more plant deaths, and thus in still more soil erosion, and so on.

Plant Death $\longrightarrow$ **Soil Erosion** $\longrightarrow$ **Plant Death** $\longrightarrow$ **Soil Erosion** $\longrightarrow$ ...

Here's another example, this one tragically familiar to some students. You do poorly in a test; this gets you a bit discouraged, and you can't face doing much work in the class; the result is that you do even worse in the next test; this makes you more discouraged, and you do even less work; and so on. Sigh.

Both of these are examples in which increase of A causes increase of B, which causes increase of A, and so on. They're cases of **MUTUAL CAUSATION**; sometimes called **POSITIVE FEEDBACK LOOPS**.

In cases of positive feedback loop, there will be a positive correlation of A and B, while A is a positive causal factor for B and B is a positive causal factor for A.

These sometimes occur; but the main point here is that you can't automatically conclude that there's mutual causation from the existence of correlation.

EXERCISE
Try to come up with a couple of examples of positive feedback loops.

ANSWER
Here are two:
A pain in the foot is a positive causal factor for limping. But limping also tends to strain the muscles in the foot, so it's a positive causal factor for a painful foot.

The more an animal in the wild eats, the stronger it tends to get. But stronger animals also have an advantage in getting food, so the stronger an animal is, the more it eats. Eating a lot and being strong are in this situation both positive causal factors for each other.

There can also be **NEGATIVE FEEDBACK LOOPS**, where increase of A causes increase of B, but increase of B causes decrease of A. The result of a positive feedback loop is continual increase; but a negative feedback loop may result in stability. For example, a governor is a device on an engine that cuts back the fuel as the engine's speed increases. This will result in a constant maximum speed. Another example: as the population of a species rises, the shortage of its food increases, which results in the population falling.

18.6 Joint Cause

In all the cases of positive correlation between A and B we've been looking at so far, one of these three situations holds:

- A causes B, but B doesn't cause A.
- B causes A, but A doesn't cause B.
- A and B are mutual causes—they cause each other.

You might be tempted to conclude that every case of correlation fits into one of these categories. After all, why do A and B tend to go together if they're not in one of these causal relations?

But this is wrong. Here's an example of a positive correlation of A and B in which it's false that A causes B, false that B causes A, and false that they both cause each other.

Imagine a certain disease, a bacterial infection, which has two symptoms: (A) your muscles ache, and (B) you break out in spots. Now there's a positive correlation between (A) muscle aches and (B) spots; but it's false that muscle aches cause spots, or that spots cause muscle aches, or they each cause each other. The reason they're positively correlated in this case is that they're both caused by a third factor: the infection. This diagram illustrates the situation:

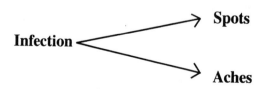

SPOTS and ACHES are positively correlated: the proportion of ACHES among people with SPOTS is larger than the proportion of ACHES among people without spots. Yet SPOTS are not a positive causal factor for ACHES, and ACHES are not a positive causal factor for SPOTS. The reason they're positively correlated is that they have a **JOINT CAUSE**: the infection.

An analogous situation can obtain where there's a negative correlation. Here's an example of this. During the summer, mosquito bites are negatively correlated with sunburn. But clearly neither is a negative causal factor for the other. Mosquito bites don't tend to prevent you from getting sunburn; and sunburn doesn't tend to prevent you from getting mosquito bites. (Neither are they mutual causes.)

EXERCISE
You might suspect that the situation here is that there is a joint negative causal factor for both sunburn and mosquito bites. Think again and try to figure out why this is the wrong answer.

ANSWER
If there is a third factor that is a negative causal factor for both sunburn and mosquito bites, then when this third factor is present there'd tend to be fewer mosquito bites and less sunburn; and when this third factor is absent, there'd tend to be more mosquito bites and more sunburn. This would mean that mosquito bites and sunburn would be positively correlated. Think about this carefully until you understand it.

We can imagine that the situation is this: dry summer weather is a positive causal factor for sunburn, and a negative causal factor for mosquito bites. (Mosquitoes breed in water, so they increase after a stretch of damp weather, and decrease after a stretch of dry sunny weather.)

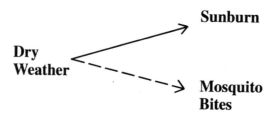

On this diagram, the dotted line represents a negative causal connection: that is, Dry Weather is a negative causal factor for Mosquito Bites.

18.7 Vitamin C and Colds

Suppose that scientists discover that people who eat lots of vitamin C catch fewer colds than those who don't eat lots of vitamin C. This means that there's a negative correlation between eating lots of vitamin C and catching colds. This does not mean that eating vitamin C is a negative causal factor for catching colds.

Can you imagine a story that accounts for the negative correlation between eating a lot of vitamin C and catching colds, but which assumes that eating a lot of vitamin C is causally irrelevant (neither a positive nor a negative causal factor) for catching colds? Draw a picture showing the causal situation.

Here's one possible story we might imagine. Colds are caused by infection by a cold-virus, and the cold-virus is spread largely via people's hands: someone who is infected spreads the virus on a door-handle or something, and you touch the door handle, and then transfer that virus into your own nose or mouth, and you get infected. Washing your hands a lot will stop the spread of the virus into you, and you'll tend to get fewer colds. So washing your hands a lot is a negative causal factor for catching colds. Here's a picture illustrating the causal situation. As before, the dotted line represents a negative causal connection—that is, that the thing on the left tends to prevent the thing on the right.

Hand Washing -------> **Colds**

Now, imagine that in the general population, certain people are health-conscious. If a person is health-conscious, that person tends wash his or her hands a lot. So being health-conscious is a negative causal factor for catching colds. But in addition, health-conscious people consume a lot of orange juice and other foods with vitamin C in them. The result is that health consciousness is a positive causal factor for both eating a lot of vitamin C, and for washing hands a lot. Here's a picture showing the causal situation:

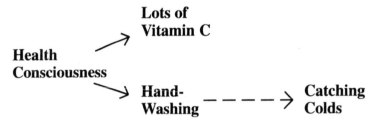

Given this situation, we'd expect a negative correlation between eating a lot of vitamin C and catching colds, despite the fact that eating a lot of vitamin C does not have any negative causal effect on catching colds—it's not a negative causal factor.

18.8 Milk and Strokes

EXERCISE

Read over this real newspaper story (from the [Toronto] Globe and Mail, May 18, 1996). How is it similar to the imaginary vitamin C case above? Explain why what the American Heart Association is reported as saying contradicts what Dr. Abbott claims the study shows (or at least may mislead us about it).

Middle-aged men who drink milk may reduce their risk of suffering the most common type of stroke, reports the American Heart Association. A 22-year study of 3,150 Hawaiian men of Japanese ancestry shows that those who did not drink milk were twice as likely to have a thromboembolic stroke as men who drank half a litre of milk a day. The research suggests that the difference was not due to calcium in milk, but possibly attributed to the men's lifestyles, says Dr. Robert Abbott, lead study author and biostatistician at the

> University of Virginia. "Milk drinkers tended to be leaner and more physically active and to consume foods that were more likely to be healthy."

STOP! ANSWER

As in the vitamin C case, there's an obvious direct causal interpretation for the observed correlation, in this case that that milk drinking is a negative causal factor for strokes.

Milk Drinking $- - - - - - \rightarrow$ **Strokes**

The American Heart Association's statement, as reported here, seems to suggest this interpretation, implying that milk drinking reduces the risk of stroke. But this is not the result of the study, according to its lead author. Dr. Abbot suggests that the real reason for the negative correlation between milk drinking and strokes is not that the milk drinking is a negative causal factor for strokes, but that rather the lifestyle which results in drinking a lot of milk also results in a leaner and more active body, and a healthier diet in general. These are actually the negative causal factors for strokes. Maybe the picture is something like this:

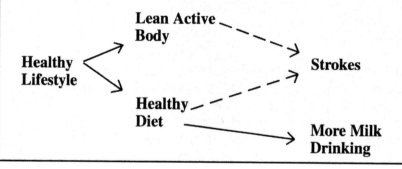

18.9 Snoring and Obesity

A real-life example (reported in the [Toronto] *Globe and Mail*, May 15, 1996) of a positive correlation that is consistent with a wide variety of causal structures is the observed correlation between snoring and obesity. A fairly obvious causal connection behind this correlation is that obesity causes snoring.

Obesity ——————————————> **Snoring**

In fact, scientists believe that an increase in fat buildup in the back of the throat results in a greater tendency to snore. But the situation is, it turns out, not that simple.

New research suggests that the fat buildup also produces a condition called sleep apnea, in which the sleeper stops breathing for a few seconds, often waking him up briefly, and leaving him sleepy the next morning. Apnea sufferers may be too tired to want to do much physical activity, and thus they may put on more weight. Thus sleep apnea, which can be caused by weight gain, may also result in weight gain:

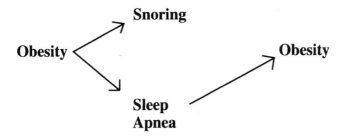

A positive feedback loop is thus set up: obesity causes apnea, which causes weight gain, which causes more apnea, and so on. All the while, more weight causes more snoring. Most unfortunate.

18.10 Sex and Prostate Cancer

A recent newspaper headline: "Men with active sex lives run higher risk of prostate cancer." Are you men alarmed? Let's look into the story. * A Swedish study reports that men with a "highly active" sex life run a greater risk of contracting prostate cancer than their more abstemious counterparts. This, we can gather, reports an unfortunate positive correlation. (The good news, however, is that there's very little correlation between prostate cancer and cigarette smoking or heavy drinking.)

---

* [Halifax] *Sunday Daily News*, May 26, 1996, p. 38.

The obvious conclusion we're tempted to jump to is that a lot of sexual activity is a positive causal factor for prostate cancer. However, cancer specialist Swen-Olof Andersson of Orebro Hospital does not recommend abstinence.

EXERCISE

Speculate on two other causal connections that might account for this positive correlation.

ANSWER

Maybe prostate cancer, in its incipient stages, causes a highly active sex life. But this is not the connection Dr. Andersson thinks accounts for the positive correlation. "We don't think it's the sexual activity in itself," Andersson commented today at the presentation of his thesis. "It might be some kind of hormonal factor that also affects sexual drive." The hormonal factor, then, would be a third factor that's a positive causal factor for both a highly active sex life and prostate cancer.

18.11 Girl's Height and Anxiety

Here's another real case in which the discovery of a positive correlation is reported:

> Girls with anxiety disorders are likely to wind up shorter than their calmer peers, according to Dr. Daniel Pine of the New York State Psychiatric Institute. He found that they were nearly two inches shorter as adults, reports Family Practice magazine.... Dr. Pine said this finding probably relates to a deficiency of growth-hormone secretion in the girls. *

There are several possibilities regarding the causal structure of the situation underlying this positive correlation.

---

*From the (Toronto) *Globe and Mail*, January 31, 1996.

EXERCISE

Give several hypotheses about the causal structure that might lie behind the correlation; diagram each.

ANSWER

STOP!

The article perhaps hints that anxiety syndrome in girls causes them to wind up shorter.

Anxiety Disorder ⟶ **Growing Less**

But the situation could be the other way around: maybe their anxiety as children is caused by the fact that they're not growing as tall as others.

Growing Less ⟶ **Anxiety Disorder**

How does a deficiency of growth-hormone secretion fit in here? I suppose that this is pretty clearly the cause of shortness, but the rest is unclear. Maybe the anxiety causes a deficiency of growth-hormone secretion, which causes shortness.

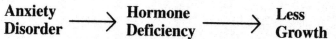

Anxiety Disorder ⟶ **Hormone Deficiency** ⟶ **Less Growth**

Maybe the deficiency of growth-hormone secretion is the joint cause both of anxiety syndrome and of shortness.

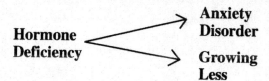

Hormone Deficiency
⟶ **Anxiety Disorder**
⟶ **Growing Less**

Maybe there's even a fourth factor which causes anxiety syndrome and deficiency of growth-hormone secretion, and the deficiency causes shortness.

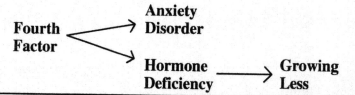

Fourth Factor
⟶ **Anxiety Disorder**
⟶ **Hormone Deficiency** ⟶ **Growing Less**

18.12 Should You Stretch Your Children's Arms?

Studies have conclusively shown that children with long arms reason better than those with short.

EXERCISE
Before you look at the answer, see if you can figure out the explanation for this.

ANSWER
They're older. *

Now, let's sum up what we've found. To simplify matters, we'll concentrate on positive correlations and possible positive causal factors. We have seen cases in which there's a positive correlation between A and B, but this does not necessarily show that A is a positive causal factor for B. There may be other causal connections that account for this positive correlation: B may be a positive causal factor for A; or both B and A may be caused by a joint cause, C. There's more to be said on this subject, but that's enough of this chapter, so we'll continue discussion in the next.

* Example from "Health Statistics May Be Bad for Our Mental Health" by John Allen Paulos, *Skeptical Inquirer* Vol. 20 No. 1 Jan/Feb 1996, p. 44.

CHAPTER 19

Causal Complications

19.1 Does Smoking Prevent Lung Cancer?

As in the case of every explanation, the only way to establish that one candidate for a causal explanation of a certain phenomenon really explains it is to rule out every other plausible candidate. Now, suppose that we have observed a positive correlation between A and B. One possible explanation for this is that A causes B. But, we've seen, there are two other sorts of plausible hypotheses: that B causes A, and that A and B have a joint cause.

An interesting case will serve as a review of the material in the last chapter, and will introduce a small new wrinkle. The new wrinkle is that we're going to look at a case that shows that it's possible that A and B are positively correlated, despite the fact that A is a *negative* causal factor for B.

It was well known for years that there was a positive correlation between smoking and lung cancer. But this fact alone did not provide good evidence that smoking was a positive causal factor for lung cancer. By now, you should realise why not.

> **EXERCISE**
> Give two other sorts of hypothesis that would also explain this positive correlation.

> **ANSWER**
> (1) Smoking doesn't cause lung cancer; it's the other way around: lung cancer causes smoking.
> (2) Smoking and lung cancer are causally unrelated: they both have a common cause.

I hasten to add here that for at least the last couple of decades scientists have been in agreement that these other two hypotheses have been conclusively ruled out. Let's imagine that we're thinking about the smoking/lung cancer correlation a few decades ago, before these other two hypotheses were definitely disconfirmed. How could they be plausible? Well, some scientists seriously argued that they were plausible. Here are the sorts of stories they imagined:

(1) It's well-known that lung cancer takes a long while to develop, and that it's undetectable by all the normal techniques of diagnosis for a long time in its early development. it just might be the case that the changes in the lungs or in the rest of the body caused by the early development of lung cancer produce a susceptibility to smoking. Maybe they make smoking a more pleasurable activity, or increase the yearning for a cigarette. Maybe the small discomforts the very early stages of cancer cause are somewhat alleviated by smoking. So it just might be the case that lung cancer is a positive causal feature for smoking. This, even in the absence of a positive causal relationship in the other direction, could produce the observed positive correlation.

(2) Let's suppose that there's a genetic factor that has two effects: it increases your tendency to smoke, by making smoking more pleasurable or increasing the desire; and independently of this, it makes it more likely that you get lung cancer. Neither of these is hugely improbable on the face of it. This, even were smoking not a positive causal factor for lung cancer, would explain a positive correlation between smoking and lung cancer.

All this should be a familiar sort of move to you, if you've mastered the last chapter. Here's an interesting twist to it however: note that if either Hypothesis (1) or Hypothesis (2) were true, and accounted for the positive correlation between smoking and cancer, it would be possible that smoking is a negative causal factor for cancer—that is, that smoking tends to prevent cancer! It would have to be a fairly weak causal factor—one not sufficient to override the stronger causal factors indicated in (1) and (2). In sum, then, there would be a positive correlation. If this were the case, then the best health advice you should give to everyone would be to go out and start smoking! Despite the positive correlation of smoking and cancer.

I repeat, however, that the falsity of (1) and (2) has now been conclusively established. So please don't go out and start smoking.*

---

* Well, don't start smoking for its health benefits. In fact it's bad for your health, but on the other hand, it's so *cool*.

19.2 Screening Off: Fred and the Birth Control Pills ▮

"Screening off" provides another complexity in the relation between cause and correlation. This topic was introduced in Section 10.7. You might refresh your memory by re-reading that section before we continue.

The point made there was that a screened-off characteristic doesn't serve as an explantion. Now, causal explanation is a variety of explanation, so you won't be surprised to hear that a screened-off characteristic isn't a cause.

The first example of screened-off properties raised in Chapter 10 was the strange case of Fred, who has been taking female birth control pills for years, and hasn't gotten pregnant; but his taking birth control pills doesn't explain his not being pregnant.

We can treat this case as an example of correlation without cause. There's a good strong negative correlation in the population of people (male and female) between taking birth control pills and getting pregnant. I don't know what the figures are here, but let's take a guess: the percentage of people who take birth control pills and who get pregnant is just about 0%; the percentage of people who don't take birth control pills and who get pregnant is, let's guess, 5%.

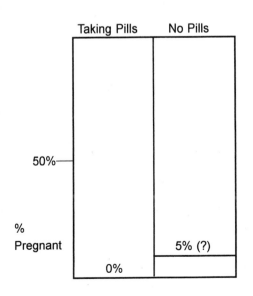

In this case, it seems that the negative correlation accompanies a negative causal factor: for the population as a whole, taking birth control pills is a negative causal factor for becoming pregnant.

But it does not follow that for every member of the population taking birth control pills is a negative causal factor for becoming pregnant. In particular, in Fred's case, his taking the pills had nothing to do with his not becoming pregnant. It was causally irrelevant.

The way we explain this in terms of "screening off" is that Fred's probability of becoming pregnant, given that he's male, is equal to the probability of his becoming pregnant given that he's male and he takes birth control pills. Both are 0%.

This same thing can be expressed in terms of correlations: for the population of males, there's no correlation between taking birth control pills and becoming pregnant. Here's the diagram showing this:

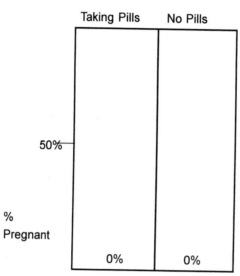

The fact that there's a smaller group (smaller than people in general) to which Fred belongs (namely, males) in which there is no correlation between taking birth control pills and being pregnant shows that the characteristic of taking birth control pills is screened off from the effect of pregnancy. Thus, despite the fact that in the general population (as well as, of course, among females) taking birth control pills is a negative causal factor for pregnancy, because among males this characteristic is screened off, and Fred is a male, it isn't, after all, a negative causal factor for Fred.

19.3 Screening Off Again: Salt and Blood Pressure

Here's another example where screening off becomes relevant. This time the example is a real-life case, involving possible links between salt consumption and high blood pressure.

It's been well known for a while that in the general population, eating a lot of salt is strongly positively correlated with high blood pressure. But a recent newspaper article* has the headline "Don't hide that salt shaker so fast." The article quotes a Canadian researcher who, after a large-scale study, concluded "Salt has little effect on the blood pressure of people under 45,

---

* The [Toronto] *Globe and Mail*, May 22, 1996, p 1.

and restricting sodium in the diet might create other health problems.... The only significant benefit of salt restriction on blood pressure was seen in people over 45."

If this were all there was to it, you could see how this is a clear-cut example of screening off. Despite the fact that in the population as a whole, reducing salt consumption is a causal factor in reducing high blood pressure, apparently being under 45 screens this effect off. If you're looking for advice on whether to cut back on your salt consumption, the answer (according to this study) depends on how old you are.

But before you start changing your eating habits as a result of this advice, you should consider a couple of things. First, critics of this study claim that it's partially funded by a food company interested in discrediting the anti-salt findings of other research. As we've seen much earlier, however, this doesn't necessarily show that the results of the study are wrong: we just have to look at it a little more attentively, to try to see if it was done right.

The second thing to consider, however, is exactly what this study is supposed to show. The newspaper article I've quoted from is a model of bad science writing, and I've quoted most of it just below, so that you can try to figure out exactly what sort of claims are being made on the basis of this study.

> Canadian researchers are challenging attempts to restrict salt in the diet of healthy people.
>
> Salt has little effect on the blood pressure of people under 45, and restricting sodium in the diet might create other health problems, according to Toronto researchers who reviewed the results of 20 years of health studies.
>
> A review of the results of 56 different diet experiments conducted over the years shows that only older people with high blood pressure would benefit from reducing the amount of salt in their diet, Dr. Alexander Logan of Toronto's Mount Sinai Hospital reported yesterday in the Journal of the American Medical Association.
>
> This conflicts with a recommendation made last week by doctors in Britain that the salt content of packaged foods be limited. The researcher, reporting in the British Medical Journal, updated a 1988 study of 10,000 people, known as Intersalt, which found a direct link between high salt consumption and elevated blood pressure.

"We say they overstated their case," Dr. Logan said in a phone interview from London, where he is on a sabbatical leave. The British study looked only at what people in different cities ate and whether they had high blood pressure, he explained.

The Canadian Group looked at whether cutting back salt in the diet changed the blood pressure of people with and without elevated levels. The only significant benefit of salt restriction on blood pressure was seen in people over 45.

But other factors, including weight, alcohol consumption and lack of exercise, can have more effect on blood pressure than diet, added Dr. Logan, who heads Mount Sinai's hypertension unit. "Salt may only be a secondary cause of high blood pressure. Studies of people who are 20 to 50 pounds overweight have found that their pressure becomes more sensitive to salt."

For healthy people, "we can no longer accept on blind faith that restricting salt intake is harmless," Dr. Logan said. Other studies not part of his review have found that in healthy people restricting sodium may make the body less able to eliminate sugar or could raise cholesterol....

Now, despite the well-established fact that in the whole population, reducing your salt intake is a positive causal factor for good health, it's pretty clear that the new Canadian study is claiming that it's not recommended for everyone, because it's screened off by certain characteristics, so it won't help everyone. But the study's claims are not at all clear in this article: which subgroups of the general population are those for which salt reduction is a positive causal factor for health, and which are the subgroups for which it isn't? Could all overweight people benefit? Or just those with high blood pressure? Or must you be over 45 as well? The article just isn't clear. The moral here is that even a comparatively good newspaper can give an incoherent or inadequate account of scientific research. Read carefully.

19.4 The Pill and Arteriosclerosis

Here's a different sort of complicated case. In this case, we imagine that A is negatively correlated with B, despite the fact that A (all by itself) might be seen to be a positive causal factor for B.

Here's the case. (As far as I know, this is true-to-life, but you shouldn't rely on a philosophy professor for medical advice!) In the population as a whole, there's a negative correlation in women between taking birth control pills and getting arteriosclerosis (hardening of the arteries). Does this mean that it's good advice for women to take birth control pills? Not necessarily. Here's the whole story. The reason that taking birth control pills is negatively correlated with arteriosclerosis is that birth control pills are (of course) a very strong negative causal factor for women's pregnancy; and pregnancy is a positive causal factor for arteriosclerosis. What this means is that women who don't take the pill are more likely to get pregnant, and women who get pregnant are more likely than others to get arteriosclerosis. Also, women who do take the pill are highly unlikely to get pregnant, and women who don't get pregnant are less likely than others to get arteriosclerosis. This explains the negative correlation between taking the pill and getting arteriosclerosis.

Notwithstanding all this, it turns out that taking the pill is (considered all by itself) a fairly weak *positive* causal factor for arteriosclerosis. This means that women who take the pill and don't get pregnant have a somewhat higher tendency to get arteriosclerosis than women who don't take the pill and don't get pregnant. This is a fairly weak phenomenon, however, and is insufficient to override the pregnancy effect. So there is in the population as a whole, nevertheless, a negative correlation.

So again one should not jump to causal conclusions about a sub-group in the population from correlations established in the whole population. For the group of women as a whole, we can say that taking the pill is in fact a negative causal factor for arteriosclerosis because it prevents pregnancy, which is a positive causal factor. But for women who are using other effective birth control measures, or who aren't sexually active, it's a small positive factor. So from the fact that there's a negative correlation among all women, one shouldn't conclude that it's a negative causal factor for every particular woman. It might actually be positive.

Is this another example of screening off? Well, maybe. Perhaps you can think of the property had by a certain sub-group as screening off the normal effect of reducing the tendency to get arteriosclerosis. What is the property that defines this sub-group? Not-being-about-to-get-pregnant? (Things get complicated here.)

19.5 Accidental Correlation

Here's an entirely different sort of example in which A and B are positively correlated, but A doesn't cause B.

I've just looked in the pocket of my pants, and I've discovered that I happen to have three dimes, one quarter, and one penny in there. The proportion of coins in my pocket that are copper-coloured is 1/5, 20%. Now consider the coins not in my pocket, but elsewhere in circulation. What's the proportion of copper-coloured coins there? It turns out that more than half—let's say 55%—of the coins in circulation are pennies. As before, let's call the coins in my pocket right now POCKETCOINS. The proportion of POCKETCOINS that are copper-coloured is .20, and the proportion of non-POCKETCOINS that are copper-coloured is .55. There's a negative correlation between being a POCKETCOIN and being copper-coloured. Is there any sort of causal connection here?

Well, it's clear that being a POCKETCOIN isn't a negative causal factor for being copper-coloured. It's also clear that being silver-coloured doesn't cause a coin to be a POCKETCOIN. I don't arrange things so that I tend to put copper coins in my pocket less than other coins. Neither is there any sort of common cause that results in this negative correlation. The whole thing is just random. It has nothing to do with any laws of nature. It's just an accidental correlation.

But compare the other positive and negative correlations we've been considering. These are, by contrast, results of the laws of nature in some way or another. They're not just accidents.

The moral here is that we expect only correlations which are matters of laws of nature to have causal explanations. Accidental correlations have nothing to do with causal relations.

Now, here's a curious fact. It seems that all of the correlations we've examined that are not just accidents—that are matters of laws of nature—have a causal explanation. For example, in every example we've looked at in which it seems to be a law of nature that As are positively correlated with Bs, there's some sort of causal connection which explains this. (Either being an A is a positive causal factor for being a B, or being a B is a positive causal factor for being an A, or both, or being an A and being a B have a joint cause.) Is every lawful positive correlation a matter of some sort of causal connection? Maybe. This is an interesting philosophical question that I'm not going to try to answer.

What's for sure, however, is that the existence of lawlike correlations does make us think that there's some sort of causal connection. When scientists find one, they try to find a causal connection that explains it. Here's a real-life example of this sort of scientific reasoning in progress:

One very active area of scientific research is the search for the causes of breast cancer. Because scientists assume that a correlation is a sign of some sort of causal connection, the first thing they do when trying to come up with causal hypotheses is often the search for correlations. So a recent very large-scale study* of breast cancer in the United States obtained information about the number of cases in each county in the country, and looked for correlations with the distributions in these counties of a large number of other factors . The following factors were positively correlated with breast cancer:

- high socio-economic status
- being Jewish
- low fertility
- being a college graduate
- having a professional job
- living near a toxic waste dump site
- living in a crowded area
- alcohol consumption

These are negatively correlated:

- early pregnancy
- being a Mormon
- consumption of fat

You can see, of course, that while this information suggests what might turn out to be causal factors, it's doesn't conclusively show anything. How is it, for example, that being a Mormon correlated negatively with having breast cancer? Is this just an accidental correlation? Or is there one of the several forms of causal connection going on here? In the next chapter, we'll talk about the techniques of confirming causal hypotheses.

---

* Rodger Doyle, "Deaths Caused by Breast Cancer, by County", *Scientific American* 273, No. 4 (October 1995) p. 32D.

CHAPTER 20

Experimental Confirmation

20.1 Gastritis and Bacteria: A Correlation

Here's a real-life scientific example involving confirmation of a causal explanatory hypothesis.

In 1979, Robin Warren, a pathologist in an Australian hospital, made a puzzling observation in the course of doing biopsies of tissue samples from patient's stomachs. Several samples had large numbers of curved spiral bacteria, but only when the stomach tissue was inflamed. This sort of inflammation was already well known; it was called chronic gastritis.

EXERCISE
QUESTION A. Warren noticed that every bit of stomach tissue he observed which had this bacterium in it also showed gastritis. What can he conclude from this?

ANSWER
Very little. Note carefully that so far, not enough information has been revealed to show that there's a positive correlation between these bacteria and gastritis even in the observed sample.

QUESTION B.
What else would Warren have to notice to establish a positive correlation in the sample, and in the population?

STOP! ANSWER

He'd have to compare proportions—for example, by finding that the proportion of bacteria-infected stomach tissue among the samples with gastritis was larger than the proportion of bacteria-infected stomach tissue among the samples without gastritis. This would establish a positive correlation in the sample. If the sample was representative, and large enough, and the differences in observed frequencies sufficiently large, then a conclusion about a correlation in the general population would be justified.

Well, by 1983 researchers had done enough work to confirm Warren's suspicion that the presence of these bacteria was strongly positively correlated with chronic gastritis in the general population.

20.2 Do Bacteria Cause Gastritis?

But now the sort of question we've been interested in—about causal connection—comes up. Warren considered three hypotheses:

H1. Maybe the bacteria caused the gastritis.

H2. Maybe the bacteria didn't cause the gastritis; instead, gastritis caused the presence of bacteria. It could be that the inflamed tissue somehow invited these bacteria to colonize there.

H3. Maybe neither one caused the other; instead both the presence of the bacteria and the gastritis had a joint cause.

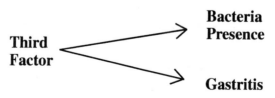

(Other hypotheses are possible too. Maybe bacteria and gastritis are *both* positive causal factors for each other. Maybe the positive correlation is just a coincidence, resulting from no causal connections at all. For the sake of simplicity, we'll ignore these alternatives.)

Now the job facing Warren and other researchers was to rule out two of these three hypotheses, and thereby to confirm what the real causal story was.

What we have here is just a special case of what's by now a familiar sort of problem: finding an explanation. In this case, the explanandum is the positive correlation of the presence of bacteria and gastritis. Three hypotheses are under consideration as possible explanations for this correlation. What can the researchers do to rule out two of these hypotheses? Examination of the details of their procedures will help us understand how this sort of thing can be done.

20.3 A Preliminary Experiment

In 1985, Warren's research associate Barry J. Marshall concocted an extremely disgusting soup consisting of a large number of the bacteria in question and drank it. Shortly afterwards, he developed a severe case of gastritis. Another volunteer drank the soup, and also developed gastritis. Both volunteers were previously healthy.

Now this little experiment, while it suggested that Warren and Marshall were on to something, didn't provide sufficient evidence that bacteria is a positive causal factor for gastritis. It's important for us to explain why.

First, let's note that a sample of two is far too small to provide any good evidence about a general population. In order to justify a conclusion about the general population, a much bigger sample is necessary. The next step was to do just this.

The article I read doesn't give all the details of the subsequent testing procedure, but let's imagine that you and I are conducting the next stage of work here. Our next step is to get a large number of healthy volunteers, say 1000, and give them all that awful soup. Now, at least, there's a large enough sample size to justify some conclusions.

Suppose that every one of these people got gastritis after drinking this soup. Now would we have good evidence that bacteria cause gastritis?

The answer is: No, not yet. It's important for us to see why. Remember that what we're interested in doing is ruling out two of these three hypotheses:

H1. Maybe the bacteria caused the gastritis.

H2. Maybe the bacteria didn't cause the gastritis; instead, gastritis caused the presence of bacteria. It could be that the inflamed tissue somehow invited these bacteria to colonize there.

H3. Maybe neither one caused the other; instead both the presence of the bacteria and the gastritis had a joint cause.

The problem with this experiment is that the results are consistent with all three hypotheses. The experimental results don't show that any of the three is false. To see why, let's consider each of these hypotheses in turn.

H1. Maybe the presence of this bacteria is a positive causal factor for gastritis. If this were true, then giving the subjects bacteria would likely produce gastritis in them (given, that is, the presence of the other causal factors for gastritis). So the result is consistent with this hypothesis. Of course, our results don't show that this hypothesis is false.

H2. Maybe the presence of bacteria isn't a positive causal factor for gastritis; maybe things actually work the other way around and gastritis is a positive causal factor for the presence of bacteria. Well, don't our experimental results show this is false? No. The reason is that we might get these results even if the hypothesis were true. Here's how this might happen. We assume that gastritis is a positive causal factor for bacteria, but not the other way around. Well, then, what's the cause of gastritis? Well, we don't know, but let's call this FACTOR C.

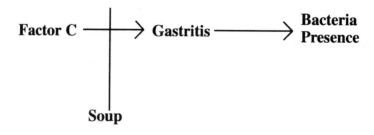

Factor C ⟶ **Gastritis** ⟶ **Bacteria Presence**

Soup

Of course, somebody could have FACTOR C already, but not yet have gastritis; FACTOR C might take a little while to bring about gastritis. Our subjects were all healthy to start off with, but this doesn't mean that they didn't already have FACTOR C; or maybe we introduced it somehow in the course of the experiment. Now, if all our experimental subjects had FACTOR C, then they would get gastritis. In this case, it would be FACTOR C, not the bacteria, that gave them gastritis. We're imagining here that

- FACTOR C, not bacteria, causes gastritis.
- All our subjects had FACTOR C.
- Gastritis causes the presence of bacteria.

If this were the case, then it would follow that our subjects would get gastritis after having been given the bacteria (though the bacteria weren't responsible for it). It would also follow that bacteria and gastritis were positively correlated in the population (because gastritis causes the presence of bacteria). So our experimental results are consistent with Hypothesis 2, as far as we know.

> H3. Maybe the presence of bacteria isn't a positive causal factor for gastritis, and gastritis isn't a positive causal factor for bacteria. The reason that they're correlated is that they're both the result of a joint cause, call it FACTOR D.

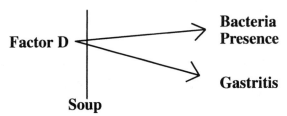

Now we imagine that the reason our subjects got gastritis was that they all already had FACTOR D, which takes a little time to give you gastritis. It was FACTOR D, not the bacteria, that gave them gastritis. We're imagining here that:

•FACTOR D, not bacteria, causes gastritis.
•All our subjects had FACTOR D.
•FACTOR D also causes the presence of bacteria.

If this were the case, then it would follow that our subjects would get gastritis after having been given the bacteria (though the bacteria weren't responsible for it). It would also follow that bacteria and gastritis were positively correlated in the population (because both are caused by FACTOR D). So our experimental results are consistent with Hypothesis 3, as far as we know.

What follows from all of this is that the experimental results are consistent with all three hypotheses; they rule out none of them.

20.4 A Better Experiment

What to do? Well, here's a suggestion: get experimental subjects who are not only healthy (i.e., no bacteria or gastritis already), but who also don't have FACTOR C or FACTOR D or anything else that would result in their getting gastritis during the experimental period. But this is no good. We don't know what the possible causes of gastritis—possible FACTORS C and D—are. If we did, maybe we wouldn't have to do these experiments in the first place, because maybe FACTOR C or D would already, all by itself, explain the correlation of bacteria and gastritis.

Here's a much better suggestion. Suppose that we divide the group of people we're going to do the study on into two parts. Call the first part the **EXPERIMENTAL GROUP** and the second part the **CONTROL GROUP**. Make sure that people are sorted into these two groups randomly. (The importance of this will be explained in a moment.) Now: give everyone in the experimental group the bacteria soup, and give it to nobody in the control group. Now observe the two groups, noting how many from each group get gastritis. If there are a lot more in the experimental group than in the control group who get gastritis, we have confirmed that bacteria are a positive causal factor for gastritis.

Why does this experimental procedure remedy the problem with the first one?

Here's why. The problem with the first procedure is that there might be some other reason—FACTOR C or FACTOR D—why our subjects got gastritis. But in this improved procedure, this doesn't matter. Let's imagine that there are such FACTORS that can give people gastritis. We're selecting the total group (experimental + control) from the whole population randomly. That means that some of them have FACTOR C or FACTOR D, in about the same proportion as these factors show up in the population as a whole. These people will get gastritis from this, whether or not they get bacteria soup. Now we divide the total group, randomly again, into the control and experimental groups. Because this is a random division, and both groups are pretty large, we can be confident enough that the proportions of FACTOR C and FACTOR D in the experimental and control groups are about the same, again approximately matching their proportions in the population as a whole. Now we give everyone in the experimental group the bacteria soup, and wait a while, observing both groups. Suppose that, at the end of this time, everyone in the experimental group gets gastritis. This fact all by itself doesn't tell us anything, as we've already seen, because maybe their gastritis is caused by FACTOR C or FACTOR D. But now, how about the people in the control group? Suppose a much smaller proportion of people in the control group gets gastritis—say only 5%. Because none of them got the soup, we know that their gastritis was caused by some FACTOR C or FACTOR D, because it wasn't caused by the soup: they didn't get any soup. So we can conclude that 5% of them had some FACTOR C or FACTOR D. Because we're confident that the same proportion of FACTOR C and FACTOR D occur in the experimental group, we can conclude that up to 5% of their gastritis was caused by FACTOR C or FACTOR D. But this can't account for the remaining gastritis in the experimental group: it must have been caused by the soup.

This is complicated reasoning, but it's important that you follow it. Go back and read that paragraph again if you're not confident you understand.

The point about this better experiment, including a control group, is that it does give us a way to rule out two of the three hypotheses. If bacteria weren't a positive causal factor for gastritis—that is, if either H2 or H3 were true, then there would be approximately identical proportions of gastritis in the experimental and control groups. The fact that the proportion of gastritis in the experimental group was significantly larger than in the control group shows that H2 and H3 are both false. An experiment utilizing a control group is a way of confirming a hypothesis about cause.

20.5 Selecting the Control Group

You'll recall that the preliminary experiments Warren and Marshall conducted involved giving bacteria soup to *healthy* people—that is, to people without gastritis and without those stomach bacteria. The experiment we imagined, using a control group who were not given the soup, would not, however, need to restrict itself to healthy people.

Suppose some of the total group already had those bacteria, or already had gastritis. They would have had these conditions in about the same proportion as the whole population (because the total group is chosen randomly). The experimental and control groups would both have these conditions in about the same proportions (because the total group is divided randomly). Thus we'd expect some gastritis to occur in both groups, and in the same proportion, because of this. (That is, because some people already have gastritis in both groups; and, if bacteria causes gastritis, then some people in both groups would get gastritis as the result of the bacteria already there.) As a result of these pre-existent conditions, there might be some gastritis in both experimental and control groups, in identical proportions. But if the proportion of gastritis in the experimental group turns out to be higher, then this must be the result of their having been fed the soup. So even if you don't check the total group for pre-existing conditions, a large difference in gastritis between the experimental and control groups still proves that the bacterial presence is a positive causal factor.

Again, this is complicated reasoning; again, you should go slowly, re-read, and make sure you understand it.

As you've noticed, the sort of experimental procedure we've been considering involves two random selections:

(1) first, you randomly get the total sample from the whole population;

(2) next, you divide the total sample into the experimental and control groups.

Of course, it's possible to do both of these tasks at once. It's important, however, that you make sure that both selection procedures are done randomly. If the total group is a representative sample of the whole population, but then you divide up this group non-randomly into the experimental and control groups, it's possible that you'll get important differences between the experimental and control groups, and the experimental results won't give you good evidence. Imagine, for example, that 5% of the population has FACTOR D, a positive causal factor for both the presence of bacteria and gastritis. You choose a random sample from the whole population, containing about 5% people with FACTOR D. Now suppose you let people volunteer for those who will drink the soup and those who won't. This is, of course, a non-random way of dividing your total subject group into experimental and control groups, and it may make a difference. Imagine that people with FACTOR D are already feeling a bit queasy, and as a result they're less likely to volunteer to drink the yucky soup. The experimental group would thus contain a smaller proportion of those with FACTOR D than the control group. Imagine that the experimental group contains only 2% with FACTOR D, but the control group contains 8% with FACTOR D. Now, if FACTOR D is the only cause of gastritis (bacteria are causally irrelevant), 8% of the control group would get gastritis and 2% of the experimental group would get gastritis. If you concluded that the bacteria were actually a *negative* causal factor for gastritis as a result, you'd be wrong. You might be led to this error by the mistake of not dividing the whole group of subjects randomly.

Of course, a non-random selection might make the results go the other way. Suppose for some reason that we got a considerably higher proportion of people with FACTOR D in the experimental group. If FACTOR D is the only cause of gastritis (bacteria are causally irrelevant), then there will be a larger proportion of gastritis in the experimental group than in the control group. This would lead you to conclude that bacteria were a positive causal factor for gastritis, and you'd be wrong.

EXERCISE

Now imagine that your division into experimental and control groups is random, but your choice of subjects from the whole population isn't. Suppose, for example, that you put an ad in the paper saying that you're looking for subjects to do experiments possibly leading to a cure for stomach problems. 5% of the population, as before, have FACTOR D. But those in the population with FACTOR D are already feeling a bit queasy, so as a result, they're more likely to sign up for the experiment, hoping that they'll find out something useful about their stomachs. Imagine that your total experimental group then contains 20% with FACTOR D. Now suppose that FACTOR D is not the only positive causal factor for gastritis; but that, in the absence of FACTOR D, the presence of bacteria is a weak positive causal factor. Predict the result of the experiment, and show how it's misleading.

ANSWER
You divide the group of subjects randomly, so 20% of the experimental group, and 20% of the control group both have FACTOR D. 20% of both groups get gastritis because of this. Now, because in the absence of FACTOR D, bacteria is a weak causal factor for gastritis, a few people in the experimental group who don't have FACTOR D will get gastritis. So imagine that your totals are: 20% of the control group get gastritis; 25% of the experimental group get gastritis. You conclude that bacteria is a weak causal factor for gastritis, but that there's some other factor which is much stronger. You're right in concluding that there are two causal factors which can independently cause gastritis, but you may be far off in estimating their relative importance in the whole population. Remember that we assumed that only 5% of the population has FACTOR D. The fact that your total group of subjects was not chosen randomly has led you to overestimate the importance of FACTOR D in the population, and to underestimate the importance of the bacteria.

20.6 Matching as an Alternative to Random Selection

If you remember the discussion in Chapters 3 and 4 concerning gathering inductive evidence about proportions and correlations, you might recall that two methods of sample selection were discussed: the random method and the "matching" method. In the "matching" method, we try to identify all the possibly relevant secondary characteristics, and then we choose our sample group so that the proportions of all secondary characteristics in the sample group are approximately the same as in the general population (or pare it down by eliminating people from the sample with the "wrong" characteristics, until the sample matches the population). This procedure has its own problems, which we noted; but sometimes it's preferable to random sample selection.

Random selection of sample (and random division into control and experimental groups) has come up here again, and you won't be surprised to hear that matching strategies are available as an alternative method here too. What we'd do to utilize the matching strategy here is the same thing, twice. First, we'd identify all the possibly relevant secondary characteristics. In the case we're using as an example, these would involve presence of bacteria,

gastritis, FACTOR C, and FACTOR D. The random selection of total subject group, and the random division of subject group into experimental and
control groups, were designed to make us confident that we had about the
same proportion of all relevant secondary characteristics in the control group
and the experimental group as occurred in the general population. When we
use the matching strategy for selection and division, we make sure that all
three groups have the same proportions of any possibly relevant secondary
characteristics we can think of.

For example, suppose we think that stress might be a positive causal factor in gastritis. Then, in order to test whether bacteria is another positive
causal factor, and if so to what extent, what we should do is to make sure that
the proportion of stressed-out people in the total subject group matches,
more or less, the proportion of stressed-out people in the total population.
And then, we should make sure that we divide the total subject group into
experimental and control groups, each containing this same proportion of
stressed-out people.

As in the case of evidence for proportions and correlations in the population, the matching strategy is risky because we can't be sure that we're able
to identify all the possibly relevant secondary characteristics in advance.

20.7 Reasoning from a Sample to the Population

Now suppose we've got our experimental and control groups selected in
ways that give us good reason to believe will result in proportions of characteristics matching the general population. (Maybe we've done this by random selection and division, or maybe by matching.) Now we run the
experiment.

Suppose that the result of the experiment is that 49% of the experimental
group get gastritis, and that 28% of the control group get gastritis. Is this
evidence that in the whole population being infected with the bacteria raises
your chances from 28% to 49% of getting gastritis? Is it evidence that the
presence of bacteria is a positive causal factor in the population as a whole, at
all?

As you might have guessed, we run into exactly the same considerations
here as we did earlier, when we were thinking about inductive evidence for a
correlation in a population. Sample size is again relevant here: this time, the
sizes of the experimental and control groups are what matters. Again we
need to calculate margins of error, assuming a confidence level. Again we

have to check possible overlap of the two regions. Here's the relevant picture in our present case, assuming a sample size of 100 in the experimental group and 100 in the control group, and a confidence-level of .95:

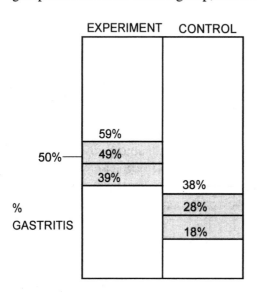

Here we can see that because there's no overlap between the margins of error, the figures we've got from our experiment are statistically significant, and we can claim that the presence of bacteria is a positive causal factor for gastritis. We can also estimate how strong this causal factor is: somewhere between (59%-18%) = 41%, and (39% - 38%) = 1%. A positive causal factor with 1% strength is very weak. One with 49% is quite strong. The small sample sizes and resulting large margins of error, result in our not being able to say anything very informative about the strength of this positive causal factor.

EXERCISE

Suppose it turns out that there's an identical proportion of gastritis in the experimental and control groups: 49% in both. Do we have evidence that the presence of bacteria is entirely causally unrelated to gastritis—that is, that it's neither a positive nor a negative causal factor? Draw the graph and answer the question.

ANSWER

Here we can't conclude that the presence of bacteria is a positive or a negative causal factor, or causally irrelevant. The best we can say is that if it's a causal factor at all, it's a pretty weak one: its maximum strength is +20% if positive, or -20% if negative.

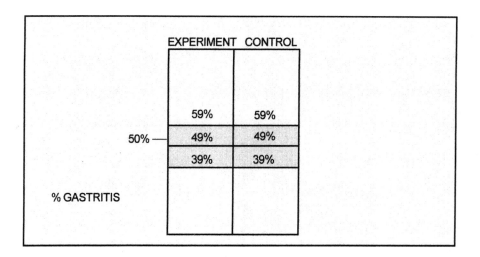

You should be able to see why the situation here is the same as when we're wondering about establishing the existence of no correlation in a population. Here, there can't be good enough evidence that there's no causal relevance of A to B. The best we can do is to estimate the possible causal relevance there might be. In this case, if there is any, it's fairly small.

20.8 Conclusion of the Bacteria/Gastritis Story

Before we leave the story about bacteria and gastritis, I should tell you some of the rest of it, in case you're interested. Experiments using a control group as we have imagined were in fact carried out, and did establish very good evidence that the bacteria Warren observed were a very important causal factor for gastritis. But much more of considerable importance was also discovered. Researchers also discovered a cheap and efficient way of curing gastritis, by using a combination of drugs. Even better, they discovered that these same bacteria also caused the majority of cases of stomach ulcers, which could similarly be cured. It had previously been universally believed that stomach ulcers were the result of acidity in the stomach, caused by stress. The standard treatment for ulcers was medication to reduce stomach acid; this treatment was safe and effective, but it was also expensive, and had to be continued indefinitely, because when the treatment was stopped, the ulcers typically returned. This new research appears to offer a way to cure ulcers cheaply, with only a week's treatment. It's a triumph.

CHAPTER 21

Experimental Procedures

21.1 How to Treat the Experimental and ██████████
Control Groups

We've been concentrating on precautions we must take in selecting the experimental and control groups, but there's something else we have to be careful about: we have to make sure that the experimental and control groups are treated identically, in all possible relevant ways, during the course of the experiment, and that the only difference between the two of them is that one gets the supposed cause and the other doesn't.

Here's an example of how things can go wrong if this care is not taken. Imagine that this is how we run our experiment testing the hypothesis that the bacterium is a positive causal factor for gastritis: we install the experimental group in the North Wing of the hospital, and the control group in the South Wing, for the duration. Both groups will be eating hospital food, but suppose one day the hospital doesn't make enough Polynesian Fruit Punch Fluorescent Blue Jell-O Brand Gelatin Cubes to feed everyone, and only people in the North Wing are lucky enough to get Polynesian Fruit Punch Fluorescent Blue Jell-O Brand Gelatin Cubes for lunch. Now, nobody knows this, but it turns out that eating Polynesian Fruit Punch Fluorescent Blue Jell-O Brand Gelatin Cubes is a positive causal factor for gastritis, and the bacterium we're testing isn't. The result, of course, will be that there will be several cases of gastritis among the experimental group (who ate the Polynesian Fruit Punch Fluorescent Blue Jell-O Brand Gelatin Cubes) and none in the control group (who didn't). We'd conclude that it was the bacteria soup that caused this difference, and we'd be wrong.

Well, it's easy to make sure that both groups get the same food; but it may be difficult to make sure that both groups are treated exactly the same in every possibly relevant way. Again the general problem arises that we have to rely on what we already know: what sorts of difference in treatment might make a difference? These are the ones we have to make sure are not present; but we can never be positive that we've identified all of them.

This problem is inevitable, because it's inevitable that different experimental subjects will be treated differently. For example, even if we do install all the subjects in the same wing of the hospital, it's inevitable that some will get their lunch a little earlier than others, and maybe this makes a difference. The best bet here is to keep the groups mixed up as much as possible. That way, any differences that do occur in the way they're treated will tend to be distributed randomly. For example, even though some get their food earlier than the others, the proportion of early-eaters among the control group won't be likely to be significantly different from the proportion of early-eaters among the experimental group.

One special problem arises because there's one way in which the experimental group must be treated differently from the control group: they have to get the supposed cause. In the case we've been using as an example, one group has to get the bacteria soup and the other one not. Of course, this difference is one that we want; but we want the bacteria ingestion to be the *only* difference. The events surrounding the process of making this difference may also introduce extraneous secondary factors. For example we'll have to get the experimental group to drink some fairly disgusting soup, and this will be an unpleasant experience, and will tend to produce some temporary nausea and disgust. Maybe nausea and disgust have some causal relevance to developing gastritis. Well, maybe it's possible to get around this problem too: concoct some equally disgusting soup without bacteria in it for the people in the control group to drink.

In all, we want to make just everything as similar for the two groups as possible. You can see that this is going to take some thought and ingenuity.

21.2 Special Problems in Experimenting on Humans ▉▉▉▉

It's now standard procedure to inform participants in research involving humans about the full details of the experiments to be undertaken, and to obtain their full and free consent. And it ought to be. * The problem here is that it's well known that the *belief* that you may be getting some treatment that's harmful can actually cause harm; and the *belief* that you may be getting some treatment that's beneficial can actually benefit. So if you tell members of the experimental group what's being done to them, this alone can result in the anticipated effect even if there's no physical effect of the procedure.

How to get around this problem of psychological effects? One way of avoiding them is not to tell anyone what's going on. But this conflicts with the ethical requirement noted above: that fully informed consent be given by every participant.

The solution routinely applied for this problem, in order to make the experimental and control groups as alike as possible, is to tell everyone that *some* of them—those in the experimental group—will be getting the potentially helpful (or harmful) treatment, and the rest of them—those in the control group—won't; and then to keep them in the dark about which group they're in. This will necessitate giving the control group what they think might be the treatment, so that they can't tell that they're in the control group. This kind of testing is called **BLIND TESTING** because the participants are "blind" to whether they're in the control group or the experimental group. Suppose it's a new drug being tested, to be administered as pills. In order to keep everyone blind, the subjects in the experimental group will have to be given something that might be the pill being tested too. So they're given a chemically inert pill—one known to have no physical effect. This kind of imitation-drug is called a **PLACEBO**.

A further factor which may result in a crucial difference between the experimental and control groups may arise even if the subjects are blind, but when those doing the testing, and administering to the subjects, are not. This may make a difference in several ways.

---

* One of the most horrible examples of medical research which violated this rule is the Tuskeege Syphilis Study, in which, from 1932 to 1970, a large number of poor uneducated black males suffering from the later stages of syphilis were examined at regular intervals to determine the course their disease was taking. They were led to believe, falsely, that they were being given proper medical care, and they weren't told that they had not been treated even after the end of the experiment. For details, see "Final Report of the Tuskeege Syphilis study Ad Hoc Advisory Panel," U.S. Public Health Service (Washington D.C., 1973), partly reprinted in S. J. Reiser et al., *Ethics in Medicine* (Cambridge, the MIT Press, 1977).

(1) If the people who come into contact with the experimental subjects know who is in the experimental group and who is in the control group, they may treat them differently. They may, for example, make special enquiries about the health of one group or the other, or treat one group with extra care.

(2) Both groups will be under observation for the effect. If those doing the observation know which subjects are in the experimental group and which are in the control group, this may have subtle effects on what they think they observe. They may tend to look for the effect more carefully at the subjects in the experimental group if they expect the effect there. They may tend to interpret what they see as the effect in the experimental group. (It's well known that observers have a tendency to see what they expect to see.) This is not fraud: it's just unconscious and inevitable psychology.

(3) And, of course, there's always the possibility of conscious fraud too. Sometimes a positive result for an experiment will be extremely important for the experimenters, and they will fudge the data a little. I know you can't possibly believe this could happen, but scientists are humans too.

For these reasons it is necessary to keep those who administer the experiments blind too: not only the people who have contact with the subjects, but also the people who work behind the scenes, preparing the experiment or interpreting the data. Of course, someone has to know which subjects are in which group at the end, in order to figure out what the experiment proved. But this knowledge is to be kept from spreading.

Experiments in which both the subjects and everyone else (except at the final stage of interpretation) are "blind" to which group any particular subject is in are called **DOUBLE BLIND** experiments.

Even when an experiment does not involve human subjects, it's a good idea to have experimenters and others blind.

The problem with using placebos and keeping subjects blind—in fact, the problem with informing them about what's going on in the first place— is that this will make all the subjects in the total subject group somewhat unrepresentative of the general population, if only because they know that something significant may be being done to them. This is a problem that there's no way around.

21.3 Harm to Subjects

In some experiments, there's potential for harm. The experimental group may be exposed to treatment that may prove harmful to them; or the control group may be deprived of a beneficial treatment. Research institutions now routinely have committees to oversee experiments, especially those using human subjects, to watch out for potential danger to subjects.

Sometimes when the anticipated harm is not great or is highly improbable, and proper precautions and warnings are given, the experiments will be permitted, but only on fully-informed volunteers. But who would volunteer to be an experimental subject when this might result in harm? Often subjects are paid, to offset the possible harm (and inconvenience) they will suffer. But when the potential for harm is significant, it's not clear that it's the moral thing to do to pay people to be subjects.

At the beginning of the bacteria/gastritis experiments, when the researchers suspected that the bacteria caused gastritis, but didn't know for sure how to kill those bacteria, it would, of course, be difficult to find people who would volunteer to be subjects, and there would be moral qualms about paying people enough to get them to do it. This may be why Marshall, the associate researcher, volunteered to be the first to ingest the bacteria soup himself.

What this all adds up to is that there are often extra difficulties imposed when experimenting on humans in potentially harmful ways, and sometimes it's just impossible. This, of course, is the main reason why animals (guinea pigs, rats, and so on) are often used in experiments instead of people. We'll discuss in the next section what sorts of problems about the validity of evidence this sort of experiment raises.

21.4 The Rat Alternative: Moral Considerations

Imagine that your laboratory has been assigned the job of testing a new preservative that a company intends to add to Yummie Cheezelike Goodies, to extend its shelf life to ten years. It's feared that this preservative might be a weak positive causal factor for cancer. How could you test it?

Well, given that this preservative might be a positive causal factor for cancer, you won't be allowed to do your testing on human beings. If you've got any moral sense, you wouldn't want to do it anyway. So you decide to do your testing on rats.

It seems pretty clear to most—not all—people that in certain circumstances we're morally allowed to do *some* things to rats which it would be impermissible to do to people. This does not mean that any sort of experimentation on animals is morally okay. There's a good deal of moral controversy about just how we should be allowed to treat animals for the sake of the scientific benefit the experiments would give to humans. Just about nobody thinks that there's absolutely nothing wrong with inflicting harm on animals, but there's some controversy about exactly what is permissible. One consideration here is just how much benefit to humans would result. In the case we're looking at here, the benefit that would result from research that proved this chemical to be harmless to humans would be that the GoodieFood Multinational Megacompany would be able to extend the shelf life of its Yummie Cheezelike Goodies. Some people might feel that this benefit is not, shall we say, earthshakingly huge. Sometimes there are experimental alternatives which don't harm animals, or not as much; but these are more expensive. Many people think that companies should be forced to use these instead.

21.5 The Rat Alternative: Considerations About Evidence

But let's look at some other—non-ethical—considerations involved with experimentation with animals.

Rats are really good for experimental studies, because they have been bred specially for laboratories. You can get a large flock of them, fairly cheaply, with confidence in the fact that they'll be genetically identical and that they've been raised under identical conditions. This is good, because now you're confident that when you divide them into experimental and control groups, there won't be any significant differences in secondary characteristics between these groups.

The first obvious problem with using the results of a rat experiment to predict what will happen to humans is that rats don't react exactly like humans in every way. We're imagining that other tests have shown that rats get cancer from chemicals they have eaten in ways fairly similar to humans. This gives us some confidence that rat experiments will be relevant to humans, though we can't be certain that they'll react to this particular chemical just the way humans would. This inevitably injects some degree of doubt into extension of the experiment's results to humans.

For this reason, tests which show that some substance is harmless to animals are often considered to give some evidence that there won't be harm to humans, but not enough. Once good animal tests give this degree of evidence of harmlessness, we might then be allowed to begin limited tests on humans for better evidence.

21.6 How Much to Feed the Rats?

Now, how much preservative should you feed the rats in the experimental group? Well, one couldn't expect any human to eat more than 10,000 Yummie Cheezelike Goodies in a lifetime. Because each Goodie contains only .1 gram of preservative, that means a maximum lifetime dose of 1000 grams of preservative for a human. Now, your rats have 1/100 the body weight of the average human, so the corresponding dose for them would be 10 grams. That's not much: about a teaspoonfull of pure chemical. You could get them to eat that.

So the idea is to feed the experimental group of rats 10 grams of additive. If they get more cancer than the control group, maybe we've got some information we can use. Of course, it may be just the fact that we're feeding them 10 grams of *something* other than regular rat food that's causing the cancer somehow. So we should, in order to make the control group as similar as possible, feed them 10 grams of some other kind of non rat food which we think is harmless to them.

But there's another problem. The suspicion is that this additive is a weakly positive causal factor for cancer in humans at normal maximum doses (1000 grams). Suppose that it's suspected that this dose would produce an additional 1% of cases of cancer—that is, 1 case per 100 more than the usual number from other causes. If this suspicion is correct, then we'd expect to find that it's a similarly weak positive causal factor—an additional 1%—for cancer in rats at a corresponding dose adjusted for their bodyweight (10 grams).

Okay, now let's do the experiment. Suppose that we give the experimental group of 1000 rats 10 grams of the chemical, and over their lifetime, 41% of them get cancer. The control group of 1000 rats gets no chemical, and over their lifetime, 40% of these rats get cancer. Just as we suspected! An additional 1% of cancer in the experimental group! A sucessful experiment, right? Wrong. Let's look at the graph.

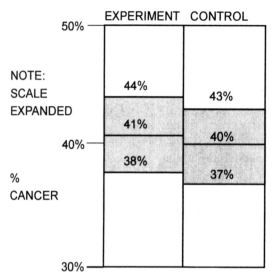

For a sample of 1000, the margin of error is ±.03. Well, unfortunately for us, the margins of error overlap, so we can't claim that the additive is a positive causal factor for cancer, even in rats.

This failure to prove that the additive is a causal factor is the result of the observation of only a small difference in frequencies between the control and experimental group. This is what we'd suspect if the chemical at this dosage is only a weakly positive causal factor.

This is not just a rare accident. In a great number of tests about possible causal factors, the thing being tested will have only a very small causal efficacy, if any. Actually, an additive that results, in fact, in 1% additional cases of cancer has a comparatively large degree of efficacy: in many known cases of positive causal factors for cancer, the degree of efficacy is much smaller. That means that it will show up in a statistically significant way only if the sample size is absolutely enormous: far too big to be practical. Given the normal practical limits on sample size, no small degree of causal efficacy can be proven by experiment.

Well, okay; what can you do about that in your lab? Here's a suggestion. Instead of giving your rats 10 grams of additive, give them 10 times as much: 100 grams. What we assume is that this will be roughly 10 times as causally effective as 10 grams. Now, let's do the experiment again. We find that instead of 1% additional cases of cancer in the experimental group (41% altogether), we get, just as we predicted, 10% additional cases (50% altogether). The graph:

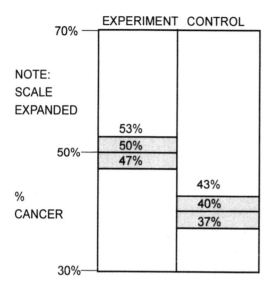

Aha! Statistical significance! We can make the claim that this larger dose is a positive causal factor for cancer in rats. It produces around 10% additional cases of cancer.

Now (on the assumption that rats react like humans) we can extend this finding to humans: a corresponding huge dose of the chemical in humans would produce around 10% additional cases of cancer in humans.

The huge rat dose was 100 grams. This would correspond to 10,000 grams for a human. This would be the amount a human would ingest from eating 100,000 Yummie Cheezelike Goodies. We can predict, then, that a group of humans who ate 100,000 YCGs would get around 10% extra cases of cancer as a result.

But this is a bit absurd. It's physically impossible for anyone to eat that many YCGs. Even if someone tried, she or he would die from Goodie Overdose long before any cancer from the additive had time to develop. Who cares if a massive overdose of this additive is a positive causal factor for cancer? Everything causes cancer if you consume impossibly enormous quantities of it, right?

Well, no, not right. It's not true that everything would cause cancer if you consumed huge quantities of it. The objection is correct in pointing out, however, that we aren't practically concerned with what would happen if someone ate impossibly huge quantities of YCGs, because nobody ever would. We're concerned with the results of eating quantities somebody actually might eat: is eating the additive *in these quantities* a positive causal factor for cancer? Can we conclude anything about that?

Maybe we can. We've concluded that eating 100,000 YCGs would produce about an additional 10% cases of cancer. But the most a real human could eat would be 1/10 that amount: 10,000 YCGs. How many additional cases of cancer would that produce? Well, it seems reasonable to say: 1/10 of 10%: 1% additional (more or less). If this conclusion is justified, then this is useful information, at last.

21.7 The Threshold Effect

What we're assuming here is that if there is a cause-effect relationship between YCGs and cancer, that it's roughly **LINEAR**. That is, that a graph relating quantity of cause (YCGs ingested) on the horizontal axis to effect (additional cases of cancer) on the vertical axis looks something like this:

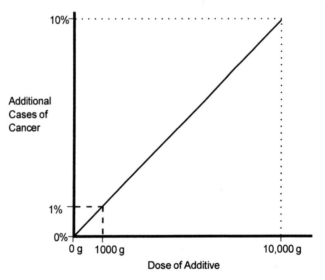

Is this assumption a reliable one? Well, it does open the study to an additional source of doubt. Maybe it's wrong. There are cases in which the usual amount of something has *absolutely* no effect, but a much higher amount does have a big effect. This is what's called the **THRESHOLD EFFECT**. Imagine, for example, that if you eat one cookie, or two cookies, or up to 10 cookies at once, nothing at all happens to your digestive system. But if you eat 11 cookies or more at once, you get a stomachache. The 11th cookie marks the "threshold" of this effect. Experiments on what happens when someone eats 11 or more cookies at once, then, would give us no information at all about what happens when someone eats one cookie.

Maybe this preservative's cancer-causing feature shows this threshold effect: it could be that even though 10,000 grams dosage would cause an additional 30 cases per 1000, 1000 grams would cause no additional cancer cases. It could be that you get no additional cancer until you reach a dose of 5000 grams:

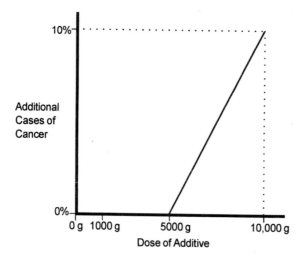

5000 grams here is the threshold. If this is the case, then the conclusion we might be tempted to draw—that a possible dose of 1000 grams causes some additional cancer—is mistaken.

Here's a real example of the threshold effect. It's widely known that consumption of a lot of alcohol by expectant mothers is a strong causal factor for a variety of problems in the fetus—the "fetal-alcohol syndrome". We might reason that if high doses of alcohol carry a high risk of damaging the fetus, then low doses carry a low risk. Even a low risk is unacceptable to some people, and they reason that they ought to stop drinking altogether when pregnant. But according to one study, none of the sixteen problems associated with fetal-alcohol syndrome show up until a pregnant woman starts regularly consuming more than three drinks a day. *

* Reported by Malcolm Gladwell, "The Tipping Point", *The New Yorker* LXXII, No. 14 (June 3, 1966), p. 36-7. Gladwell remarks on his having as a child mused on the threshold effect when trying to encourage ketchup out of a bottle by hitting the bottom; his father summed up this non-linear relation with this couplet:

Tomato Ketchup in a bottle—
None will come and then the lot'll.

21.8 Non-Linearity

A more general possibility is that the effect is related to the cause **NON-LINEARLY**. A fairly common way this can happen is if more cause means more effect at every level, but the relation between the two is not simple. It might be the case that, up to a certain level, increasing the cause a little increases the effect a little, but above that level, a similar small increase in the cause produces a much larger effect.

Here's a picture of how a non-linear connection between cause and effect might look:

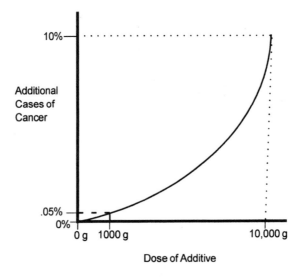

On this picture, you can see that increasing the dose from 0 to 1000 increases the additional cases of cancer a little, but not 1/10 of what 10 times that dose causes. Instead of 1%, on this graph it's much less: .05%.

What we want to know, then, is whether it's reasonable to think that food additives would show a threshold effect, or some sort of non-linear relation to cancer. If a lot of a substance causes a lot of incidents of cancer, can we conclude that a little of it causes a few incidents of cancer? You can see why this question is difficult to answer. It's not easy to get good evidence for the claim that something has a small effect. Some cancer-causing agents do show the threshold effect. Some have a non-linear relation to effect.

21.9 Risk

But suppose that a suspected cancer-causing agent does result in a substantial increase in cancer when administered in very large doses. Suppose in addition that we have reason to think that the effects of this agent are linear. We can conclude, then, that the ordinary small dose of that agent—of the size that people are likely to run into in everyday life—will have some cancer-causing effect.

This is not, however, necessarily a cause for alarm. It depends on how much effect that agent does have in ordinary doses. If, for example, it's likely that an ordinary dose of that agent might cause one additional case of cancer in ten million people, we are probably rational to ignore that information. It wouldn't make sense for someone to go out of his or her way to avoid exposure to that chemical. An extremely small risk can rationally be ignored. Suppose, for example, that you just love YCGs, and that your life would be significantly poorer if you stopped eating them. The really tiny risk to you of cancer would not make it worthwhile for you to stop.

The moral here is that we don't, can't, and shouldn't try to avoid *all* risk. After all, you incur some risk of death or injury every time you cross the street, but that doesn't mean that you should never cross a street again. The risk is very small, and the benefit of crossing streets is substantial. It's worth it.

Experimental studies that show a significant bad effect from an outlandishly high dose or frequency of some suspected agent are used when the ordinary quantity of cause produces tiny or rare effects. You always have to ask yourself, when the results of these tests are given, whether this tiny or rare effect is so tiny or rare that it should be ignored.

Sometimes statistics about danger to health are given in a way that makes them unduly alarming. Suppose that it's discovered that eating one kumquat a month would increase your risk of cancer of the toenail—a very rare cancer—from one in ten million to one in a million. If you're a kumquat lover, a headline announcing that eating a kumquat a month would make it TEN TIMES LIKELIER that you get cancer of the toenail would scare the hell out of you. Perhaps then you'd swear off your favourite fruit forever.

EXERCISE
Explain why this is not rational behaviour, and why the newspaper headline says what's true, but is unduly alarmist.

ANSWER
The risk of cancer of the toenail is multiplied by ten; but even ten times the normal risk is so tiny that if you love kumquats that much you can ignore it altogether.

21.10 A Real Example

In 1977, women who dye their hair were alarmed by an announcement from a researcher that there's a good chance that the chemicals in hair dye caused cancer. This researcher based his warning on the following reasoning: many of the chemicals in hair dye weren't tested on humans, but some of them were in the same chemical family as known cancer-causing agents. When several chemicals in hair dye were applied in very large doses to laboratory animals, there was a significant increase in cancer in these animals.

In 1996, however, a radio science program decided to check back with this researcher to find out if there had been any developments in this story. * The researcher said that he was mistaken back then to issue the warning. He said that it had later become clear to him that very many substances administered in huge doses cause cancer: about one-half of the substances tested in huge doses in laboratories show this result. Later studies of other sorts on hair dye showed that the risk of cancer from using hair dye is in fact so tiny that it ought to be ignored. In the next chapter, we'll take a look at the form these other tests took.

---

* "Quirks and Quarks", CBC Radio, May 1996.

CHAPTER 22

Non-Experimental Methods

22.1 When You Can't Experiment ████████

We've seen how experimental procedures can give reliable information about causes which is not provided merely by correlations. But experiments can't always be done. Why not?

Here are some examples of questions scientists might have about causes, when experiments are out of the question.

A. What causes dormant volcanoes to erupt? Suppose that geologists observe that most of the dormant volcanoes that erupt are in areas where there tend to be frequent earthquakes: there's a positive correlation between eruption of dormant volcanoes and earthquakes. Is this just a coincidence? Are the earthquakes a positive causal factor for the eruptions? Are the eruptions a positive causal factor for the earthquakes? Are they both positive causal factors for each other? Are they both caused jointly by something else?

EXERCISE
Imagine an experiment to test these hypotheses.

ANSWER
Choose 1000 locations on the Earth, at random. Divide these at random into 500 experimental sites and 500 control sites. At each of the 500 experimental sites, make some dormant volcanoes erupt. Observe to see whether there are a higher proportion of earthquakes at these sites than at the control sites. If the proportion is the same, then we've ruled out the hypothesis that

> eruptions cause earthquakes. If there is a higher proportion, then we've ruled out the other hypotheses, and we can conclude that eruptions cause earthquakes.

Well, of course, this is silly. We have no way of making dormant volcanoes erupt. Nor could we cause earthquakes, to see if this increases the incidence of eruptions.

B. The spotted Albanian anteater is a seriously endangered species: there are only 10 of them known to exist. What's the cause of this species dying out? Obviously, again, experimentation on the spotted Albanian anteater is out of the question. There aren't enough of them to conduct experiments on—we couldn't get statistically significant results. Anyway, suppose you want to test the hypothesis that their young are being eaten by the striped Albanian jackal. To test this, you'd presumably have to put some of their young in the same enclosure as some striped Albanian jackals, to see what happened. But the success of this experiment would mean that there are even fewer spotted Albanian anteaters left in the world. Don't do it!

C. There's a strong correlation between development problems in infants and their being fed on an exclusive diet of Yummie Cheezelike Goodies. It's not likely that the fact that an infant is suffering development problems causes their eating only YCGs. Are the Goodies causing the development problems? Maybe; but maybe there's a joint cause: any parents who are giving this as an exclusive diet to their infants might also be mistreating them in any number of other potentially harmful ways. Okay: feed an experimental group of infants exclusively on YCGs, and compare what happens to a control group who get a normal diet.

You don't really want to attempt this vicious experiment on a bunch of innocent infants, do you? Even if you did, there are Ethics Panels at most scientific institutions that need to approve any experiment involving humans, and they (fortunately) wouldn't let you do it. And even if they did, you'd never get parents to volunteer their children to be in this experiment. And even if you did, they'd likely be a rather unfair sample of the population, since they wouldn't mind your interfering with their children's diets in this horrible way.

D. What caused the dinosaurs to become extinct? The problem with doing experiments on dinosaurs at the moment is obvious.

E. (REAL CASE) You may recall the preliminary study (mentioned in Chapter 8) designed to test the hypothesis that car accidents cause neck pains and headaches. A classical experimental test of this hypothesis would take a group of experimental subjects and subject a randomly-selected portion of them to car accidents; then see if they develop more neck pains and head-aches than the rest of the group—the control group. Yeah, well, good luck on getting people to volunteer to be experimental subjects.

F. (REAL CASE) It's fairly well-known that there's a positive correlation between snoring and obesity. However, as we noticed in Chapter 19, this correlation is consistent with a number of different causal hypotheses, two of which are:

(a) obesity is a positive causal factor for snoring;
(b) snoring is a positive causal factor for obesity.

Just one of (a) and (b) might be true, or both, or neither (if snoring and obesity have a joint cause). An experiment to test (a) would make people in a randomly selected experimental group get fat, and then observe whether they snore more as a result. We know how to make people fat (for example, by feeding them a lot of those Yummie Cheezelike Goodies we've got left over from that other experiment); but this is not a practical research program, for obvious reasons. An experiment to test (b) would make the randomly se-lected group snore, and see if they gain weight; but since the causes of snor-ing are not very well known, it's hard to see how this could be accomplished. But a study did find out reliable information about the causal structure here. Can you imagine how they did it? I'll tell you a little later.

G. What's causing so many of the Airbarge airplanes to crash? Perhaps it's that the particular wing design makes the plane unstable when flying through high winds. But we wouldn't want to fly a lot of these through high winds, in case we produce a lot of crashes this way.

22.2 Experiments Using Modeling

I'm sure that in at least some of these examples, alternatives to the experiments which are ruled out have occurred to you.

Sometimes other sorts of experiments can give indirect evidence. The procedure we imagined earlier for testing the potential carcinogenic effects of YCGs might be applied to case C, above, using rats or some other animal. In case B, it happens that there's another animal, the mottled Transylvanian anteater, that's very closely related to the spotted Albanian anteater, but which is not endangered. In fact, there are too many of the damned mottled Transylvanian anteaters, and the Transylvanians are trying to get rid of them. We could see whether those jackals would eat some mottled Transylvanian anteater young. If the jackals won't touch them, and if they're a great deal like their Albanian cousins, then we have some reason to rule out this causal hypothesis.

What we're doing in these cases is to experiment on something other than what we're directly interested in, and we take this something else to be a **MODEL** of what's of direct concern. What happens to rats fed YCGs is taken to model what happens in humans. The word 'model' here isn't used in its most literal sense: the model isn't usually a scale model we build, like a model airplane. In some cases, a literal scale model might be used, however. In case G, for example, we might use a suitable model Airbarge in wind-tunnel experiments; if these little models crash, it's no big loss. In case E, some information about what happens to people in car crashes might be gained by using models—crash-test dummies. While this information might be helpful, it can't answer all our questions. For one thing, while carefully designed dummies might suffer physical head and neck damage in a similar way to humans, dummies can't feel neck pain or headaches. So our questions can't be answered directly. In case A, we might consider building some huge models of the terrain out of concrete, and trying out various procedures on these models; but it would clearly be very hard to build a model that could be expected to perform the way the real thing does. Computer "modeling" perhaps offers a better possibility. Perhaps we know enough about the dynamics underground to produce some equations relating some phenomena to others; and maybe we can use these equations in a computer program in which we change variables in several ways and see what results. Computer "modeling" might be helpful with some of the other questions too. But maybe not enough is known about the mechanisms involved to give us a reliable model; anyway, as we've noticed, this sort of indirect experiment introduces doubts about the conclusion.

22.3 The Observational Alternative to Experimentation

Sometimes there's just no way that experiments using modeling can give us very good information. There is a way, however, in which a kind of non-experimental observation can sometimes give us some reason to believe causal hypotheses.

Consider this real-life example. For a long time, it was known that there was a positive correlation between smoking and heart disease. Even though people suspected that the explanation for this was that smoking was a positive causal factor for heart disease, you should remember from earlier discussions about smoking and cancer that a correlation doesn't prove anything about causal connections. Experiments on humans couldn't be done to investigate the causal connections directly, for several reasons. For one thing, it would be hard to get an experimental group that you make smoke cigarettes. People who already smoked would of course be willing to be in this experimental group, but non-smokers would be reluctant to start smoking. For another, researchers who suspected that smoking really was a positive causal factor for heart disease were understandably reluctant to induce large experimental groups to take up the habit. Modeling experiments using rats didn't work very well. Rats can't be trained to smoke cigarettes (not even by getting them to watch Humphrey Bogart and Lauren Bacall movies to show them how cool smoking is). You could fill their cages with cigarette smoke instead, but this would reduce the value of the model: smoke in the air is somewhat different from smoke directly puffed out of a cigarette. But the main problem was that a positive causal factor with a comparatively low degree of causal efficacy, which smoking is, won't show up in samples of practical size. It proved impossible to give rats really large doses of cigarette smoke in the air. This is the problem that we talked about in the YCG/rats case in Chapter 21.

Here's the way this problem was solved. The study that finally did establish the causal connection was not an experimental study at all, but rather a careful and extensive set of observations of samples. You might wonder how this could be. Observations of a sample, no matter how large the sample is, and no matter how careful the observation, can only give evidence for cor-relations. How in this case it gave evidence for a causal connection needs some explanation.

In order to see how this can work, let's simplify matters somewhat. Let's suppose that there are only two plausible causal hypotheses which could account for the well-known positive correlation between smoking and heart disease:

- Smoking is a positive causal factor for heart disease.
- Smoking and heart disease are both caused by a third factor.

The second hypothesis may seem implausible to you, but in fact it was not completely implausible at the time. Some people take up smoking, and some don't. It's not unlikely that there's something about the ones who do (other than merely their environment and personality) that is a positive causal factor for this. Maybe, for instance, there's a certain genetic factor that makes them more prone to become smokers. We already know that cer-tain genetic types are more prone to get certain kinds of heart disease. So maybe there's a certain genetic type that is the joint cause of both.

Here's another way the second hypothesis might be true: (1) imagine that city people tend to smoke more than country people, just as a cultural matter. So living in the city is a positive causal factor for smoking. (2) Cit-ies of course provide an environment different in many ways from the coun-try. Imagine that some environmental factor of city life—for example, the higher stress level, or the different diet, or the air pollution from car exhaust, is a positive causal factor for heart disease. So putting (1) and (2) together means that living in the city is a joint cause of both smoking and heart dis-ease.

Here's still another way. Poor people tend to smoke more than rich ones. Poor people also live in more crowded conditions, have poorer diets, and so on. Maybe something here is actually the positive causal factor for heart dis-ease. Then poverty could be a joint cause of both smoking and heart disease.

Another: men smoke more than women. Men also are more prone to heart disease. Maybe being male is somehow a cause both of smoking and of heart disease, and explains the correlation.

What we've been doing here is hypothesis creation. We've been spelling out the second hypothesis:

- Smoking and heart disease are both caused by a third factor in greater particularity, by hypothesizing about what this third factor might be.

So far, we just have a partial list of hypotheses about this third factor. It's easy to see how we might add some more possible third-factor hypotheses; but what we're interested in is getting a list of *all plausible* possibilities for this third factor. Obviously, this is going to take a great deal of thought and research. What sorts of other features might be associated with smoking, and causally connected to it in various ways? We've thought of a few (genetic makeup; living in the city, lower economic status). What others could there be? Is it at all plausible that these might also have a causal connection to heart disease?

Suppose we now have a satisfactory list; we're reasonably confident that we've added all possible third factors which have any plausibility.

Now we can begin our observations. We need an enormous sample of the population, and we need to collect an enormous amount of information about each member of this sample, including, of course, whether each of the people in the sample gets heart disease. Note that this may mean keeping track of them for a long period, to see if heart disease develops. What we're interested in doing is ruling out each of our third-factor hypotheses. Let's look at one of these and see how the information about correlations in our enormous sample might serve to rule it out.

One of our hypotheses was that living in the city was a positive causal factor for both smoking and heart disease. Now let's look at the enormous pile of data on the sampled individuals. Divide the individuals into two piles: those that live in the city, and those that live in the country. Now we have to make sure that these two piles match reasonably well with respect to all the other relevant secondary characteristics *and with regard to amount smoked.* In order to match these two groups, we may have to discard data from a large number of individuals. When we've created these two groups, they will have identical proportions of each possible secondary factor we can think of, and will differ only with regard to where they live. If these groups are pretty close with regard to the proportions of heart disease, then this will show that the causal efficacy associated with city/country location is small or none—not enough to account for the substantial positive correlation of smoking and heart disease.

Next, the individuals need to be divided into two (or more) groups based on level of income; again, these groups are matched with regard to the other characteristics including amount smoked; and again this factor can be ruled out if the proportions of heart disease are fairly close.

This process must be gone through to rule out all the other hypotheses. If, at the end of all this, we're left with no hypotheses except that smoking is the cause, we're entitled to claim that this is the right one.

This is a real-life, not a hypothetical example. The study I'm referring to is called the Framingham Study, sponsored by the National Institutes of Health in the U.S. The study chose over 5000 people from Framingham, Massachusetts, gathered all sorts of data about them (to divide them into groups on the basis of possible third causes) and kept track of the health of their hearts for 24 years. This famous study produced highly reliable results: smoking is in fact a significant positive causal factor for heart disease. *

22.4 The Snoring/Obesity Study

You may remember the discussion in Chapter 18 of the causal hypotheses to explain the positive correlation between snoring and obesity. I mentioned there that a study has been done to try to confirm the real causal story here. I'll quote a newspaper article reporting it: **

> NEW ORLEANS—Zzzzzzknx. Sknrf. Zzzzzzknx.
> That could be the sound of a kilogram or so gathering around your waist.
> Older men who snore gain more weight than silent sleepers, a study has found.
> Many people who snore also stop breathing for a few seconds, a condition called sleep apnea. The lack of breath wakes the sleeper—often so briefly he does not realise it—and can leave him feeling sleepy during the day.
> Previous research has indicated that obesity can contribute to sleep apnea; one possible explanation is that the sleeper's fat pushed down on the airway, interfering with breathing.

---

* You can read the details of this study in *The Framingham Study : an epidemiological investigation of cardiovascular disease*. Bethesda, MD: U.S. Dept. of Health and Human Services, 1968- (RC667 F813).

** Excerpted from the [Toronto] *Globe and Mail*, May 15, 1996, p. A8.

The new research indicates that sleep apnea may also cause weight gain, said Dr. J. W. Weiss, lead author of a study presented yesterday at a meeting of the American Thoracic Society and the American Lung Association.

Dr. Weiss theorized that apnea sufferers are too tired to want to do much, and start putting on the weight.

"It makes us rethink the way we look at obesity and sleep apnea," said Dr. Normal Edelman, the ALA's consultant for medical affairs and a professor of medicine at the State University of New York at Stonybrook.

Sleep apnea affects 4 to 5 per cent of adult men. For some reason, men appear twice as likely as women to develop the disorder.

The research involved 508 veterans taking part in a long-running Veterans Administration study on aging. They ranged in age from 47 to 90 at the start of the research on snoring and obesity.

In the early 1990s, Dr. Weiss and three other Boston-area doctors added questions about sleep. The questions were asked whenever a participant visited his doctor. Participants were weighed then, and again three years later.

After taking into account the veterans' ages and initial weight, the researchers found that after three years the snorers gained a kilogram or two more on average than the quiet sleepers.

Other questions indicated that the symptoms of sleep apnea dated back many years for many of the men. "If you can extrapolate back, it's likely that the cumulative weight over time may well be substantial...."

Sleep apnea is not the only cause of sleepiness, and many things can contribute to weight gain. However, since many of the people in the study were retired, work schedules and second jobs were not causing the sleep problems, Dr. Weiss said.

Dr. Edelman said the study suggests that weight gain and sleep apnea increase each other: "The whole thing kind of feeds on itself in a loop."

We haven't been given all the details of this study in this short newspaper article; to be fair in criticising the study, we should really look at the account of the study written by the scientists involved. But never mind. What the hell: let's just think about it on the basis of the details we're given in this article.

It was apparently already accepted among scientists that there were positive correlations between snoring and obesity, and between snoring and sleep apnea; and that one causal connection involved was that obesity was a positive causal factor for snoring and for sleep apnea. What this study wants to establish is that sleep apnea is a positive causal factor for obesity (thus setting up the positive feedback loop). Do the observations, as described, make this causal connection likely?

Here's what was (apparently) done. A large number of veterans were observed over several years. The ones who snored gained a significant amount more weight than the ones who didn't.

EXERCISE

The question we should ask is whether the causal hypothesis under investigation—that sleep apnea causes obesity—is the only plausible one to account for this observation. Remember that it's already established that obesity causes sleep apnea. Could this alone, without the addition of the hypothesis under investigation, account for the observation?

ANSWER

It could. Suppose that obesity causes snoring and sleep apnea, but that sleep apnea does not cause weight-gain. Now, this study first identifies those veterans who snore and those who don't. Presumably, some significant number of the snorers do so because they are overweight. What's causing them to be overweight? Well, it's not necessary to speculate on this, but whatever it is, it's reasonable to think that these causes are still there during the study period, and the overweight people will continue to add weight. Thus we can predict that the snorers— who are more likely to be overweight— will gain more weight than the non-snorers during the period of the study.

What this reasoning shows is that it's plausible to think that the observations in this study could be accounted for by what's already known, without having to assume the causal hypothesis under investigation. Thus, the observations (at least, as described in this article) do not support the hypothesis under investigation.

22.5 The Cost of Teen Mothers ████████

Here's a real-life example that illustrates a number of things recently discussed. Note that in this case scientists gave up when faced with the difficulty of identifying all the possible third factors, and instead produced an ingenious way of automatically matching two groups that differed only with respect to the hypothesized cause.

> It's standing room only for those waiting to denounce teen childbearing.... At every turn, liberals vie with conservatives in condemning teen childbearing as the source of social ills. And they would have us believe that irrefutable scientific evidence points to enormous social costs of childbearing by teenage mothers....
>
> The question policy-makers and social scientists need to answer is whether social problems would be alleviated if the women who become teen mothers postponed childbearing. This is difficult to investigate scientifically. The same women cannot have their first births twice, nor can we do a true controlled experiment. Instead, analysts must try to approximate an experimental approach by comparing teen mothers with older mothers who otherwise resemble them in every possible respect. But we know that those who will become teen mothers differ from the larger population in countless and consequential ways. For example, teen mothers are far more likely to have grown up in extremely impoverished circumstances and to have experienced failure in school. To assess the effects on social problems of teen motherhood per se, we must consider whether an already disadvantaged group is further disadvantaged by early motherhood, or any conclusions we draw are apt to be misleadingly dire.
>
> The Robin Hood Foundation commissioned a number of studies of the social problems hypothesized to be caused by teenage childbearing. The methodologically strongest study explores the effect of teen childbearing on long-term economic outcomes, including recourse to welfare. In it University of Chicago economist Joe Hotz compares teen mothers with teens who miscarried and then went on to have their first birth when they were older. Since the second group would have become teen mothers if not for the accident of miscarriage, they can be thought of as comparable to the teen mothers in important ways. The authors conclude that over their adult

lives, teen mothers are no more likely to participate in welfare programs or to suffer seriously reduced earnings then if they had post-
poned childbearing. *

In a sense, this observational method uses random selection of the two
groups. By comparing teen mothers with teenagers who would have become
teen mothers if it weren't for the miscarriage, they believe they have groups
which automatically match for all relevant third factors. When they discovered no difference between the two groups in economic prospects, they concluded that being a teen mother has no significant causal influence on
economic prospects. Note that even with this ingenious solution to their
problem, the investigators weren't freed from the necessity of identifying
possible third factors. They had to have some idea of what they were, so they
could be sure that having a miscarriage wasn't causally connected to any of
them.

22.6 Comparing the Two Methods

In general, the "observational" method should be used only when the experimental method is not available. One disadvantage of the "observational"
method is obvious: it is a much more labourious process. Huge groups of
subjects are necessary, especially when the causal efficacy under investigation turns out to be small. A labourious process of matching sample groups
is necessary; this means either that it will be difficult to find subjects with the
"right" characteristics, or that data will have to be discarded to get groups to
match.

The main problem with the observational method is, however, that it relies on your having identified and ruled out all the other possible causes of
the effect in question; and thus, it requires that you identify them in advance.
So it always runs the risk that there's another cause of the effect which you
haven't checked for. It relies, in other words, on your having thought of all
the possible other causal factors; and, of course, there's always some doubt
that you've left some out.

You should understand why the experimental method doesn't run this
risk. In a sense, it automatically rules out other variables, without your having to think about them.

---

* "Mothers of Invention" by Arline T. Geronimus, in *The Nation* Vol 263 No. 5, August
12/19, 1996, p. 6.

22.7 Prospective and Retrospective Designs

The observational studies attempting to confirm causal hypotheses which we have looked at have worked this way. First, they find a large bunch of subjects (usually people) to be the group observed. Within this group, they distinguish those that have the supposed cause from those that don't. (These groups must be carefully matched for other possibly causally relevant variables.) Then both groups are followed around for a sufficient length of time for the presumed cause to produce the effect. If the group with the supposed cause shows significantly more of the effect than the group without it, then the causal hypothesis can be thought of as confirmed.

This kind of study is called **PROSPECTIVE** because after identifying the two groups, it looks forward, into the future, to see whether there's a difference in effect. The contrast here is with a sort of study called **RETROSPECTIVE**, which looks backward, into the past. A retrospective study identifies the two groups by sorting them into those who show the *effect* and those that don't. (The groups should be otherwise matched, as before.) Now the investigators look into the *pasts* of the two groups, to see whether the ones with the suspected effect had more of the suspected cause, in the past.

As we've noticed, observational tests of causal hypotheses look for correlations between C, the supposed cause, and E, the supposed effect. The prospective test hopes to find that the percentage of E among Cs is greater than the percentage of Es among the non-Cs. The retrospective test hopes to find that the percentage of Cs among Es is greater than the percentage of Cs among non-Es.

You may recall that either of these discoveries is sufficient to show a positive correlation between C and E. It's necessarily the case that whenever one of these facts holds, the other will also. One can show then that C and E are correlated by doing either a prospective or retrospective test. (Bear in mind, however, that a positive correlation between C and E doesn't alone show that C is a positive causal factor for E. It's the careful matching of the two observed groups that rules out other causal hypotheses and allows us to be justified in concluding from the correlation that there is a causal connection between C and E.)

▆ 22.8 Two Ways of Doing a Prospective Study

Often it takes a while for effects to show up. So often in prospective studies, the first step is to find a group of individuals who have the (supposed) cause, and those who don't, before any of them show the effect; the next step is to keep track of them for the time it's thought it would take for the effects to appear. So, for example, in the Framingham study, two groups, smokers and non-smokers, both free of heart disease, were identified, and they were all kept track of, with health checks every two years, for twenty years.

The way I've defined a 'prospective study' above, it merely involves the comparison of the percentage of supposed effects in groups with and without the suspected cause. So this need not take twenty years at all: you might accomplish it in a much shorter time by finding a group of people who have already been smoking for years and a group who haven't been smoking, and then examine the two for signs of heart disease.

The first way of performing this study—in "**REAL TIME**"—has its problems. When it's suspected that the cause can take a long time to produce the effect, the study takes a long time to complete. If it's on a group of people, it can be expected that it will be difficult to find people who'd be willing to commit themselves, in advance, to a study that will take that length of time. And, of course, over that length of time, you'll lose track of some proportion of the people in the study when they move away, or just get tired of participating. It's a costly and difficult way to do a prospective study.

But nevertheless, this sort of "real time" prospective study gives more confidence in its findings than the second sort, which we can call an "**AFTER-THE-FACT**" prospective study. The reason why "after-the-fact" prospective studies can't be counted on to provide as good evidence is that if you choose groups with and without the cause only after the effects have shown up, it's not so likely that these groups will be representative of the population as a whole. You can see why this is the case by considering prospective studies involving smoking and heart disease. Consider the second sort of prospective study, where we identify the groups as having smoked, or not smoked, over the past twenty years. Suppose that smoking really is a positive causal factor for heart disease. In that case, some smokers over the past twenty years will have gotten heart disease, and will have died or gone into the hospital, or be otherwise unavailable for the study. This will make it likely that the group of smokers you do get for the study will contain less heart disease than the real population of smokers. Another reason why this method may produce an unrepresentative sample is that some of the smokers in the study will already have heart disease, or think they do or might. This fact might make them feel guilty about their smoking, with the result that they would unconsciously underestimate the amount they smoked in the past.

You can see that it's more likely to produce a representative group of smokers and non-smokers if you start with healthy people in both and then keep track of them for years to see what happens.

22.9 Comparing Prospective and Retrospective Studies

A retrospective study would choose, for its two groups, a bunch of people with heart disease and a matched bunch without heart disease. It would compare these two groups with regard to the percentage of smokers in each.

In this sort of study, just like the "after-the-fact" prospective study, the whole study takes place after effects have shown up.

In an after-the-fact prospective smoking/heart disease study, you would find two groups (those who have smoked and those who haven't) and compare the percentage of heart disease. In a retrospective smoking/heart disease study, you find two groups (those who have heart disease and those who don't) and compare the percentage of people who have smoked in each.

We saw some reasons why a real-time prospective study is more likely to provide good evidence than an after-the-fact prospective study. For the same reasons, a retrospective study often produces less confidence in its results.

Now read over the account in the previous section of why, in the example of the smoking/heart disease studies, a real time prospective study was probably better than an after-the-fact prospective study. Also, see why these reasons apply as well to a retrospective study.

EXERCISE

Here are two hypotheses:

A. Watching a lot of violent TV shows while a teenager is a positive causal factor for criminal behaviour when people reach their twenties.

B. A period of substantial immigration into a region is a positive causal factor for a period, a few years later, of higher than usual unemployment there.

For each of these hypotheses, answer the following questions:

1. Imagine an experimental test of this hypothesis. Why is this out of the question?

2. Describe "observational" tests of this hypothesis of all three kinds: (a) Real-time prospective test (b) After-the-fact prospective test (c) Retrospective test.

3. Is the real-time prospective test likely to give better evidence than the other two sorts?

ANSWERS

A1. To do an experimental test of this hypothesis you would get a large number of teenagers to participate, and divide them into experimental and control groups. Then you would make the experimental group watch a lot of violent TV shows, and restrict the violent TV-watching of the control group. It's doubtful that you could manage to do this.

A2. (a) Identify a number of teenagers who now watch a lot of violent TV, and a number who don't, but none of whom are currently involved in criminal activity. Years later, when all have reached 30, check the criminal records of both groups to find out if the violent TV-watchers have more incidents of criminal records the rest.

(b) Identify a number of 30 year-olds who, when teenagers, watched a lot of violent TV, and a number who didn't, but were as closely matched as possible then in criminal record and other respects. See if the incidence of criminal record now is higher among the TV watchers.

(c) Identify a number of 30-year-olds who now have criminal records, and a number who don't, but are as closely matched as possible in other respects. Check to see if the former group used to watch more violent TV than the latter when teenagers.

A3. The causes of crime are notoriously difficult to pin down, and it would be difficult to figure out what respects one had to match these groups in. It would also be difficult to match the TV watchers with the non-watchers, or the ones with criminal records with the ones without, because (one would guess) they would tend to differ in all sorts of other relevant respects. In any case, (a) seems like a somewhat better study than (b) or (c), because by the time the supposed effect has shown up, the ones with criminal records might be unavailable for study (because in jail) or unwilling to participate in your study; or might, for various reasons, over- or underestimate their TV time when teenagers. There's really no way we can do a really good study of this hypothesis. That's why, when people go around claiming that TV watching has this or that bad consequence, they're whistling through their hats.

B1. To do an experimental test of this hypothesis you would choose several regions (matched in relevant respects) and divide them into experimental and control groups. Then you would make a lot of immigrants arrive in the experimental regions, and restrict immigration in the control regions. Well, no: you couldn't do this unless you had the power of a government, and then there'd be obvious reasons why you wouldn't want to do this, just for the sake of experiment.

B2.(a) Identify a number of regions that now have a high level of immigration and a low level of immigration, but are as closely matched as possible in current unemployment levels and in other respects. A few years later, check these regions to find out if the high immigration regions have a higher level of unemployment than the rest.

(b) Identify a number of regions that a few years ago had a high level of immigration and a low level of immigration, but were as closely matched as possible then in unemployment levels and in other respects. Check these regions to find out if the high immigration regions have a higher level of unemployment than the rest.

(c) Identify a number of regions that now have a high level of unemployment and a low level of unemployment, but are as closely matched as possible in other respects. Check these regions to find out if the high unemployment regions had a higher level of immigration a few years ago than the rest.

B3. Maybe none of these tests would provide a really good test for the hypothesis, because it's very hard to do the matching, to rule out other factors. But anyway, it doesn't seem that (a) would be significantly better than (b) or (c).

One of the morals of this exercise is that just about everything here is very doubtful science. When you can't experiment, it's often difficult or impossible to establish evidence for or against causal hypotheses.

22.10 Hair Dye and Cancer, Revisited

You'll recall the real-life example which was mentioned in the last chapter, involving the researcher who terrified many hair dye users in 1977 with the warning that experimental tests had shown that some of the ingredients in hair dye were likely cancer-causing.

When he was interviewed again in 1996, he reported that a very large-scale prospective test on hair dye use was carried on after that, following around an astounding 99,000 women for over a decade. You can see that even a tiny causal effectiveness would show up from a careful prospective test with this many subjects. He reported that this test showed that there's nothing to worry about: using hair dye carries no risk that anyone should worry about. So you can breathe easier, and continue to colour your hair that attractive shade of fluorescent orange.

What's interesting about this case for our purposes is that, despite the costs and doubts which observational tests inevitably bring with them, in this case the results were much firmer and more reliable than the original experimental test.

CHAPTER 23

The
Truth

23.1 Mrs. Smith Again ████████

We've come a long way from Mrs. Smith's advice to scientific tiny tots. Let's summarize the areas in which we've gone beyond her naïve empiricist view of science.

Mrs. Smith's idea of scientific knowledge was a vast and somewhat random collection of individual observations: a stamp collection. We've seen several ways in which this is an inadequate view.

Merely walking around with your eyes open is not the way to go. Science always needs some guidance about where to look. Scientists almost never merely look around at random: they start with questions. And what counts as a question worth investigating is a matter which can be decided on the basis of what we already know, and what we want to know, and what's of value to know.

Science is more concerned with general facts about groups of things, than with particular facts about particular single items. General facts are not obtained merely by pasting together a large number of individual observations. We saw in our discussion of the inductive procedures for confirming statements about proportions and correlations in populations that in the usual case, it is impossible to observe the relevant characteristics of everything in the group we're interested in. We have to make do with observation of only a sample. The right way to collect a sample, and the right sort of reasoning from what's observed in this sample to what we're justified in saying about the whole group, are important here. Of course, individual observations are vital, but they're not all there is to the story. Observations are not merely gotten by a sort of walking-around-with-your-eyes-open and piling them up.

There are systematic ways that we must go about seeking the relevant sorts of observations, and systematic rules we must observe in using the information gotten from observation to reach our general conclusions.

An important consideration in reasoning from a sample to a general conclusion is how much evidence is good enough. The use to which a generalisation is to be put will be relevant to how strong the evidence must be; so a scientist must not ignore practicalities. It makes no sense merely to advise a scientist to seek the truth; what we want to know is how close to the truth we need to get, and with what level of confidence. This is one place where values come into science: a value-free Smithian scientist wouldn't be able to begin to answer these questions.

But generalisations aren't all we're interested in. Only some generalisations are laws; and these are the ones science is interested in finding out. We need to be able to distinguish laws from mere generalisations, and to look for the former.

Laws are relevant to science because they figure in explanations. Finding an explanation is hardly something you can do merely by keeping your eyes open. We noticed that a vital step in explaining was the creation of a list of hypotheses in advance of observation. The place of imagination and creativity—even of prejudice and preconception—in the formation of hypotheses was emphasized. Again we saw that a scientist would get nowhere if she or he started with an empty mind and just looked. But imagination and creativity are not all there is. A great deal of prior knowledge and experience is necessary in order that someone can create a good hypothesis list, and make a good judgment at the start about which hypotheses are plausible enough to warrant investigation.

In order to produce good explanations, we need to use the right set of categories. A good set of categories is the one that creates the sort of science we want, that explains the phenomena in which we're interested, and that deals with the areas we think are morally relevant. This is a further point at which the naïve empiricist view is inadequate.

The use of experimental method also shows the incompleteness of Smithian science. What *causes* something is not a bit of knowledge you can get merely by walking around at random, with your eyes open, scooping up facts. Very often we can find this out only by interacting with the world, by making things happen in a carefully arranged experiment.

An important non-Smithian characteristic of science which came up everywhere was its cumulative nature. We found that in order to find out something new, you already had to know something. Indirect observation, using instruments, always involves interpretation of what the instruments tell you; so we already have to know what the instrument readings have to do with the reality they indirectly reveal, and we already have to believe that they're reliable indicators of what reality is like. Reasoning from observations of a sample to generalisations about proportions or correlations in a population involved subsidiary beliefs about whether or not the sample was random, or about the relevance of secondary characteristics to be used in matching samples to the population. Testing hypotheses while searching for an explanation characteristically involves having prior beliefs about what we would observe, under certain conditions, if a hypothesis were true.

23.2 Science and Truth

All these considerations have a common theme: that real science can be undertaken only when you start from a position quite different from the empty-mindedness Mrs. Smith urged on us. A scientist must come to the process with a whole lot of mental baggage, including values, ideas about proper method, and a great deal of prior knowledge about what others already claim to have discovered.

Mrs. Smith was well aware of the dangers posed by having this mental baggage. Values can distort findings, and can lead to our believing falsehoods. Using traditionally accepted methods can lead us astray. Conventional scientific wisdom can turn out wrong. That's why she thought that the search for truth must discard all of this dangerous baggage.

The empiricists started from the right idea. What science is after is truth. What it needs is an objective method for finding out truth. That method would let the outside world determine what we believe. This, after all, is the only way of reliably finding out what's going on out there. And the way the outside world acts on our minds is through our senses. Look and see!

As we've seen throughout this book, however, there's very little if anything that we can find out just by looking and seeing.

Does this mean that science cannot be objective? that there's no hope of finding out real truth? that anything it tells us might be totally wrong?

23.3 Scientific Objectivity

Well, there's only one kind of science that's even possible, and it relies on using the scientist's own values and those of the scientific community and the community at large; it relies on the methodological techniques that are set down in manuals such as this one, and on the accumulated claims of previous science. And this kind of science, while in its very nature it sometimes goes astray, can't always be wrong. It works. The predictions we make using it mostly turn out true. The things we use it to build work. No doubt it's wrong here and there. But there's also no doubt that most of what science says is true, and that as time goes on, it accumulates more new truths and fixes up more of its prior mistakes.

The reason science works so often is not that it's a completely passive, empty-minded fact accumulator. The reason it works is that it provides places for the outside world to tell us what it's like. Despite the necessity of cultural and individual variables in science, it retains objectivity in a certain sense: in complex ways, intermixed with our own presuppositions, categories, and values, science determines what our beliefs are when it is done well. It's not totally up to us.

We can look at science as a big factory for making true statements. As time goes on, it refines its tools, and its products get better and better. Whenever it's been discovered that some of the products are defective, there's a retooling to make its machines work right. The methodology we've been looking at is the result of centuries of improvements to this truth factory.

The position we're advocating has stressed all along that science has subjective (non-objective) elements in it. This means that it can come up with the false answers. Anything scientists believe just might be wrong. But given the truth finding, testing mechanisms of science, which let the outside world take a hand in determining what we think, a good number of our mistakes will eventually get corrected. All this leads to a sort of optimism about science: it will eventually move closer to the truth.

What was behind Mrs. Smith's position was her profound commitment to truth. She thought of scientific technique as a way of letting the universe outside us determine what we believe. The argument throughout this book has been that her view of scientific method was naïve in some ways; but her central commitment to truth has not been rejected. Despite the fact that scientists cannot act and think in the simple empirical ways Mrs. Smith advised, nevertheless the complicated techniques we've been looking at are designed to get things right as much as possible. Mrs. Smith was giving us an over-simple and misleading view about what goes on in the truth factory; but she was right after all about the important thing: truth is what we're after.

Index